JUSTICE,
AND ONLY
JUSTICE

JUSTICE,
AND ONLY
JUSTICE

A Palestinian Theology
of Liberation

NAIM STIFAN ATEEK

ORBIS BOOKS

Maryknoll, New York 10545

The Catholic Foreign Mission Society of America (Maryknoll) recruits and trains people for overseas missionary service. Through Orbis Books, Maryknoll aims to foster the international dialogue that is essential to mission. The books published, however, reflect the opinions of their authors and are not meant to represent the official position of the society.

ORBIS/ISBN 0-88344-540-9
0-88344-545-X (pbk.)

This book is dedicated

to the memory of my father and mother
Stifan and Nevart Ateek
who instilled in their children faith in God and a sense of justice

to the memory of my brother
Michael

and in honor of my brother
Saleem
and my sisters
Hanneh, Hilda, Huda, Neda, Fida, Naomi, & Selma

Contents

Foreword

Father Naim Ateek's presentation of a Palestinian liberation theology is written in an extraordinary spirit that unites justice and love. One finds in this testimony to his faith as a Palestinian Christian both the dignified claims of truth and righteousness against injustice and the peacemaking extension of the hand of forgiveness to those who have injured the Palestinians, once the wrongs are acknowledged. It is a liberation theology that comes, first and foremost, from the heart and mind of a pastor, who lives in the midst of the tragedy of one victimized people suffering at the hands of another historically victimized people.

The claim of empowerment in the name of security for the one people, the Israeli Jews, has been purchased at the expense of the just claims to the land of another people, the Palestinians. The claims of both sides seem mutually exclusive, and so the conflict appears irresolvable. Yet, to the mind of a Christian faith rooted in the ethic of Christ, it becomes apparent that each people can live in the land both claim only by the deepest mutual affirmation of each other. As Ateek puts it, the Israeli Jews seek peace with security, and the Palestinians seek peace with justice. Palestinians must come to acknowledge Jewish fear and need for security, while Israeli Jews must recognize that the only authentic security for them is through justice to the Palestinians.

This testimony to a Christian faith, incarnated in the midst of this most poignant human historical conflict, must be heard by Christians, Jews, and Muslims, by all people of faith. Its simple and direct message has explosive and transformative significance for us all. While not wishing once again to make exaggerated claims for the specialness of the "Holy Land," one cannot help but feel that the sheer historical weight of this place that the three monotheistic faiths call "holy" has a uniquely paradigmatic significance.

The rival claims of these three major religions, that each find their roots in Palestine, has been, in a sense, a curse rather than a blessing for those who are indigenous to this region. For five millennia armies have fought over this land for its strategic location as the bridge connecting three continents. But for three millennia they have also fought over it because of its symbolic meaning. Muslims claimed it in the seventh century as the land of their father Abraham and the site of Mohammed's heavenward journey. Christian crusaders slaughtered Jews and Muslims, as well as Eastern Christians, to get it in the Middle Ages. Tens of thousands of Jews and Arab Christians and Muslims have died for it in the twentieth century.

This land of three faiths cursed by its "holiness" can become a land of blessing only when it becomes clear to all three that it is a land that cannot be claimed by one people only. It is a land of two peoples, Israeli Jews and Palestinians. It is a land of three faiths, Judaism, Christianity, and Islam. The key to peace is the acknowledgment that this land must be shared. The path to blessing is to learn how to share it.

For Christian liberation theologians the advent of a Palestinian liberation theology calls for a profound paradigm shift in the way in which much of this type of theology has been done by Christians in other lands. For such Christians the language of Exodus and the promised land, the election of Israel as God's people, and redemption as the empowerment of the oppressed has been unquestioned. Christians of Latin America, Asia, and Africa have used such motifs from the biblical story as paradigms of their own situation.

A Palestinian liberation theology reveals the dangerous, shadow side of these images of liberation from former oppression. Palestinians are victims of a Zionist liberation theology and ideology. The Jewish exodus from oppression in Europe is the rationale for their conquest. The Jewish claim to the promised land is their dispossession from their land of Palestine. Jewish peoplehood excludes the existence of Palestinians as a people. Jewish redemption is Palestinian oppression.

This testimony to the oppressive underside of the biblical motifs of God's liberation of one chosen people must call us all to question exclusivist concepts of peoplehood and God. It must call us back to the universalist direction of the three faiths, not as imperialist denial of particularity, but as the global context in which particularities of peoplehood, culture, and nationalism can be reconciled and we can learn to live as neighbors sharing one land, sharing one earth.

The critical issue for every liberation theology, every liberation movement, is not simply how to throw off oppression and empower the formerly victimized, but how to do so in a way that does not simply make the former slaves into new slave masters. How do we end violence to one people in a way that does not create new violence to another people? How do we cease to let our guilt toward one people be used to stop our ears to the cries of another people? How can we end the cycle of violence?

For Father Ateek the answer to that question is justice, but more than justice. It is a justice tempered by mercy and forgiveness. We must learn to love, not just our neighbors, but our enemies. This does not mean accepting injustice from them. But it does mean trying to understand their hurts, the story behind their fears and their need to dominate. This is indeed the deep meaning of *metanoia,* the conversion of two people's hearts to one another. This happens when we cease simply to testify to our own wounds at the hands of the other and also begin to feel the wounds inflicted on the other as if they were inflicted on ourselves. This is the ethic and spirituality called compassion.

Only justice rooted in compassion can save us from repeating the cycle of violence, from empowering one oppressed people only to make them oppressors of another people. This may seem like too high an ethic to expect from any group of political communities. Reinhold Niebuhr taught Christians in the nineteen thirties that the ethic of love and compassion is possible only between individuals. It can never be expected between political communities who can only be motivated by power and self-interest. ''Rough justice,'' or the balancing of power claims, is the most we can expect in political ethics.

Perhaps what makes the Israel-Palestine conflict so profound and so paradigmatic for the world is that here even 'rough justice' will be possible only through the birth of compassion or fellow feeling. What is true of Palestine is finally true of the whole earth. As Father Ateek affirms, the earth belongs finally to God and not to us as private property. We can learn to live in peace only when we cease to claim it as our own against others, and learn to share it as sisters and brothers, children of one God who created us and chooses us all.

ROSEMARY RADFORD RUETHER

Acknowledgments

I would like to acknowledge with gratitude the support of many friends and relatives, without whom it would have been extremely difficult to complete the manuscript for this book:

Dr. Marc Ellis, of the Maryknoll School of Theology, made the initial contact with Orbis Books, and has been throughout a hospitable friend and advisor;

The Maryknoll Fathers and Brothers, who invited me to live at Maryknoll while completing this book. The warmth of their welcome made me feel very much at home.

The executive director and the staff of Orbis Books, especially Eve Drogin, my editor, who was always open, encouraging, and helpful, and Geraldine DiLauro, who typed my manuscript many times over.

In Jerusalem, Bishop Samir Kafity and fellow clergy, especially those who took my place in the parish ministry of the Church during my absence. Kenneth Bailey of Tantur, for his advice and encouragement. And Brother Gilbert Sinden of St. George's College, who reviewed parts of my manuscript with great patience and offered valuable suggestions.

In San Francisco Abla Aranki, who was a great help to me while I was writing my dissertation in Berkeley, California—much of which went into the present book—in the early nineteen eighties.

Most significantly, my own family—my wife, Maha, and our children, Stifan, Sari, and Nevart—who stood by my side with unflinching love and understanding, and bore the pain of our separation especially while I was away from them, completing the writing of the manuscript at Maryknoll, and they were in Jerusalem at the height of the *Intifada*.

Above all, it is to God that I owe greatest and deepest thanksgiving for laying on my heart the writing of this book, and for making its actual writing possible; without God's grace and mercy I would never have had the courage to accomplish this task. Any and all errors and shortcomings in it are mine; to God alone be the glory and honor.

Introduction:
Dimensions of the Conflict

One of the most excruciating disputes that has occupied the minds of millions of people in this century, and that still staggers their imaginations and frustrates their actions, is that of Israel-Palestine. This conflict has drawn the attention of people all over the world because of its many dimensions—the political, the religious, and the historical, no less than the emotional. From its inception, the conflict has driven people apart. It is charged with emotions and sentiments that do not bow to reason or to logic.

As the years have passed, the main issues of the conflict—instead of receding or moderating—have sharpened and deepened. Five wars and an *Intifada*, the uprising of the Palestinians on the West Bank and in Gaza that began in December 1987 and continues even as this is written, have only exacerbated tensions. As a way of introducing this book, I would like to make three important points.

THE RELIGIOUS VIEWPOINT

Although scores of books have been written about one or more aspects of the conflict as seen from Palestinian, Jewish, or other positions, and some writers have alluded to religious questions, very few have concentrated on the biblical and theological issues of the struggle. I am writing as a Palestinian Christian who has lived most of his life in Israel-Palestine. I write mostly out of my own personal experience, trying, above all, to reflect on the conflict both biblically and theologically. I am not writing primarily for scholars or theologians, but for people from all professions and walks of life. I hope, at the same time, that the main theological section (chapters 4 and 5) will not deter those who have not had any theological training from reading on. If it does, I hope that they will skim through it and keep going, returning, eventually, to read it more slowly and carefully; I strongly believe that such reading can illuminate the biblical and theological issues underlying today's painful realities.

More specifically, I would hope that this book will appeal and reach out to four categories of readers: the Palestinians themselves, both Muslims and Christians; a Jewish readership, both inside and outside of Israel; the wider Christian community in the West; and all people of good faith, throughout the world.

I am very conscious that Palestinian Muslims are seldom mentioned in this study, largely because of its nature—a Palestinian Christian theology of liberation. Nevertheless, Muslims make up the vast majority of the people of Palestine who, together with the Christians, have been very much in solidarity in the struggle for justice and peace. While this book reflects a Christian perspective on the Palestine problem, I hope that Palestinian Muslims, Druze, and others in the Arab population will find it useful.

Another segment of the Palestinians whom this study addresses is Palestinian Christians. This community is, I believe, in desperate need of a proper and adequate understanding of the theological meaning of the Palestinians' experience with the State of Israel. Many Palestinian Christians have been exposed, in one way or another, to a dangerous religious abuse of the conflict. Many of them have been agonizing, hoping that the Church would be able to develop and articulate a Palestinian theology of liberation that comes to grips with the excruciating problems of its existence amid the political turmoil. But the existing theologies of the various Christian churches in Israel-Palestine have either remained stagnant for decades or have been imported from abroad. Much of this theology addresses issues that are no longer relevant to the contemporary life of many people. For the Church hierarchy, the pastoral ministry has been the primary concern. Yet it has barely succeeded in training enough clergy to serve existing churches. There has been no time to set theology within a regional context beyond what a few members of the clergy have achieved on the parish level. And at times the Church has been reluctant to venture opinions on sensitive political issues. For these reasons, no indigenous theologians have emerged from the Palestinian Christian churches—or, if they exist, their voices have not been loud enough. The local clergy continue to mutter their discontent with existing theologies, reacting vehemently against political misuses of the Bible and voicing protests against injustice. But the need for a contextualization of theology for the Church in Israel-Palestine remains; it is of the utmost importance.

Jewish readers, inside as well as outside of Israel, both religious and nonobservant, might not agree with the Christian perspective of my interpretations. I trust, however, that they can recognize a human spirit trying to reach them, talking about the real possibilities of peace and appealing for the realization of justice for all the peoples of Israel-Palestine. I hope that this book will, in a unique way, reach Jews of influence and prominence who can, out of concern for Israel's peace and health, assume their prophetic role and do all in their power to bring justice to the Palestinians; for in that alone lies the genuine security of the State of Israel.

This book will, I hope, clarify for many people in the wider Christian community in the West the nature of the Palestinian problem as seen through the eyes and experiences of a Palestinian Christian, as I attempt to elucidate those crucial issues that have confronted the Christians of Israel-Palestine.

Included among the Western Christian audience are the so-called Christian Zionists and some Christian fundamentalists, who have at times unknowingly contributed to the agony of Palestinians and Jews in the Middle East. Instead of deterring injustice, they have exacerbated it by encouraging Israel's militancy. Increased awareness will, I hope, lead them to play a more constructive role.

Finally, this study is addressed to all people, Christian or not, who consider themselves concerned citizens of our global village—those who care about the well-being of people everywhere and who realize that the Arab-Israel conflict holds the potential of a superpower confrontation that could lead to global catastrophe. It is extremely important for all people of goodwill to exert the pressure that is needed for the achievement of justice, peace, and reconciliation for all the peoples affected by the Israel-Palestine conflict.

STATISTICS AND TERMINOLOGY

Although it will be made clear later on exactly who the Palestinians and the Israelis are, I would like to offer some statistical data that can help keep things in perspective.

At least five major groups of Palestinians live in different areas of the world under different conditions:

1. Approximately 800,000 Palestinians are Israeli citizens and live in the State of Israel.
2. Over 1.3 million Palestinians live in eastern Palestine, commonly known as the area lying on the West Bank of the Jordan River and hence referred to, after 1948, as the West Bank; it was also called the West Bank in relation to the East Bank of the Jordan River, the Hashemite Kingdom of Jordan, and the city of Gaza and its region (a strip of land in the southwest of Palestine on the Mediterranean Sea which after 1948 came under Egyptian rule). These territories were occupied by Israel in 1967 and their inhabitants have been living under military rule ever since. They are not citizens of Israel.
3. Almost 1 million Palestinians live in the Hashemite Kingdom of Jordan and hold Jordanian citizenship.
4. About 300,000 Palestinians live in Lebanon, most of them in refugee camps.
5. Approximately 1 million Palestinians live in the diaspora—both in the Arab world and in various countries of the West.

These groups make up a Palestinian population of 4-5 million people; most of them are Muslims, but about 10 percent are Christians.

In some parts of this book readers will notice that I am dealing with Palestinians, both Muslims and Christians, who have become Israeli citizens; as I was brought up in that milieu, this is the group with whom I am most familiar. Gradually, however, I move to encompass Palestinian Christians in the West Bank and Gaza. When I discuss a future solution, however, I have all segments of the Palestinian population equally in mind.

According to Professor Roberto Bacchi, head of the Statistics Department of the Hebrew University in Jerusalem, there were 16 million Jews in the world before World War II. Today, there are approximately 13 million. Three and one-half million Jews live in Israel; 9.5 million live in the diaspora, most of them in the United States and the Soviet Union.

One of the difficulties I encountered while writing this book was that of terminology. On the whole, I have chosen to use "Israel-Palestine" to identify the land that is the source of the conflict.

This term incorporates all of geographic Palestine under the British mandate before 1948. For me, Israel-Palestine expresses both acceptance and hope: acceptance of the existence of the State of Israel in western Palestine (pre-1967 Israel) and my hope for the establishment of a Palestinian state in eastern Palestine (the West Bank) and Gaza.

Furthermore, except in a very few places I have intentionally not used the term "Holy Land." It conjures up in some people's minds the past more than the present; it is a catchy term that speaks to tourists more of holy sites than of the people who live there now and struggle together for peace. I am not suggesting that the term is all negative and should never be used. For my purposes, however, "Israel-Palestine" is more precise and specific.

I have also avoided using the word "problem" when describing the conflict in Israel-Palestine. In many people's minds, the Palestinians have become a problem and the conflict the "Palestine Problem." I have also reduced to a bare minimum the use of the term "Arab-Israeli." When it is used, it generally refers to the wider conflict or relationship between Israel and all the Arab states.

There is also a difficulty in referring to Israel and Jews. To say "Israeli" when talking about Jews in Israel, as some people do, is not very precise. There are about eight hundred thousand Palestinian Arabs living in Israel as Israeli citizens; they are Israelis, too. To use the word "Jews" when talking about Jews living in Israel is to risk misunderstanding, since most Jews live outside Israel; a number of them are not Zionists and do not identify with the policies of the State of Israel. I have chosen to use, instead, "Israeli Jews" or "Jews in Israel." When the term "Jews" is used, I usually intend a general, inclusive meaning—all Jews inside and outside of Israel.

WHY A THEOLOGY OF LIBERATION FOR PALESTINIAN CHRISTIANS?

For some of the world's Christians, and especially for many Eastern Christians in the Middle East, a "theology of liberation" might seem odd and unacceptable.

Liberation theologies have been perceived by some Christians to be influenced by Marxism. This assumption, rightly or wrongly, leaves such theologies open to criticism and even makes them taboo. Because it is essential to examine one's presuppositions, I would like to say clearly that the theology found in this book is firmly based on the Bible. It is an attempt to contextualize theology, to make it meaningful to Palestinian Christians, but this theology stems from biblical roots. Moreover, it is a theology that struggles with certain ways in which the Bible itself has been misunderstood, misinterpreted, and misused by many people.

Some of my fellow Eastern Christians argue against a theology of liberation on theological grounds. For them, it is superfluous, since liberation has already been achieved in the redemptive work of Christ—in his crucifixion, death, and resurrection for the whole world. There cannot be one theology of liberation for Africa and another for Latin America, no black or women's theologies of liberation—because all have been radically liberated by Christ, and in Christ all Christians are one. To those who hold such views I can only say that this book does not create a brand-new, unique, and separate theology for Palestinian Christians. It is really an attempt to rediscover the liberation that Christ has already accomplished and of which we should be aware.

This theology, therefore, calls attention to the heart of the biblical message. It emphasizes the liberating aspect of the Word of God—that has been there in the Bible all along but that, unfortunately, has been neglected—and it helps us to focus on it. It brings the Word of God to us in our daily lives, attuning our ears to what God is saying to us today and to what God wants to do through us in this world that God loves and to which God has sent Christ. A theology of liberation is a way of speaking prophetically and contextually to a particular situation, especially where oppression, suffering, and injustice have long reigned. God has something very relevant and very important to say to both the oppressed and the oppressors in the Middle East.

It is with these things in mind that I invite the reader to go with me through the pages of this book. I hope that you will find it not only informative but challenging, calling you to active participation in the work of justice and reconciliation so that the peoples of Israel-Palestine might live as peaceful neighbors and God be glorified and honored by all.

1

The Encounter

You will know the truth, and the truth will make you free.

John 8:32

A FIRST EXPERIENCE OF ISRAEL

I am a Palestinian. I had just turned eleven in 1948 when the Zionists occupied my hometown, Beisan (Beth Shean).[1] We had no army to protect us. There was no battle, no resistance, no killing; we were simply taken over, occupied, on Wednesday, May 12, 1948.

Our house was on the main street, so as a boy I watched the Zionist troops, the Haganah, come into town past our door, watched them enter every house in the neighborhood, looking for weapons. They searched our house, too, but did not find any. My father had never owned a gun; he did not believe in doing so.

In the early 1920s my father had left the city of Nablus, where he was born, and moved to Beisan with his wife, their two small children, and his aged father. He had learned to be a silver- and goldsmith, but since Nablus already had several goldsmiths, my father decided to establish his business in a town where there were none. Beisan seemed a good choice. Situated about 30 kilometers (20 miles) south of the Sea of Galilee, its population was approximately six thousand. All the people were Palestinians, most of them Muslim, but there was a small, flourishing Christian community;

7

relations between the religious groups were good. Beisan was accessible to many of the Bedouin tribes, and most came to Beisan to do their shopping and trading.

My father's business prospered. Within a few years of his arrival, he was able to buy a good piece of land located on the main street of town. There he built the first house for his family, then another, and finally a third to accommodate a few women who were sent by the Church Missionary Society (CMS) from England to do mission work in Beisan. The homes were not fancy by any means, but they were adequate and comfortable.

The good Lord blessed my father with a large family of seven girls and three boys. I was the eighth child. After work, or early in the morning, my father enjoyed tending the garden around our house. He planted many vegetables, and almost as many fruit trees: banana, pomegranate, fig, grapefruit, orange, lemon, and mulberry. Beisan had an abundance of water and a small irrigation canal went through our garden. I still have many fond memories of helping my father till, plant, and irrigate the garden.

My father, who was brought up as an Eastern Orthodox Christian,[2] decided early in life to take his faith seriously. Our house was a center of Christian activity, Bible study, and Sunday school. On Sundays the family would go to the Orthodox church for the liturgy, and the congregation would then send their children to Sunday school in our house and would themselves attend Bible study there. Through the influence of the CMS missionaries, father became more active in the Anglican Church. He was later instrumental in building a small Episcopal (Anglican) church in Beisan. Since a priest came only once a month from Nazareth for the service of Holy Communion, father acted as a lay reader.

When the soldiers occupied our town in 1948, our simple and unpretentious life was disrupted. Some members of both the Muslim and the Christian communities fled their homes, horrified when news of what the Jewish soldiers had done in Deir Yasin reached them. Deir Yasin was a small town on the outskirts of Jerusalem. When the soldiers occupied it, they massacred 254 persons, including women and children and threw their bodies in a well.[3] I remember the many friends and neighbors who came to store their valuables with us before leaving town. Some even left their house keys, asking us to look after their homes while they were gone. They expected to be away, staying with relatives in less dangerous areas, for a few days or weeks. Many friends tried to convince my father to leave. They said, "The Jews will kill you; escape with your life and your family!" I recall my father's repeated response: "I have nowhere to go with my large family. We will stay in our home. If we have to die then we will die here together." My father referred not only to his own immediate family, but also to his extended one. My oldest brother, his wife, and their baby were living in the house next door. My second oldest sister, who had lived with her husband and two little daughters in the Haifa area, had fled with them to our home in Beisan a few days before. There were seventeen of us in all.

Our town was occupied on May 12, 1948. (The State of Israel was proclaimed two days later.) We lived under occupation for fourteen days. On May 26, the military governor sent for the leading men of the town; at military headquarters, he informed them quite simply and coldly that Beisan must be evacuated by all of its inhabitants within a few hours. My father pleaded with him, "I have nowhere to go with my large family. Let us stay in our home." But the blunt answer came, "If you do not leave, we will have to kill you."

I remember vividly my father's return from headquarters to give us the bad news. With great anguish he said, "We have been given no choice. We must go." The next two hours were very difficult. I can recall with great precision what happened, almost minute by minute.

My father asked us to carry with us whatever was lightweight yet valuable or important. The military orders were that we should all meet at the center of town in front of the courthouse, not far from my father's shop. My oldest brother and sisters had each carried a few items to the center of town, hoping to leave them there and return to the house for more. Yet when they got to the courthouse, they found that the soldiers had fenced in the area so that whoever reached there was not allowed to leave again. I recall that my father and mother were quite upset because my brother and sisters had not returned. I was asked to run and hurry them back. So I ran to the center of town, only to be caught with them; the same thing happened to both my father and mother when they came themselves. I discovered later—I was not told at the time—why my parents were so terribly anxious: they realized that in one of the baskets left in front of our house to be picked up later was some of the gold we were trying to take with us. In another basket was some fresh bread my mother had been baking that morning when my father came home with the bad news. My brother Michael was worried about a small Philips radio—one of his most precious possessions—that he had bought just before his marriage. When the soldiers occupied Beisan, they ordered people to turn over their radios. It was so difficult for my brother to part with his radio that he hid it in our garden.

My father and brother pleaded with the troops to let them go back to the house to pick up a few more things, but to no avail. Later, however, when we were on the bus passing our house on the way to Nazareth, my father asked the driver to stop for a minute. He did, and we saved the fresh bread, the gold, and the radio. My brother, taking with him a wool blanket from one of the beds, wrapped it around the radio and so smuggled his treasure out of Beisan.

As people gathered at the center of town, the soldiers separated us into two groups, Muslims and Christians. The Muslims were sent across the Jordan River to the country of Transjordan (now Jordan). The Christians were taken on buses, driven to the outskirts of Nazareth, and dropped off there, since Nazareth had not yet been occupied by the Zionists. Within a few hours, our family had become refugees, driven out of Beisan forever.

Rudyard Kipling has written in his famous poem "If":

> If you can meet with Triumph and Disaster
>   And treat those two imposters just the same;
> If you can bear to hear the truth you've spoken
>   Twisted by knaves to make a trap for fools,
> Or watch the things you gave your life to, broken,
>   And stoop and build 'em up with worn-out tools . . .[4]

At the age of fifty-seven my father had to stoop and, with or without worn-out tools, begin all over again. I am sure he found great comfort in the words of the Psalmist:

Why are you cast down, O my soul,
and why are you disquieted within me?
Hope in God; for I shall again praise him,
my help and my God.[5]

Life in Nazareth during the ensuing months was difficult. Palestinians flooded the city—either fleeing or expelled from neighboring towns and villages. Church institutions had to open their doors to thousands of refugees. The rest stayed with relatives or friends or had to manage as best they could in miserable living conditions.

Our family found refuge with some friends, who gave us two rooms in their own house near Mary's Well; the seventeen of us lived there for several weeks until we moved into the Episcopal primary school building for the summer. Almost from the beginning, my father, though himself a refugee, worked with church organizations collecting clothing and food for other refugees.

On July 19, the Jewish soldiers occupied Nazareth, again with no battle fought. My father hoped that we would be allowed to return to Beisan. But it became evident that our exile was permanent.

On the whole, our family was more fortunate than many others. None of us was killed. We did not stay in refugee camps. We had been able to take most of the gold with us, and my father had a good profession. After that summer of 1948, Father was able to rent a small house belonging to the *Waqf* (religious endowment property) of the Episcopal church in Nazareth and, with my brother, began to rebuild his business.

The wounds of that war were not only physical; the psychological agonies were at times greater. Borders were closed, and many families were divided on different sides of the armistice lines. People worried about their loved ones—a father or mother, brother or sister, aunt or uncle. Fear, uncertainty, anxiety, anger, bitterness—all these became part of the life of the humiliated and demoralized Palestinian community. In those days, people's anger was directed more toward the Arab countries for their inability to protect and save Palestine than toward the Jews. The dispersion of the Palestinians had started. Unable to return to their homeland, they were forced to live in the surrounding Arab countries, in Western Europe, in North America, and even in Australia.

As second-class citizens of the new state, we lived under military law. We could not travel from one place to another without a military permit. And since Beisan had no Arabs left to live in it, it was out of bounds. It was ten years later, on Israel's Independence Day in 1958, when Israeli Arabs were permitted on that day only to travel freely without a military permit, that my father took us all to Beisan. Israeli Jewish families were living in Palestinian homes. Some homes had been pulled down. Our little church was used as a storehouse. The Roman Catholic church and its adjacent buildings had become a school. The Orthodox church was left to rot. The Beisan we knew was left to gradually become a ruin while a new Israeli Jewish town was sprouting on the edge of it. Our homes were still standing and several families were occupying them. I still remember that when we asked permission to go inside, just to take a look, our request was turned down. One occupant said very emphatically, "This is not your house; it is ours."

Shortly after our return to Nazareth my father had a stroke, followed by another a few months later that immobilized him. Whether the stroke was brought on by the fateful visit to Beisan, I will never know. But I do know that the visit was very traumatic for all of us, especially for my father and mother.

On July 10, 1959, with the blessing of my father, now partially paralyzed, I left Nazareth for the United States to begin my university education. Father knew that I was going to study to be a priest, as I had always hoped, and it delighted him. One year later, on September 4, 1960, just before I started my second year of college in Texas, Father died in Nazareth. The telegram I received from my brother Michael a few days later said simply, "With deep sorrow we inform you that on September 4th your father went to be with the Lord. The family sends you its condolences. We pray for you and wish you well."

A few weeks later, Mother sent me a note that she had found inside my father's Bible. I could tell from the handwriting that it was written during his illness. It read, "To my son Naim: read Psalm 37:5." I looked it up and read, "Commit your way to the Lord; / trust in him, and he will act." This was my inheritance, my father's last will and testament to me, a very precious and meaningful one. From that moment on, this verse has been my favorite.

Six years later, my mother came to Berkeley, California, to attend my seminary graduation. She and Father had long looked forward to that day. I returned with Mother to Nazareth to be ordained and to begin my ministry among my people.

THE SHATTERING OF STEREOTYPES—WHO AM I?

It is easy for humans to stereotype one another. It is even easier for them to live out those stereotypes. Once we label people, we go on about our lives feeling comfortable, since we have defined, analyzed, and catalogued them—they have been captured and caged.

As a person who comes from the Middle East, I embody the different stereotyping to which my people has been subjected. Once I define or introduce myself, a number of contradictory images surface in the minds of many people. Some are curious; others are stunned. It is important, then, to begin by dispelling the myths and shattering the stereotypes. When that happens, freedom ensues; both parties are liberated.[6]

There are four important words that, cumulatively, make up my identity: I am a Christian, a Palestinian, an Arab, and an Israeli. If I wanted to add to the confusion of the reader and complete the picture, I would add that I am an Episcopalian (Anglican) and a clergyman.

Each of the first four words can be charged with myths; each has been the object of much stereotyping. Stereotyping can be the consequence of sheer ignorance or wrong impressions, but it is more often the result of propaganda and disturbing prejudice. Let me elucidate the apparently contradictory aspects of my identity and do away with some myths.

A Christian

Two questions are immediately asked when I identify myself as a Christian: When did you convert? Are there Christians in the Middle East? Many inquirers often forget that Christianity originated in the Middle East. Jesus Christ was born in Bethlehem and lived most of his life in the Galilee. He was crucified, died, and resurrected in Jerusalem. The Church was born on the day of Pentecost in Jerusalem and spread to the uttermost parts of the Earth from there. Today, there are no less than twelve million Christians in the Middle

East whose roots date back to the early centuries of Christianity. They have remained true to their faith despite centuries of difficulties, minority status, and, at times, persecution. They belong to the ancient historic churches of the Middle East, churches with a long and rich heritage that goes back to apostolic times.[7] Therefore, so far as I know, my Christian roots go back to the early Church in Palestine.

A Palestinian

To identify myself as a Palestinian poses a greater problem for many people. How can a Christian be a Palestinian? Worse still, how can a Christian clergyman be a Palestinian? Are not all Palestinians terrorists? Tragically, this is the way many people have come to perceive the Palestinians. How did this happen? Is it the result of propaganda? What about the Palestine Liberation Organization (PLO)? Is it not a terrorist organization?

Palestinians have been labeled as terrorists by the State of Israel and its friends so that Israel might seem right and justified in its actions against the Palestinians. And some Palestinians have been guilty of acts of terror. One needs to understand that the Palestinians have cried out to the world for many years (long before the establishment of the PLO) that they are victims of injustice. They have wanted to tell the world their story, but many people have not wanted to listen. Out of frustration and despair, some Palestinians have resorted to violence, and engaged in acts of terror, to attract the world's attention to the justice of their cause. It is a tragic commentary on our broken world that many people do not listen as carefully to the quiet voice of truth as they do to the loud noise of bombs. Many oppressed people have not been able to communicate their grievances effectively except through acts of violence and terror.

Having said that, let me hasten to add that the huge majority of Palestinians are not terrorists, nor have they at any time advocated terrorism. Palestinians are a people who call the country of Palestine their home, the land of their ancestors. For many centuries Palestinian Muslims, Palestinian Christians, Palestinian Jews, Palestinian Druze, and, more recently, Palestinian Baha'is have lived side by side. They belonged to different religious faiths, but they were all Palestinians. The most numerous of them, before the creation of the State of Israel, were the Palestinian Muslims. Palestinian Christians composed the second largest group until the 1920s, when European Jews began flocking into Palestine. Other religious groups, including Jews, constituted small minorities and lived for centuries in a few areas. Today there are approximately 4 to 5 million Palestinian Arabs. About 2.1 million live inside the State of Israel and the occupied territories of Gaza and the West Bank. The rest live in the diaspora.[8]

An Arab

A third part of my identity is as an Arab. In the minds of many Westerners, to be an Arab is synonymous with being a Muslim. However, Arab Christianity predates Islam. Muhammad was born in the year 570 *after* Christ. Christianity had already passed through six hundred years of existence in the Middle East before Islam appeared, and by then many Arab tribes had already become Christian. Moreover, when the Arab Muslims swept through the Middle East in the seventh century, most of the Semitic peoples in the region who had already been Christian for centuries gradually became Arabized.[9]

The association of Arabism with Islam and the confusion that such an association produces prevails not only among Westerners but among many Muslims themselves, whether they are ethnically Arab or not. Many of them do not accept (some would even refuse to accept) the fact that there are Arab Christians. They, too, think that "Arab" is synonymous with "Islam"—although they agree that the reverse is not true, for there are many non-Arab Muslims. In fact, the rise of Arab nationalism was in part an attempt to transcend the religious provincialism that infests the Middle East by giving the Arabs a wider and broader base and by making them share a common allegiance to the homeland *(watan)* that would contribute to their well-being regardless of their separate religious allegiances.[10]

Moreover, Arab Christianity before Islam was neither marginal nor peripheral, but a movement that had penetrated and affected the lives of many Arab tribes long before Muhammad. Some Christians, under Islamic domination and pressure, eventually converted.

Others gradually moved to the northern part of the Arabian peninsula, where they integrated with other Christians.

Today, the Arab Christians of the Holy Land are a mixture of many peoples, the true melting pot of a faith that knew no boundaries of ethnic or racial origins. They are the offspring of the Canaanites, the Syrians, and the Phoenicians; of the first Christian communities, that came out of the Jewish, Samaritan, Greek, Roman, and Arab populations; and, later, of the Crusaders and probably a dozen other indigenous ethnic groups who lived in the area. All mixed together and all eventually became ethnically Arabized.

My own ancestors are from Nablus, today the largest city of the West Bank. I often wondered why our family name is "Ateek." *'Atiq,* in Arabic means "old," "ancient," or "antique." A number of years ago, I happened to meet the leader of the Samaritan community in Nablus. He turned out to be a classmate of my father in their early childhood in Nablus. He told me that the name Ateek signifies that our family was one of the oldest Christian Arab families in Nablus. Whether this is true or not is difficult to ascertain, but the mere thought of it filled me with great joy and pride.

An Israeli

The term "Israeli" refers to my citizenship in the State of Israel. As will be made clear later, the Palestinian Arabs who remained in Israel of their own volition, or who were allowed to remain by the Jewish Israelis, were given Israeli citizenship. In Acts, the apostle Paul, although of Jewish background, enjoyed Roman citizenship because he was born in Tarsus, a Roman city.[11] Likewise, since 1948 all Palestinian Arabs born in the State of Israel became Israeli citizens. This has had practical advantages as well as disadvantages. In response to anti-Semitism and the Holocaust, many countries in the world have shown great friendliness toward the State of Israel. Many times I have been in the awkward position of being mistaken for an Israeli Jew. Sometimes, assuming I am Jewish, someone will deliver a long, virulent tirade against the ugly Arabs and the terrorist Palestinians, only to turn red-faced and apologetic when confronted with my true identity.

There are about eight hundred thousand Palestinian Arabs living in the State of Israel today, making up approximately 18 percent of the population; all are Israeli citizens. Included among them are approximately one hundred thousand Christian Palestinian Arabs.[12]

Obviously, it is not important to emphasize my Christian denominational affiliation. I mention it only to complete the cycle of complexity. The Episcopal (Anglican) Church in Palestine and other Protestant churches did not emerge in the Middle East until the second part of the nineteenth century. Western missionaries came to convert both Muslims and Jews. Very few of either community were in fact converted. Those who became Episcopalians or joined other Protestant churches were already Christians who belonged to the historic churches of the land.

Some readers might wonder whether I have dealt with these four aspects of my identity in an order of priority, and whether I attach certain significance to that order. I hasten to say that the order is arbitrary and can be altered. I have chosen to begin from the position of faith, the traditional means of identification in the East; and as a clergyman dedicated to the ministry of the Church, I find it significant to begin there. Yet I do so not out of fanaticism, radicalism, or prejudice. I have been brought up to respect other faiths and religions. I pray continually for greater tolerance, understanding, and mutual acceptance among the different religionists in the Middle East. I abhor all religious fanaticism; it is detrimental to the sanity of human beings, disrespectful, and an insult to God. Religious extremists are guilty of stereotyping God. Unfortunately, many areas in the Middle East are infested with this type of extremism and intolerance.

At the same time, I realize that some people would begin by identifying themselves as Palestinians or Arabs and then as Christians. I have participated in lively discussions where young people hotly debated whether they are *Christian* Palestinians or *Palestinian* Christians, *Christian* Arabs or *Arab* Christians. There were good arguments on both sides, depending upon which part of one's identity was being threatened, for that which is threatened receives greater emphasis. However, if I wanted to begin with the general and proceed to the particular, I would have to say that I am an Arab, a Palestinian, a Christian, and a citizen of the State of Israel, in that order.

2

An Arena for Strife:
The Political-Historical
Background

Thus says the Lord: "Let not the wise man glory
in his wisdom, let not the mighty man glory in
his might, let not the rich man glory in his riches;
but let him who glories glory in this, that he understands and knows me, that I am the Lord who
practice steadfast love, justice, and righteousness
in the earth; for in these things I delight," says
the Lord.

Jeremiah 9:23–24

The one single problem that has had the most devastating impact
on the life of the Church in Israel-Palestine, on the life of all the
people of Palestine, and on the whole of the Arab East throughout
this century is the Arab-Israeli conflict. This conflict remains the
most excruciating of problems, overshadowing all others—the fundamental, basic source that feeds and nourishes other disputes that
directly or indirectly derive from it.

It has become almost impossible to be objective about the Arab-
Israeli conflict. Every proponent claims objectivity, yet this is
achieved only up to a certain point. Beyond that point, objectivity
is clouded by the emotions of the proponents and their convictions

that are based on varying interpretations and appropriations of the facts.

In essence, the problem results from the claim of two peoples to the same piece of real estate. Although this claim is drawn out of thousands of years of history, the conflict itself is really a modern phenomenon that is not quite a century old—a conflict rooted in political and nonpolitical factors that originally had nothing to do with the area in dispute but began far away in Europe. Gradually, this small land of about ten thousand square miles became an arena of strife, violence, and wars resulting in massacres, expulsions, and misery for hundreds of thousands of people, conditions that still plague the area with continual instability and tension. One Arab writer has said, "The holy land has become more holy by the shedding of the blood of martyrs on its soil." [1]

Palestinians try to distinguish between the conflict over Palestine and the Arab-Israeli conflict. The latter is only the result of the former. The late Dr. Fayez Sayegh, son of a Presbyterian minister, put it in the form of an allegory:

A child is playing in front of his home. A group of strangers approaches. They grab him and try to spirit him away. He resists, kicking and screaming. Attracted by the tumult, his brothers rush out to rescue him. One of the kidnappers picks up the child and flees, while the others stay behind to engage the brothers and obstruct the chase. A fierce fight ensues.

A crowd soon gathers around. A policeman intervenes to separate the combatants. Every now and then they clash again— and again they are separated.

Some of the bystanders, weary of the protracted quarrel, leave the scene, indifferent to its outcome. Others urge the brothers to go back into the house, hoping that peace will be restored. A few offer proposals for settling the conflict. Meanwhile, the policeman dutifully keeps careful count of the blows and maintains a meticulous record of who does what to whom. But all appear to be either ignorant of the abduction that caused the fight or oblivious to the fate of the victim.

All the while, however, the brothers protest that the only reason for a quarrel at all is the kidnapping of their brother, and announce that there will be no peace until he is freed. But this announcement is misconstrued as an expression of intransigence and pugnaciousness.[2]

The quarrel between the brothers and the kidnappers in the allegory symbolizes the Arab-Israeli conflict, while the dispute over Palestine is symbolized by the abduction. For Arabs, Palestine is an Arab country, an integral part of the Arab world. Since the seventh century, Arabs have comprised the majority of its population. For many Jews, however, Palestine is a Jewish country. Throughout their long history, some Jews have lived in the land—for brief times constituting the majority of its population, at other times comprising a very small minority—and they have never totally abandoned it. It was remembered as the land of their forebears and the focus of their hope of return, expressed quite clearly in their worship and liturgy.

While the attachment of the Jews to Palestine has never been in question, the Zionist movement, which began at the end of the nineteenth century, did not arise primarily from religious motives; it was a nationalist political movement, influenced by a number of significant factors.

MODERN ANTI-SEMITISM

Although its roots lay in earlier centuries, modern anti-Semitism did not come into being until the 1800s.[3] Anti-Semitism is a Western phenomenon directed against Jews as Jews. It has nothing to do with individual Jews, their faults or virtues. It manifested itself in Europe in discrimination, prejudice, and pogroms. Moses Hess (1812–1875), the real father of Jewish political nationalism, was appalled at the presence of anti-Semitism in his native Germany. As he wrote in 1862 in *Rome and Jerusalem:*

We Jews shall always remain strangers among the nations. . . . It is a fact that the Jewish religion is above all Jewish nationalism. . . . Each and every Jew, whether he wishes it or not, is automatically, by virtue of his birth, bound in solidarity with his entire nation. . . . Each has the solidarity and responsibility for the rebirth of Israel. . . .[4]

It is significant that Hess, who fled from Germany to France, advocated to the French a sort of mandated Palestine for the benefit of the Jews, so that it would eventually become a Jewish state.[5]

THE RISE OF NATIONALISM

In the nineteenth century, various national movements arose in eastern Europe. Poles, Czechs, Slovaks, Serbs, Croatians, Lithuanians, and others began agitating for national independence. Each was dreaming of a nation-state of its own, characterized by its own language and culture. "Each new state was conceived as a reincarnation of ancient glories, of the resurrection of some ancient state or empire in which that particular people had stamped its imprint on history."[6] Zionism was launched on the important assumption that all the Jews in the world constituted a nation in the European sense, a group of people who identify themselves with a political state, either existing or to be established.[7]

JEWISH EMANCIPATION

Beginning with the French Revolution (1789), the Jewish communities in western Europe achieved equality of rights and citizenship. The Jews of Westphalia, for example, gained their emancipation in 1808; the Jews of Prussia, in 1812. In England, the last discriminatory restrictions against the Jews were removed in 1858.[8] Emancipation, however, created serious problems. When the ghetto walls in western Europe were torn down, Jews were free to enter fully into public life—a new experience for most of them. The response was diverse, with some seeking to assimilate into the Christian Church.[9]

David Friedlander (1750–1834), a disciple of Moses Mendelssohn, proposed a mass conversion of Jews to Christianity on the condition that Jews who accepted baptism would not be required to believe all the Christian doctrines. Indeed, some traditionalist rabbis actually opposed the emancipation of the Jews for fear that entry into the dominant culture would eventually lead to acceptance of the dominant faith.[10] Poet Heinrich Heine (1797–1856) called his own acceptance of Christianity an "entrance ticket to European culture."[11]

But emancipation also brought the evil of anti-Semitism into full view. One famous example was the 1894 court-martial of Alfred Dreyfus, who, although innocent of the charge of espionage against him, was nevertheless convicted because he was Jewish.[12] Enlightened Jews thought that emancipation would mean tolerance, but the Dreyfus affair showed that anti-Semitism was not subsiding. Indeed, it was this event that drove Theodor Herzl (1860–1904) to finally discard the idea of assimilation and to write *The Jewish State* (1896), which set forth his ideas for political Zionism.

COLONIALISM

The Zionist movement found inspiration in the spirit of nineteenth-century European colonialism, which had not yet fully showed its exploitative character. Most Europeans still viewed it in a positive light, as bringing civilization and culture to backward peoples. For Herzl, Palestine was to be "a part of the rampart of Europe against Asia" that "would serve as an outpost of culture against barbarism."[13] When Chaim Weizmann (1874–1952), later the first president of the State of Israel, was projecting the shape of things to come in Palestine and planning his program of Jewish settlement, he wrote in early 1917 that "the Suzerain Government [that is, any government, Allied or otherwise, in command of the territory] shall sanction a formation of a Jewish company for the colonization of Palestine by Jews. . . ."[14]

Professor Edward Said of Columbia University has shown the connection between Zionism and European colonialism in his book *The Question of Palestine.* Although Zionism was born in an era of virulent Western anti-Semitism, it also emerged during a period of unparalleled European colonization in Africa and Asia. "It was as part of this general movement of acquisition and occupation that Zionism was launched initially by Theodor Herzl. . . . Zionism never spoke of itself unambiguously as a Jewish liberation movement, but rather as a Jewish movement for colonial settlement."[15] This was further illustrated when the Second Zionist Congress, held in Basel, Switzerland, in August 1898, established the Jewish Colonial Trust Limited, out of which, in 1901, came the Jewish National Fund.[16]

Although the Zionist movement was similar in most respects to European colonialism, it differed in one major tenet. Whereas the colonialists' mission was to bring culture and civilization to the natives of the colonized areas—who were viewed as inferior, marginal, and irrelevant—this was not so for the Zionists. Herzl wrote in his diary on June 12, 1895, that "when we occupy the land . . . we must expropriate gently the private property on the estates assigned to us" and "try to spirit the penniless population across the border."[17]

Zionism was explicitly secular in character. This is evident in its early stages, for Palestine was not considered the only country that could provide a solution to the dispersion of the Jews. Even before the official launching of the Zionist movement, Dr. Leo Pinsker (1821–1891), a noted Russian Jew who turned ardent Jewish nationalist as a result of the pogroms of 1881–2 in Russia, advocated a national home in either Palestine or Argentina. He wrote that nations respect one another as long as they can anticipate reciprocity in extending hospitality, that is, as long as they all have homelands of their own: "The anomaly of the Jews consists in their lack of a homeland. As a nation without a homeland they create a ghost-like impression among their host-peoples . . . and there is a general fear of ghosts. . . . Let the Jews acquire a homeland of their own and become like all other nations."[18]

In fact, Theodor Herzl, founder of the Zionist movement, was willing to consider places for a Jewish home as divergent as Argentina, Uganda, Cyprus, and El-Arish (northern Sinai).[19] Before long, however, Palestine became the focal point of attention, the place that embodied all of the hopes, heritage, and history of the Jewish people.[20] A Jewish state in Palestine was a stirring proposition, and not only for Jews. It could play on the emotions and garner the support of many Western Christians, who saw in the Jews' return to Palestine a sign of the approaching *eschaton,* the coming again of Christ, and the fulfillment of God's scheme for the future.

A NATION WITHOUT A COUNTRY

As early as August 17, 1840, an editorial appeared in the *Times* of London recommending a plan "to plant the Jewish people in the land of their fathers" and grant rights and privileges to the Jewish settlement that would be "secured to them under the protection of a European power." The referent here was Britain.[21] This plan was advanced by the Earl of Shaftesbury, a deeply religious Christian who looked forward to the fulfillment of biblical prophecies and the return of the Jews to "their own land." On May 17, 1854, the Earl wrote in his diary:

> The Turkish Empire is in rapid decay; every nation is restless; all hearts expect some great thing. . . . No one can say that we are anticipating prophecy; the requirements of it [prophecy] seem nearly fulfilled; Syria "is wasted without an inhabitant;" these vast and fertile regions will soon be without a ruler, without a known and acknowledged power to claim domination. The territory must be assigned to some one or other; can it be given to any European potentate? to any American colony? to any Asiatic sovereign or tribe? Are there aspirants from Africa to fasten a demand on the soil from Hamath to the river of Egypt? No, no, no! There is *a country without a nation; a nation without a country*. His own once loved, nay, still loved people, the sons of Abraham, of Isaac, and of Jacob.[22]
>
> Wrote this day to Sir Moses Montefiore, to learn, if I could, the sentiments of his nation respecting a plan I have already opened to Clarendon, and Clarendon to Lord Stratford, that the Sultan should be moved to issue a firman granting to the Jewish people power to hold land in Syria, or any part of the Turkish dominions. This would be analogous to the Decree of Cyrus. Surely no one can say, "you are precipitating events"; they are rushing upon us; we desire simply to meet them.[23]

The Earl of Shaftesbury was always working for Israel's temporal as well as spiritual welfare. His biographer, Edwin Hodder, wrote:

> The position of affairs in the East [in 1854] revived the hopes that the time was at hand when a way would be opened for the return of the Jews to their inheritance in the Land of Promise. . . . Lord Shaftesbury never had a shadow of doubt that the Jews were to return to their own land, that the Scriptures were to be literally fulfilled, and that the time was at

hand. . . . His study of the prophetic Scriptures led him to associate the return of the Jews with the Second Advent of our Lord, and this was the hope that animated every other.[24]

The Zionists were hoping to capitalize on such religious sentiments as well as on political ones. The idea of a Jewish commonwealth in Palestine as an outpost of the British Empire was considered as early as 1840. Lord Palmerston, the British foreign secretary, was the stepfather of Shaftesbury's wife and also his very close friend.[25] Palmerston thought that a Jewish settlement in Palestine would be helpful to the Ottoman Empire. He wrote to his ambassador in Istanbul:

There exists at the present time, among the Jews dispersed over Europe, a strong notion that the time is approaching when their nation is to return to Palestine. . . . The Jewish people, if returning under the sanction and protection and at the invitation of the Sultan, would be a check upon any future evil designs of Mehemet Ali or his successor. . . . I have to instruct your Excellency strongly to recommend [to the Turkish government] to hold out every just encouragement to the Jews of Europe to return to Palestine.[26]

Significantly, Shaftesbury expressed these sentiments half a century before the formal emergence of Zionism. Some Western Christians were from the beginning a potential source of support for Zionist aspirations. Protestants, in particular, proved themselves very effective in this regard. With the Bible as their sole guide, and observing the dispersion of the Jews, many Protestants applied certain exilic and post-exilic prophetic statements to their own times, thereby uncritically accepting the necessity of the return of the Jews to Palestine.

There is both anomaly and contradiction between Christian and Jewish religious responses to Zionism. Many Christians were ready to support the Zionists in their endeavor because it fitted their own schemes of prophetic history. However, religious Jews—both Orthodox and Reform—opposed it vehemently, attacking Zionism as a nonreligious, even an antireligious, movement.[27] For the Zionist, religion stood as an obstacle to the rejuvenation of the people of

Israel; the Orthodox believed that only the Messiah would lead the Jewish people back to the Promised Land. Almost all the Orthodox leaders rejected Zionism and denounced Herzl, saying that the establishment of a Jewish state and the "ingathering of the exiles" were reserved exclusively for the Messiah.[28] The evil of Zionism was seen precisely in that it shifted this responsibility from the shoulders of a Messiah to the shoulders of the Jewish people.[29]

Reform Jews, who stressed the universalistic character of Judaism, also attacked Zionism. They believed in the "mission of Israel," the spreading of the knowledge of ethical monotheism among humankind. They did not regard themselves as a "nation." In 1885 Reform Jewish rabbis met in Pittsburgh, Pennsylvania, and adopted the "Pittsburgh Platform," which read, in part:

> We recognize, in the modern era of universal culture of heart and intellect, the approaching of the realization of Israel's great Messianic hope for the establishment of the kingdom of truth, justice and peace among all men. We consider ourselves no longer a nation, but a religious community, and, therefore, expect neither a return to Palestine, nor a sacrificial worship under the sons of Aaron, nor the restoration of any of the laws concerning the Jewish state.[30]

A Country Without a Nation?

The early Zionist leadership, which met for the First Zionist Congress at Basel in 1897 and included Theodor Herzl, had not visited Palestine or learned much about its inhabitants; they must have assumed that the country was vacant. In the 1880s Palestine had an Arab population of no less than six hundred thousand,[31] while by the beginning of this century the number of Jewish settlers did not exceed fifty thousand.[32] In fact, Jewish philosopher Martin Buber tells in one of his books an anecdote about Max Nordau, one of the most famous German Jewish personalities of the Zionist movement. Upon hearing for the first time that Palestine was inhabited by Arabs, Nordau, deeply shocked, ran to Herzl exclaiming, "I didn't know that! We are committing an injustice."[33]

Conflicting Agreements

Zionism's most important aim at the turn of the century was to achieve "a publicly recognized and legally secured Jewish home in Palestine." [34] This meant finding a sponsor who would adopt their scheme and become their patron. Herzl devoted his time and energy to this goal, making direct representations to Germany, Turkey, Italy, the Vatican, England, and others. On May 17, 1901, Herzl went to Istanbul and was received by Sultan Abd-el-Hamid, not as a Zionist delegate but as a journalist. During his two-hour visit with the sultan, Herzl offered the assistance of world Jewry in solving Turkey's chronic financial problems in exchange for a charter of autonomy for the Jewish people in Palestine. The visit ended in failure. [35] Contacts with Kaiser Wilhelm, the Russian czar, the pope, and the king of Italy yielded the same result. [36] Herzl also turned to England and met with Joseph Chamberlain, the colonial secretary. Herzl asked for the establishment of a Jewish settlement in Cyprus, in return for ". . . five million pounds; the Greeks would gladly sell their lands at a good price and migrate to Athens or Crete." [37] This visit also proved futile.

At the time, two objectives were being pursued simultaneously. The first was the encouragement of Jewish immigration to Palestine in order to buy land and build settlements. The second was to work tirelessly to achieve the legal charter. This latter goal was finally achieved on November 2, 1917, with the Balfour Declaration communicated to Lord Walter Rothschild by Lord Balfour, the British secretary for foreign affairs:

Foreign Office
2 November 1917

Dear Lord Rothschild,

I have much pleasure in conveying to you, on behalf of His Majesty's Government, the following declaration of sympathy with Jewish Zionist aspirations which has been submitted to, and approved by, the Cabinet.

His Majesty's Government view with favor the establishment in Palestine of a National Home for the Jewish people, and will use their best endeavors to facilitate the achievement of this object, it being clearly understood that nothing shall be done which may prejudice the civil and religious rights of existing non-Jewish communities in Palestine, or the rights and political status enjoyed by Jews in any other country.

I should be grateful if you would bring this declaration to the knowledge of the Zionist Federation.

(signed)
Arthur James Balfour[38]

Some two years before the Balfour Declaration, the British had conducted secret negotiations with the Arabs, trying to induce them to rise in rebellion against Turkey and enter the world war on the side of the Allies. It is clear from the correspondence between Sir Henry McMahon, the British high commissioner in Egypt, and the Sherif Hussein of Mecca (eight letters in all) that in return the Arabs would receive the independence of all Arab land in Asia (with the exception of Aden). "Palestine fell clearly within this British pledge of independence, dated October 24, 1914."[39] The last assurance from McMahon came on February 12, and the Arab revolt erupted in the Hejaz, in western Arabia, on June 4, 1916.

During the war years (1914–8) Britain entered into three separate agreements that contradicted one another. Besides the McMahon-Hussein agreement with the Arabs and the Balfour Declaration addressing the Jews, on May 16, 1916, Britain reached a secret understanding with France and Russia, which became known as the Sykes-Picot Agreement, stipulating that the Ottoman Empire was to be divided among the three countries. Most of the Arab lands were to be the spoils of England and France.[40] It was the Turks, in February 1918, who revealed these secret agreements to the Arabs in an attempt to prompt them to recant their allegiance to the Allies. In alarm, Hussein checked with the British government. Balfour replied, "His Majesty's Government confirms previous pledges respecting the recognition of the independence of the Arab countries."[41] Thus, Britain was guaranteeing the integrity of the Mc-Mahon-Hussein agreement and reaffirming its commitment to Arab independence.

These conflicting agreements became the source of strife, suspicion, and distrust that have plagued the Middle East ever since. For the Arabs, they were clearly acts of betrayal intended to replace the repressive Turkish rule—under which, in certain places, the Arabs enjoyed partial autonomy—with a non-Islamic European colonization embedded in France, England, and, eventually, the Zionist state.

After World War I, the Zionists were moving toward the achievement of their goal. One of the signals confirming the British government's commitment to Zionism was the appointment of Herbert Samuel as the first British high commissioner (1920–5) of mandated Palestine. Samuel was a British Jew and an ardent Zionist.[42] At the time of his appointment the population of Palestine, according to the 1921 census, included 590,000 Muslims, 84,000 Jews, and 89,000 Christians.[43]

ZIONIST ADVANCES, ARAB RESISTANCE

During the period 1918–47, relationships among Arabs, Jews, and British deteriorated. Palestinian Arabs increased their resistance against the colonial government, for its tolerance of Jewish immigration, and against the Zionists, who gradually became more outspoken about their real intention: the creation of a Jewish state. The Arabs' opposition to this was expressed in both political action and armed resistance—strikes, demonstrations, and violence ensued, most notably in the rebellions of 1920, 1921, 1929, 1933, 1936, and 1937–39.[44] The underlying cause of all these uprisings, as the British Royal Commission of July 1937 found, was the desire of the Palestinian Arabs for national independence and their fear of the establishment of the Jewish homeland as a state.[45]

The Zionists were working from within Palestine as well as from abroad. Both legal and illegal immigration of Jews into Palestine was taking place. Hitler allowed Jews who left Nazi Germany in 1933 to take their money with them. They contributed much of their resources, their skills, and their intelligence to the building of the Jewish homeland. The tragic events of the Nazi Holocaust forced the emigration of more Jews from Europe to Palestine, and attracted worldwide sympathy and support for them. Germany subsequently paid billions of dollars in restitution to Israel. In one of the horrible ironies of history, it may be said of Adolf Hitler that "he contributed more than any other man to the establishment of the State of Israel."[46]

During the 1930s and 1940s, Zionist armed forces within Palestine became strong and effective. Most had been trained by the

British and many had fought in World War II. Likewise, the Palestinian Arabs were resisting the increased immigration of European Jews into Palestine. The British were caught between the two fires. Having sown the wind during World War I, Britain was reaping the whirlwind of rebellion and strife after World War II. This unrest led the British to issue a new interpretation of their promises to the Arabs and Jews, only to follow these by counterinterpretations—a chain of new policies, statements, and commissions. All told, eighteen different commissions—each of them issuing policy statements and position papers—were set up to study Palestine. These included the Churchill White Paper of 1922, the Passfield White Paper of 1929, the MacDonald Letter of 1931, the Palestine Royal Commission (Peel Commission) of July 1937, the British Statement of Policy of November 1938, the White Paper of 1939, the Anglo-American Committee of Inquiry of 1946, among others.[47] But the whole of Palestine was so polarized that none of these was acceptable to all factions.

The situation in Palestine by the mid 1940s was out of control. Ernest Bevin, Britain's foreign secretary, announced on February 14, 1947, that the British government had decided to refer its Palestine problem to the United Nations. Britain was no longer able to administer the mandate because of the rising tension in Palestine and the continued illegal Jewish immigration. The United Nations set up a Special Committee on Palestine (UNSCOP) composed of representatives of eleven member states. Its report and recommendations for the partition of Palestine were published on August 31, 1947.[48]

PARTITION AND PANIC

According to the partition plan, Palestine would be divided into separate Jewish and Arab states and an "international corpus separatum" would exist in Jerusalem and the surrounding villages and towns.[49] The adoption of this recommendation by the United Nations on November 29, 1947, was preceded by prolonged doubts and hesitation, overcome only "after inordinate pressure was put by the United States on several dependent countries."[50] In one case $75,000 in cash was paid to the representative of a Latin American country to make him change his vote and support the partition plan.[51] The Zionists accepted the partition plan, while the Arabs rejected it. Consequently, the Zionists have sought to advance the argument that Palestinian Arabs, having refused to be satisfied with half of Palestine (which they believed was wholly theirs), had forfeited their right to any part of that whole. As one erudite Arab scholar commented: "Proponents of this argument would make poor Solomons, indeed. For the proverbial wisdom of Solomon lay not in proposing that the contested baby be cut into two, but in drawing the right conclusion from the different reactions of the two 'mothers,' rightly inferring that it was precisely she who *opposed* the partition of the baby who was the true mother."[52]

It seemed illogical as well as tragic to the Arabs that the Jews, who owned about 6 percent of the total land area of Palestine and comprised only 33 percent of the population, were granted a state consisting of over 56 percent of the country. Moreover, the proposed Jewish state was to have more Arabs (509,780) than Jews (499,020) under its jurisdiction. By contrast, the recommended Arab state was to contain only 10,000 Jews in its population of 735,000.[53]

Faced with rising strife and bloodshed in Palestine, the General Assembly of the United Nations suspended the partition plan less than six months after its adoption and submitted an alternative proposal calling for a temporary trusteeship over an undivided Palestine. This proposal was accepted by the Arabs but adamantly rejected by the Zionists. A special session of the assembly was called to reconsider the partition plan.[54] During this period, the Zionists took matters into their own hands. As the British were ending the mandate and their troops were withdrawing, Zionists began occupying town after town. The Palestinian population either fled in terror or was evicted by force, as was my own family. The particularly atrocious events at Deir Yasin (recounted in chapter 1) left an indelible mark of horror in Palestinian memory. This tragedy—carried out by Menachem Begin's Irgun and the "Stern Gang" (Begin gave a boastful account of it in his book *The Revolt*)[55]—caused the panic-stricken Arabs to flee, in what became a twentieth-century exodus of tragic proportions.[56] The Zionist forces occupied not only the areas allotted for the Jewish state under the partition plan but parts of the Arab state as well.[57] By mid May 1948 more than three hundred thousand Palestinian Arabs had left the country—all of this before even a single soldier of the neighboring Arab countries had entered Palestine.[58]

On May 14, 1948, the Zionists proclaimed the establishment of the State of Israel. At the same time, the United Nations General Assembly concluded its consideration of the issue by suspending the partition recommendation and ordering a halt to its implementation. A mediator, Count Folke Bernadotte, was appointed to "promote a peaceful adjustment of the future situation in Palestine,"[59] but he was assassinated by the "Stern Gang" on September 17, 1948. It was only after the State was proclaimed and the British Mandate expired that the armies of the neighboring countries entered Palestine to aid their fellow Arabs. However, they were outnumbered: General Glubb Pasha (of the Arab Legion) estimated that the combined Arab soldiers numbered 55,000, whereas the Israelis had an army of 120,000, many of them tough, seasoned soldiers and determined men.[60]

By the end of the war with the armistice of 1949, the total Palestinian Arab exodus amounted to about 750,000 people.[61] Reflecting on the tragedy, Arnold J. Toynbee observed on January 31, 1961, that "the treatment of the Palestinian Arabs in 1947 (and 1948) was as morally indefensible as the slaughter of 6,000,000 Jews by the Nazis." Dr. Toynbee went on to say that the Arabs had been "robbed" of their territory and cruelly treated: "Though not comparable in quantity to the crimes of the Nazis, it was comparable in quality."[62]

The Pandora's box was now fully opened, and only more injustice, misery, fear, and bloodshed were awaiting the Palestinians.

THOSE WHO REMAINED:
THE PALESTINIAN ARABS IN ISRAEL

Approximately 150,000 Arabs remained in that part of Palestine that on May 14, 1948, was proclaimed the State of Israel. Most of the social, political, economic, and intellectual elite of the Palestinian community had left the country for the West Bank, Gaza, or the neighboring Arab lands. Of the 150,000 who remained in Israel, 30,000 were refugees displaced from one area within Israel to another.[63] It must have thrilled the Zionists to see the exodus of

panic-stricken Arabs; Weizmann described it as "miraculous sim-
plification of Israel's tasks." Ben-Gurion said, "For decades we
collected pennies to buy a scrap of earth. Now we have millions of
dunams to dispose of."[64]

Repeated resolutions of the United Nations after 1948 for the
repatriation of the refugees were futile. The vacant Palestinian villages and towns posed a problem for the Zionists—they were obviously an incentive to the refugees to return. But Israel's policy
discouraged this in two ways. First, those villages that were not
wanted were destroyed; out of more than 550 Arab villages in the
territory occupied by Israel only 121 remained.[65] The rest were
bulldozed completely, in order to foil any attempt at repatriation.
Second, new Jewish immigrants were housed in Arab homes in the
different towns and cities as was the case with my family home. In
the first massive wave of immigrants, approximately 200,000 Jews
were able to obtain immediate housing by moving into "abandoned" Arab houses. "In 1954, more than one third of Israel's
Jewish population lived on absentee property and nearly a third of
the new immigrants (250,000 people) settled in urban areas abandoned by the Arabs."[66]

As I reflect on the history of the Palestinian Arab community in
Israel since 1948 and evaluate its development, it is apparent to me
that it has passed through three different stages: shock, resignation,
and awakening.

A People in Shock (1948—55)

Israel's Palestinians were stunned when, within a short period,
they had become a minority in their own land. The catastrophe was
too great to be believed. Intense bitterness and hatred also developed. On the one hand, profound feelings of recrimination against
both the Arab countries and the Zionists were constantly, although
privately, expressed. On the other hand, divided families were trying
to establish contact with their relatives. Thousands of people attempted to cross the armistice lines in order to be reunited with
their families or to return to their homes. Moshe Dayan estimated
that between 1949 and the middle of 1954 there was an average of
one thousand cases of infiltration per month along the various fron-
tiers, this at the risk of being killed, jailed, or in most cases thrown

back across the border.[67] It was also a nightmare for the remnant of the Palestinian community in Israel. Many of the refugees inside Israel, like my family, although only a few miles away, were forbidden to return to their towns and homes. Even the urban dwellers who had stayed in their homes were forced out and resettled in assigned "ghettos" within the cities, while their original homes were occupied by Jews. In many instances, several families had to live in the same house, each huddled in one room, all sharing the same facilities. Food was scarce and living conditions were appalling. Two actions by the Israeli government contributed to this nightmare. The first was the imposition of martial law on October 21, 1948. The military administration was aimed at controlling and restricting the movement of Israeli Palestinians. No Palestinians were permitted to leave their places of residence without a permit from the military governor of the district. This proved to be a very powerful weapon of control, since it reduced the interaction of Palestinians with one another—it literally fragmented our community. For example, in the early years of military rule the Galilee was divided into over fifty military districts.[68] Every Palestinian needed a permit in order to pass from one district to another. These travel permits specified not only the dates on which they were valid, but also the destinations, the routes to be taken, and the time of return. A report submitted to the United Nations Commission on Human Rights stated that "Arab children died in the arms of their mothers while waiting in the corridor of the Governor for a permit to go to see a doctor."[69] Many areas were totally off-limits, especially those Jewish towns that had been Palestinian before 1948.

In addition to the military administration, Israel also retained the Emergency Defense Regulations of the British Mandate that suspended the rights of individuals. For example: "Articles 109 and 110 give power to enter anyone's home at any hour, day or night; article 119 empowers the Military Commander to destroy a house if under his suspicion [sic]; article 120 gives the power to confiscate private property; article 121 gives the power to expel from the country."[70] When the Jewish community was suffering under the atrocious regulations, which were used by the British against both Palestinians and Jews after World War II, a leading Jewish lawyer, Yaccov Shapiro, who later became Israel's minister of justice, described them as "unparalleled in any civilized country; there were no such laws in Nazi Germany."[71]

The second level of repression that the new State imposed on its Arab population proved even more potent and vexatious to the Palestinian community in Israel: the expropriation of its land. In 1950, Israel enacted the Absentee Property Law, under which the State was able to confiscate Palestinian land—not only that of these Palestinian Arabs who had left Israel, but of those who had remained within it. Many Palestinians stayed in Israel during the 1948 war; they did not leave their homes but were dislodged from them, as were my family and I. Nevertheless, they were deemed by the State to be "absent" in the legal sense. Even more tragically, many of those who never were displaced from their homes suffered under this law, which was popularly referred to by Arabs as the "present/absent law," calling attention to its paradoxical nature.[72] It has been estimated that "approximately one-half of the Arab population of Israel was subject to categorization as 'absentee.' "[73] Indeed, during the 1948 war, many kibbutzim exploited the victory of their armed forces by seizing the land of their Palestinian neighbors.[74] Between 1948 and 1953, 370 new Jewish settlements were established, 350 on land classified as "abandoned." At least 250,000 *dunums* (62,500 acres) so classified were in fact owned by Palestinians who were given absentee status.[75] Indeed, by 1965 the Absentee Property Law and similar laws enabled the State to confiscate 12,500,000 *dunums* (approximately 3,125,000 acres) of Palestinian land, more than 60 percent of it belonging to Palestinians who never left Israel.[76] This included the Muslim *Waqf* (religious endowment), hundreds of thousands of *dunums* of agricultural land and urban real estate, and thousands of houses, businesses, and shops designated for the benefit of the Muslim community. All were placed at the disposal of new Jewish immigrants.[77] This systematic confiscation of land, begun in 1948, was to continue, as I discuss below.

Some Palestinians in Israel were offered compensation under the Land Acquisition Law of 1953, but these payments were so minimal that many refused them. However, pressure was exerted on some people to accept these nominal reparations, especially those who were desperate for the return of their families or who needed a work permit or other vital assistance.

During this period, the passage of Israel's Law of Return (1950) and the Nationality Act (1952) allowed further discrimination against the Palestinians in Israel and perpetuated their status as second-class citizens. Under these laws every Jew had an automatic right to settle in Israel, and Israeli citizenship was conferred upon entering the country.[78] At the same time, no Palestinians in Israel could gain citizenship until certain requirements were met and documentary proof given that they had never left the country.[79]

The period of shock lasted into the second half of the 1950s, during which time the Israeli Palestinians saw the immigration of over nine hundred thousand Jews into Israel, while Palestinians who had inhabited the area for centuries were denied admission.[80] For the Palestinians, being prevented from returning to their homes was clearly a stark injustice, and the international community clearly failed to redress it.

A Community Resigned (1956–67)

In 1956, Israel's collusion with Britain and France resulted in the Suez Crisis and the attack on Egypt. Israel was able to occupy the Gaza Strip and Sinai but was eventually forced by U.S. President Eisenhower to withdraw. The youthful state, however, was on its way to becoming a full military power, thus fulfilling the wishes of its minister of education, who in 1950 called on all Israelis to become a "nation of soldiers" rather than a "nation of priests."[81] Israel was still defying international resolutions and imposing its will and *faits accomplis* on the land and its inhabitants.

For the Palestinian community in Israel, this second period was characterized by a more realistic, though reluctant, attitude of adjustment and acceptance of the unresolved conflict. Its life was clearly that of a minority, considered foreign and basically unwanted. The policy of the Jewish state was to control the Palestinians rather than to eliminate, integrate, absorb, or develop them.[82] Palestinians were living on the sufferance of Israeli Jews. Even their identity was threatened: on the new identity cards that were issued to them, the word "Palestinian"—that had so far designated their nationality—was deleted and replaced with the more generic term "Arab." They became known as Israeli Arabs. Golda Meir, the Israeli prime minister, could blatantly declare: "It was not as though there was a

Palestinian people in Palestine . . . and we came and threw them out and took their country away from them. They did not exist."[83]

In addition to such physical and psychological restraints, the State also issued cultural and educational restrictions. In the curriculum used in schools for Israeli Arabs, there was an intentional avoidance of themes, events, and personalities reflecting the Arabs' contributions to the culture and history of the area. By contrast, there were explicit attempts to instill pride in Jewish history. In fact, Palestinian children spent more time studying the history of the Jews than they spent studying their own.[84] There was no real interest in teaching about the "interregnum" period of Palestinian history, A.D. 135–1948; Israeli Jews considered it irrelevant. The epitome of this attitude, in its extreme form, was David Ben-Gurion's demand after the 1967 war that the walls of the Old City of Jerusalem be razed because they did not represent the ancient Jewish era but were a reminder of the medieval Turkish phase of Palestinian history.[85]

During this period of resignation there was a general feeling among the Israeli Arabs that no solution for the Israel-Palestine conflict was in sight. Many of them were impressed by the development, progress, and vitality of the new state. Besides the millions of dollars pouring in from the United States, billions of dollars came from West Germany as reparations, restitution, and loans.[86]

Any attempt to organize the Palestinian community in Israel politically was immediately repressed. The political quiescence of the Palestinians and their seeming docility were perplexing to the late James Pike, Episcopal bishop of the diocese of California, who was a strong supporter of Israel. "The problem I have not understood yet is why the Arabs in Israel do not organize politically more than they do. It would seem that with this many voters something could be done."[87] In a study of the Israeli Arabs, Ian Lustick found that

the failure of Israel's Arab minority to "organize itself" and the minimal significance, to date, of the communal segmentation of Israeli society for the operation and stability of the Israeli political system, are due to the presence of a highly effective system of control which, since 1948, has operated over Israeli Arabs.[88]

Lustick goes on to emphasize that the system of control in Israel is different from apartheid in that it is not recognized in the legal framework of the State. On the contrary, Israel's Declaration of Independence declares:

> [The State] will promote the development of the country for the benefit of all its inhabitants; will be based on the principles of liberty, justice and peace as conceived by the Prophets of Israel; will uphold the full social and political equality of all its citizens, without distinction of religion, race, or sex; will guarantee freedom of religion, conscience, education and culture.[89]

Although the Declaration is not legally binding, in the continuing absence of a constitution it supposedly guides judicial interpretation of Israeli law, so Israel can claim that the Arabs and Jews are equals. Nevertheless, the State of Israel has developed a sophisticated "system of control" by which to manipulate the Arab minority and control it effectively. The three components of this system of control are segmentation, dependence, and cooptation.

> "Segmentation" refers to the isolation of the Arab minority from the Jewish population and the Arab minority's internal fragmentation. "Dependence" refers to the enforced reliance of Arabs on the Jewish majority for important economic and political resources. "Cooptation" refers to the use of side payments to Arab elites or potential elites for purposes of surveillance and resource extraction.[90]

At the end of this period, the sobering and chilling facts were quite clear: the world saw the "Palestinian problem" as a problem of refugees. Those Palestinians living in Israel had become isolated from their fellow Palestinians and had resigned themselves to the life and status of a minority.[91]

A Nation Awakening (1968—88)

Paradoxically, the third period had its stirrings in the aftermath of the 1967 war. To most observers, the lightning-fast, crushing victory of 1967 was seen as striking the deathblow to the hopes and aspirations of the Arabs in confronting Israel. From the vantage point of Israel, the war pushed the Arabs back, militarily, for a long time. Israel hoped that the war's incredibly swift conclusion would bring the Arabs to a point of surrender and would compel them to accept peace on Israel's terms. After the war, Moshe Dayan remarked that he was "waiting for the Arabs to ring his telephone."[92]

As it turned out, a new awakening sprang from this tragic and humiliating defeat that saw the deaths of thousands of Arabs and seven hundred Israeli soldiers.[93] By the end of the 1960s, and especially after the March 1968 battle of Karameh, when the Palestinian Arabs engaged in direct battle with the Israelis and inflicted heavy losses on them, there was a rebirth of Palestinian consciousness and a renewed dedication to the rightness of the Arab cause. The Palestine Liberation Organization (PLO) was recognized by the Arab countries as the sole representative of the Palestinian Arabs.

Many people have come to see the PLO as merely a terrorist organization. But for almost all Palestinians the PLO is their national-liberation movement. Brought into being in 1964 by the Arab League, the PLO had its first meeting in Jerusalem in May of the same year, when 422 Palestinians from various Arab countries met and outlined the basic structure of the organization. It was created as a political body whose purpose was to bring together the fragmented segments of the Palestinian people scattered in so many parts of the world. The PLO created a framework that would integrate the cultural, social, educational, economic, political, and military activities of the Palestinians. So its aim from the very beginning was not only the achievement of the national political rights of the Palestinians, but also the reconstitution of a healthy society for their shattered community.

The PLO is best known for its military wing, which is divided into eight separate groups, with *al-Fatah* being the largest. But very few realize the extent of the civilian services the PLO provides. It employs thousands of people who run schools, hospitals, and health clinics, publish books and periodicals, promote literacy programs, operate radio stations, work at economic development, and so on. Its Palestine National Council (PNC), or parliament, is composed of 428 members. Represented in the PNC are unions and syndicates of

Palestinian writers and journalists, workers, women, students, teachers, engineers, lawyers, doctors, painters and artists, and peasants. The PLO has an executive committee of fifteen members, elected by the PNC, who in turn elect a chairperson. Each member of the executive committee has a portfolio covering foreign affairs, education, health, finance, or other areas. The PLO has political representation in approximately one hundred countries and in various agencies of the United Nations.

> Thus the PLO may be quite legitimately thought of as a "proto state" or a government in exile, although it has never formally so proclaimed itself. Regardless, however, of how it is defined, its achievements are remarkable and surely indicative of the determination and ability of this community of people to transform themselves into a viable nation-state. The degree of sophistication of PLO political institutions, the processes of bargaining and negotiation, the politics of consensus building (in the context of high levels of political consciousness and political participation), combined with the extensive civilian institutional infrastructure, provide the basis for a government, and bode well for the successful operation of a state once it is constituted.
>
> Moreover, the existence of the civil institutions of the PLO and the extent of their activities, in addition to the political institutions and processes of interaction in the play of Palestinian politics, are testament to the fact that the PLO is not only a military organization. Indeed the military activities of the PLO pale in magnitude, sophistication, and complexity in comparison with its civilian activities.[94]

Thus, the PLO helped link together the scattered Palestinian communities and focus their hopes and aspirations.

For the Israeli Arabs, it helped to raise their consciousness as Palestinians. They suddenly realized that they were part of a wider entity, a greater whole. They recovered their lost identity, which had haunted them for twenty years. This holistic view brought hope and life to what had been a fragmented, dismembered community. The word "Palestinian," which had been taboo in Israel, was suddenly resurrected. Many Israeli Arabs no longer saw themselves as an isolated minority, but as a part of a larger Palestinian entity with dignity and inalienable rights.

Moreover, the 1967 war—which many Westerners saw bringing salvation to the Jewish people, vindicating their cause, and averting another Holocaust—exposed Israel's militarism and its expansionist policy. The war also revealed to many a vision of the plight of the Palestinian people, who had unjustifiably borne the consequences of Western anti-Semitism.

Since the inception of the State of Israel, the number of Palestinian Arabs in Israel has been growing at a phenomenal rate, with the birth rate increasing by 4 percent annually—twice that of the Jewish population and one of the highest in the world.[95] Between 1948 and 1977 the Israeli Arab population more than tripled, rising from approximately 150,000 to 574,000.[96] Of the Palestinians living in Israel, 60 percent lived in the Galilee; 20 percent in the Triangle, a cluster of Arab villages bordering the West Bank northeast of Tel Aviv; and 20 percent in urban centers (this including Bedouins in the Negev).[97] During this period the standard of living of the Israeli Arab community rose, reflecting the general economic boom in the country. Deprived for so long, many Israeli Arabs were caught up in the pursuit of wealth and possessions. Some built beautiful and expensive villas; others seized the opportunity to travel abroad. Wealth became a symbol of status, success, and authority. It tended to corrupt its possessors, especially when it was accumulated quickly. Affluence produced waste and moral decadence; it was not used for the development of the Arab community but for self-enhancement and self-aggrandizement.

During the periods of shock and resignation, the Israeli Arab work force was largely blue-collar, "hewers of wood and drawers of water." Most of those who aspired to white-collar jobs found themselves teaching in private or public schools. A relatively small number worked as clerks in various government or government-related agencies. In 1950 there were only ten Palestinian Arab students enrolled in Israeli universities. At the end of the 1950s it was easier to receive a scholarship from an American school and to travel abroad than to be accepted into one of the local universities. Most of those who left Israel made the West their permanent home. Gradually, the prospects of Israeli Arab students improved—in 1977 there were approximately twenty-one hundred, mainly at the Hebrew University in Jerusalem and the University of Haifa. Nevertheless, the number of Arab students had never exceeded 4 percent of the total university student body, while the Arab community comprised 15 percent of the country's population.[98]

At the end of the 1960s, the presence of Israeli-educated Arabs began to be felt in the community. Surprisingly, their education in Israeli universities did not make them pro-Israel; on the contrary, they became more nationalistic. These students, whose views were formed within the Jewish setting, became the most vocal exponents of justice, equality, liberty, and self-determination for the Palestinians. They were joined by a new crop of Israeli Arab university graduates returning from the Eastern European countries. Sent under the joint sponsorship of the Communist party (RAKAH) and the host countries, their program of study was well-organized and managed, and proved valuable. Unlike their counterparts who settled in the West, students had no choice but to return home once their education was completed. Doctors, lawyers, engineers, architects, teachers, accountants: together with those Palestinian Arabs educated in Israel, they formed the backbone of the nascent thinkers, organizers, and conceptualizers of the Arab community in Israel. Initially, because of a lack of channels to express their views, these professionals and university graduates turned to the Communist party, which was ready to provide an outlet for them. Many were not Communists, nor did they desire to become Communist. They aligned themselves with the Party because they felt it was the only real champion of the Palestinian people. The Party encouraged such affiliation, hoping to assimilate the Israeli Arabs into its ranks and keep them under its wing. In fact, in order to accommodate this new phenomenon, RAKAH incorporated itself under a new name, the Democratic Front for Peace and Equality. This proved a significant development for the Arab community in Israel for a few years. Gradually, however, many Arab intellectuals became disenchanted and broke with the Democratic Front. These people, together with some progressive Jews, organized themselves into the Progressive List for Peace, which first appeared in the 1984 Israeli elections, attracting approximately 18 percent of the Arab votes. Today, both the Democratic Front and the Progressive List have staunch and avid supporters, and at election time they compete strongly for Arab votes.[99] Moreover, a new Arab party has emerged, making its debut in the last Israeli election, of Nov. 1988.

Many Israeli Arabs still consider the famous Land Day of March 30, 1976, as a real watershed, when they collectively and courageously expressed their awareness of a national identity. The Israeli authorities had revealed their intention to expropriate 1.5 million *dunums* (350,000 acres) of Arab land in the Galilee and the Negev. It was clear to Israel's Arabs that this was an attempt to Judaize the Galilee, whose population was over 70 percent Arab. On March 30, 1976, a strike took place in which the whole Arab population of Israel participated; they were joined in a general strike by Palestinians in the occupied territories. Arab teenagers blockaded roads and threw stones at the Israeli soldiers. By the end of that day, seven Arabs had been killed and scores were injured on both sides.[100]

A few months later the Arab community was even more concerned when a secret memorandum written by Israel Koenig, a member of the National Religious party, the senior Arabist of the Ministry of Interior, and the district commissioner of the Galilee, was made public. Koenig's memorandum, "Handling the Arabs of Israel," identified a number of troublesome demographic, political, and economic trends within the Arab sector. In order to meet the rising tide of nationalism among the Arabs, he proposed to reduce the Arab population through such measures as giving them only 20 percent of the available jobs and limiting the number of students in the universities, restricting their choice of study, facilitating their studies abroad, and obstructing their return or employment. In essence, he advocated the adoption of "tough measures at all levels."[101]

Israel's policy makers have always disagreed on how to deal with the Arab minority in Israel. Some have advocated a relatively positive, integrative approach; others have opted for harsher and stricter methods. The fact is that since 1976 there has been an awakened consciousness among the Arabs in Israel. This can be called their "Palestinianization." They have rediscovered and revivified their roots.

This new conscientization of the Israeli Arabs steadily increased in the 1980s. Israel's invasion of South Lebanon drew Palestinians everywhere together and further raised their consciousness. In spite of some Israeli leaders' protests to the contrary, the invasion of Lebanon was Israel's Vietnam—a disaster that killed 19,000 Arabs,

most of them Palestinians, and no less than 654 Israeli soldiers.
Apart from the battle of Karameh in March 1968, when the Palestinians fought the Israelis, many people felt that the war in Lebanon
was the first war in which Palestinians actually engaged the Israeli
army. As a result, the myth of Israel's military invincibility was
shattered.

The invasion of Lebanon was the only war that Israel's leaders
had really had to justify to their own citizens and to people abroad.
The war was waged on the pretense of bringing peace to the Galilee, but its results were not easily discernible.[102] Many Israelis were
vocal in their opposition to the war. In July 1982, approximately
one hundred thousand Israelis marched through the streets of Tel
Aviv demanding the withdrawal of troops from Lebanon. Moral
questions were asked about the war, the most difficult ones raised
by the massacre of Palestinians in the Sabra and Shatila refugee
camps in September 1982. Between seven hundred and eight hundred
men, women, and children were slaughtered by Lebanese Christian
Phalangists with the full knowledge, support, and, some say, encouragement of Israel's Defense Minister, Ariel Sharon, and some
other high army officials.[103] In September 1982, an estimated four
hundred thousand Israelis again marched in Tel Aviv to protest the
massacres. The Palestinian community inside and outside Israel joined
with thousands of others to hold special memorial services at mosques
and churches. The tragedy drew attention to the gravity of the injustice suffered by all Palestinians. It accentuated the tragic dehumanization to which Israel has subjected the Palestinians and Israel's intention to push them as far away from Palestine as it can—
into oblivion, if possible. Palestinians were able to detect and feel
this and it brought them closer together.

INTIFADA: THE UPRISING

The revolt of the Palestinians on the West Bank and in Gaza in
December 1987 has completed the circle of their conscientization.
After twenty years of life under occupation and military rule, the
Palestinians began to purposefully resist the forces of occupa-
tion.

The *Intifada* began as the spontaneous reaction of an oppressed
people. Perhaps it can be compared to a volcano that finally erupted,

or to a pot that boiled over after having been on the fire for too long. The Palestinians felt that they had nothing to lose except their humiliation and oppression.

On December 6, 1987, an Israeli Jewish salesman was stabbed to death in Gaza. This was not the first stabbing of its kind; there had been similar incidents both in Gaza and the West Bank since the beginning of the occupation. Gaza, in particular, was known as a dangerous place, and Israelis were discouraged from going there. On the day of the stabbing, a curfew was imposed on a large part of Gaza as the army searched for the killer. Two days later, an Israeli Jew driving a semi-trailer at the entrance to Gaza swerved suddenly and crashed into two cars, killing four Palestinians and injuring seven others. The Palestinians believe that this was not an accident but an act of revenge. Protests erupted in the Jabaliah refugee camp in Gaza on December 8 and again on December 9, when thousands of Palestinians attended the funeral of the victims. Palestinians threw stones at Israeli soldiers, who responded with live ammunition. A seventeen-year-old boy was killed. The *Intifada* had begun.

The demonstrations, protests, and rioting that started in Gaza gradually spread throughout the West Bank. At first, the *Intifada* was lived a day at a time. Many Palestinians were not sure themselves whether it would last. The military government increased the number of its armed forces and police on the West Bank and in Gaza but the rioting did not stop.

On December 15, Ariel Sharon, now minister of industry and known for his open anti-Palestinian sentiment and extreme views, announced that he would move into a house in the Muslim quarter of the Old City of Jerusalem. Palestinians saw this as a clear act of intimidation and provocation, signaling a potential takeover of more areas of the Old City. The Palestinians of East Jerusalem reacted with commercial strikes. Sharon's provocative act was more fuel to keep the flame of the *Intifada* burning.

Stone throwing became a daily occurrence and Palestinian casualties mounted. On December 21 there was a general strike on the West Bank and in Gaza, and the Arabs in Israel joined it. By Christmas the mood of the whole people was one of pain, anger, and a clear determination to persevere. Christian celebrations in all the churches were limited and subdued. The customary congratulatory visits among the heads of the church communities during the Christmas season were canceled.

With the coming of 1988, the momentum of the *Intifada* increased and military policies became harsher in response. These included severe beatings—crushing hands to prevent stone throwing, clubbing shoulders, legs, abdomens, and heads—the use of tear gas, rubber bullets, and live ammunition; arrests, night raids on homes, detentions, sieges of refugee camps, curfews, deportations, harassment, and humiliation. The press covered the news of the *Intifada* well and the world became aware of what was going on. Gradually, the military government began to prevent newspeople from entering the areas of conflict, thus curtailing the effective reporting of the uprising. In spite of all this, the Palestinians persisted in their strikes, boycotting Israeli goods and products, throwing stones, rioting, burning tires, blocking roads, and raising the Palestinian flag. At the same time secret committees were being organized in each town and village, and an overall committee composed of the different political factions of the Palestinians was supervising events and periodically issuing guidelines and directives to the people. The *Intifada*—which means the sudden rising of a person to shake off something that has stuck—was the grassroots reaction of a people who had lived for twenty years under occupation. It was their way of shaking off occupation and crying out for their rights.

On a Friday noon in mid January 1988, as Muslim worshippers were finishing their prayers at the Al-Aksa Mosque and the Dome of the Rock (one of Islam's holiest sites), they were attacked by soldiers who beat them and used tear gas to disperse them. Many people were injured. Two days later a similar incident took place in the courtyard of the Church of the Resurrection (the Church of the Holy Sepulcher) as Christian worshipers left on Sunday morning.

On January 22, 1988, in an almost unprecedented move, the heads of the Christian communities in Jerusalem issued a statement against injustice and oppression, calling upon all Christians to pray, fast, and give generously to meet the dire need of those who were already suffering in the camps from shortages of food and supplies. By May, about two hundred people had been killed and thousands were both injured and detained, but the determination was still there to resist the force of occupation. Through the *Intifada,* the Palestinians did more for themselves than others have done for them in the last forty years. The uprising was multidimensional in its effects. It brought Palestinians hope, unity, organization, and self-respect. It dissipated fear and gave them confidence and strength. It lifted their morale and increased their determination to pursue the path of resistance through relatively nonviolent means.

Through the *Intifada,* the Palestinians were able to communicate to the world in a more emphatic way their demands: (1) an end to occupation; (2) recognition of the PLO as their sole and legitimate representative; and (3) their right to self-determination.

The Palestinians were not calling for the destruction of the State of Israel but for the creation of their own state. As one Palestinian put it, ''a people not fighting to destroy its neighbor, but a people fighting for the right to be a neighbor.'' [104]

For Israel, the uprising brought confusion into the ranks of its people and its government. It caught them by surprise. The Israeli leadership had studied the Arab mentality well; it thought it knew precisely how to deal with them and control them. The uprising shattered all these preconceptions. The long-used system of control that had proved to be so successful in the past has now, finally, failed. The Palestinians showed great unity and solidarity. The geographical segmentation imposed by Israel's policies proved inadequate to suppress their high morale. Their spiritual sense of identity transcended the physical boundaries of the West Bank and Gaza to reach far beyond, to all Palestinians living in their own diaspora.

Gone was the Arabs' total dependence on Israel's economy. Instead, a good measure of independence was achieved through people's willingness to sacrifice and rely on local products, which in turn damaged the Israeli economy. Instead of cooptation, the uprising brought a soaring spirit of nationalism, where Palestinian collaborators with Israel expressed their repentance publicly and many who had worked for the military governments on the West Bank and in Gaza submitted their resignations.

The Israeli soldier has been well-trained to fight wars, to bomb refugee camps in Lebanon, to preempt Arab strikes and acts of aggression, to surprise the ''enemy''; but the uprising introduced new factors that the soldiers were not trained for. They had to resort to beatings, tear gas, and live ammunition to defend themselves. It was not only the Palestinians who were suffering; the Israelis themselves were feeling mental and psychological stress and anguish.

The *Intifada* has also opened the eyes of the world to the real tragedy of the Palestinians. The myth of a beleaguered Israel, constantly threatened, always the victim of aggression by its neighbors, was shattered. The roles have now been reversed. In 1967, Israel was depicted as little David trying to survive against or overcome giant Goliath, the Arab states. In 1988, Israel, with its fine war machinery, resembled the giant Goliath, harassing little David, whose only weapon was the stone. The sympathy of many people throughout the world has begun to shift. Even Jews themselves—outside as well as inside Israel—have become critical of Israeli policy. To a few, Israel has become an embarrassment, perhaps even a liability.

Since 1968, there has been a gradual awakening of the Palestinian national consciousness. Within a forty-year period, Palestinian Arabs in Israel have moved from humiliation and shock to despair and resignation and on to raised consciousness and awakening. From isolation and fragmentation to entity. From a people robbed of its very identity to one that has regained it. If the establishment of the State of Israel was the antithesis of the Holocaust, then the *Intifada* of 1988 was the beginning of a process antithetical to the 1948 tragedy of Palestine. Even if the uprising is momentarily quelled, it will remain a turning point in the awakened consciousness of the Palestinians, bringing a new understanding of themselves and a new view of Israel. In fact, Palestinians have already started dating events as pre- or post-uprising. Undoubtedly, a new period in their long struggle for justice and peace has begun.

As the Palestinians stand on the threshold of this new period in their history, many questions begin to surface. How will or can Israel suppress or control the awakened Palestinian consciousness of the Israeli Arab community within the State, as well as that of the Palestinians on the West Bank and Gaza? Will the Arab leadership in Israel have the resilience to survive with a distinctively Arab Israeli identity and clear a political path for themselves within the Israeli system? Can they play a constructive role in the advancement and development of their Arab constituency in Israel? Can they be a bridge between Israel and the occupied territories, taking part in the achievement of justice and peace for their fellow Palestinians on the West Bank and in Gaza? Can the Palestinians on the West Bank and in Gaza sustain an active yet nonviolent resistance against the occupation and military rule, thus putting greater pressure on Israel? Will the awakening conscience of world Jewry exert the right kind of pressure on both the U.S. government and the State of Israel to recognize the right of the Palestinians to self-determination? Can the superpowers help bring about the desired international conference under the auspices of the U.N. in order to find the appropriate solution to the Palestine conflict?

These are only a few of the barrage of crucial questions that await answers during the coming months and years.

3

Being Palestinian and Christian in Israel

> But we have this treasure in earthern vessels, to show that the transcendent power belongs to God and not to us. We are afflicted in every way, but not crushed; perplexed, but not driven to despair; persecuted, but not forsaken; struck down, but not destroyed; always carrying in the body the death of Jesus, so that the life of Jesus may also be manifested in our bodies.
>
> 2 Corinthians 4:7–10

A FRAGMENTED BODY OF CHRIST

The Middle East is where Christianity began. Since then, both Christianity and the Middle East have seen many drastic changes. The Church has passed through excruciating times of persecution, but nowhere has the third-century Church father Tertullian's comment, "the blood of martyrs is [the] seed of the Church," been more apt than in the Middle East. Although the number of Christians multiplied in many places there, after Constantine the Church was caught in some bitter controversies that eventually left it weak and fragmented. These controversies were theological, but they were magnified by cultural and national tensions. For example, the predominantly non-Greek inhabitants of Egypt and Syria passionately resented the power of the Byzantines.

After the first four ecumenical councils of the Church (in 325, 381, 431, and 451), most of the Eastern Christians, who were mainly Semitic in background and committed either to the Nestorian or Monophysite Christological positions, separated and formed their own ecclesiastical communities. Although excluded from the mainstream of Christian orthodoxy, these Christians maintained their life of faith under their own patriarchs and carried on missionary activity outside the areas in which they were living. They comprised most of the Christian populations of Egypt, Syria, Armenia, and Persia, as well as of Ethiopia and India. Christians who remained loyal to the Orthodox faith were pejoratively referred to by their opponents as Melkites, because they retained their allegiance to the faith of the king (in Arabic, *Melek*), in this case the Byzantine emperor. The number of Melkites in the patriarchate of Alexandria was very small. Most of them lived within the area of the patriarchates of Antioch and Jerusalem.

The fragmentation of Eastern Christianity was a great blow to Christendom. Bitterness, hostility, and animosity did not end with the councils, but grew with the passage of time to drive deep and lasting wedges among the Christians of the East.

Two major factors, both political and religious in nature, contributed to sustaining and defining this Eastern schism. The first was the Arab Islamic conquest of the seventh century. Eastern Christians welcomed the Semitic Muslims as liberators freeing them from the yoke of the Byzantines. Consequently, Christians enjoyed a good measure of tolerance and prestige in the early period of Arab rule. Gradually, with successive changes in ruling dynasties, intolerance toward Christians and Jews set in. Christians began to migrate from one area to another and to congregate as their numbers were depleted through apostasy to Islam.

The second great blow to Eastern Christians were the Crusades. They affected not only the life of the Monophysites and Nestorians but the strength of the Eastern Orthodox Church. The Crusades challenged the authority and supremacy of the Greek Orthodox patriarch by establishing a Roman Catholic (Latin) patriarchate in Jerusalem that conducted vigorous missionary activity among the native Eastern Christians. Since the time of the Crusades, seven groups have entered into communion with the See of Rome, thus upsetting further the precarious life of the Eastern churches. The bodies going into "uniateship" with Rome were the Maronites, in 1180; the Chaldeans (from the Assyrians, or East Syrians), who were Nestorians and are called the Ancient Church of the East, in 1672; the Greek Catholics (Melkites), in 1724; the Catholic Armenians in 1742; the Catholic Syrians (from the Jacobites, or West Syrians), who were Monophysites, in 1783; and the Catholic Coptic Church in 1895.

More annoying than all of these to the Orthodox was the creation, in 1099, of a native Roman Catholic (Latin) Church, whose members were solicited from the Orthodox and other Eastern churches.[1]

In addition to these conflicts within the Church, which left Eastern Christians suspicious of collaboration with the West, the bitter legacy of the Crusades upset the lives of all the Christians of the East vis-à-vis their Muslim neighbors. The Crusades' heritage of distrust and suspicion would in the future inflict much undeserved suffering on the Christians of the East.

As was mentioned earlier, the first rift in Christendom occurred in the fourth and fifth centuries when a large segment of the Eastern Christians of the patriarchates of Alexandria and Antioch separated from the main body of the Church. About six hundred years later, in 1054, there was a second schism that affected the two great Sees of Constantinople and Rome, thus separating the Roman Catholic Church from the Eastern Orthodox, that is, the Latin from the Greek.[2] The next great rift took place about five hundred years later (sixteenth century) with the Protestant Reformation in western Europe, which split the Roman Catholic Church and eventually brought numerous Protestant denominations into existence.

By the nineteenth century, this last group of separated brethren did not have a foothold in the Holy Land. With the rise of the missionary movement, however, Anglicans, Lutherans, Presbyterians, and other Protestant missionaries began to converge on the Middle East and to establish new Christian denominations out of the historic churches, thus completing the picture of a fragmented body of Christ in the land from which the voice of the Gospel was first heard nineteen hundred years before. These churches, the ancient and the modern, with their centuries-old controversies, were converging not in a spirit of repentance and a search for unity, but seeking to lay claim to the spot of their spiritual origin, to the place of their roots. Their physical proximity in Jerusalem, instead of contributing to their healing, was often the cause of bitter friction.

CHRISTIAN ROOTS IN PALESTINE

The history of the Christians who live in Israel-Palestine today goes back to the first centuries of Christianity.[3] By the time of Constantine the Great, Palestine had become a mainly Christian country, with only scattered Jewish settlements and a small community of Samaritans.[4] After the Arab-Islamic conquest of Palestine in the seventh century, the Christians were gradually Arabized and eventually became a minority. This demographic fact was not changed until the 1920s, when because of the large migration of Jews into Palestine, the Jewish population exceeded that of the Christians:[5]

Population of Palestine, 1918—44

Year	Muslims	Jews	Christians
*1918	574,000	56,000	70,000
**1922	589,177	83,790	88,907
**1931	759,700	174,606	88,907
*1939	797,133	445,457	116,958
**1944	1,061,277	553,600	135,547

The creation of the State of Israel in 1948 placed the Jews on top of the demographic ladder, with Muslims and Christians trailing behind. It is significant, however, that the ratio of Christians to the Muslims who remained in Israel after 1948 was much higher than that which existed under mandated Palestine.[6] Forty percent of the Christians remained (about 30,000), as compared with only 20 percent of the Muslims (about 120,000). This is because, during the last weeks of the 1948 war, with the collapse of Arab resistance in the north, the majority of the Arabs in the Galilee (Nazareth as well as the upper Galilee), half of whom were Christians, remained behind Israeli lines.[7] The areas of Palestine that were hit the hardest by the Christian exodus were the New City of Jerusalem, Jaffa, Ramla, Lydda, and Haifa. The following table illustrates this point:[8]

*estimate
**census

The Christian Exodus from Israel

City	Population 1931		Population 1961	
	Arab	Christian	Arab	Christian
New Jerusalem	19,223	11,526	2,313	1,403
Haifa	34,560	13,827	9,468	6,663
Jaffa	44,657	9,132	5,886	2,481
Ramla	10,345	2,184	2,166	1,302
Lydda	11,250	1,210	1,582	363

Today, Israeli Arab Palestinians are divided into three main groups: Muslims comprise 70% of the total Arab population, about 600,000; Christians, 13%, or 100,000; and Druze and others, 10%, or 75,000.[9] Christians are more urbanized than the Muslims or the Druze. In 1967, the Christian population of Israel numbered about 55,000. Of this number, 85% were concentrated in the Galilee; 61% lived in towns and cities, the rest in twenty-five villages.[10] Because of a high birthrate, the number of Christians has almost doubled since 1967. The Christian population has been consistently better educated than its Muslim counterpart, owing mainly to its greater urbanization and the consequent availability of church and mission schools.

The largest Christian denomination in Israel is the Greek Catholic Church. It numbers about 45,000 Arab members, most of whom live in Haifa, Nazareth, and the Galilee. One of the Uniate churches and popularly identified as the Melkite Church, it is fully indigenous in leadership; the archbishop resides in Haifa and all of his clergy are Arab. An increasing cadre of Greek Catholic clergy are receiving a good education, including some training in France or Italy.

The Greek Orthodox Church is the second largest denomination in the country, with adherents numbering about 35,000. Although the church's membership is Arab, its hierarchy, including some of its lower-echelon clergy, is Greek (the church has long suffered from a shortage of indigenous clergy). Almost all of the Arab clergy have had little theological training; the pastoral care of congregations, especially in the villages, has suffered in consequence.

The Roman Catholic (Latin) and Maronite (a Uniate church) groups are third and fourth in size of church membership. The former, numbering twelve thousand, enjoys an influence far greater than its size might warrant because of its many institutions and religious orders long established in the land. Although most of its laity is Arab, only a small percentage of the clergy and religious are indigenous. The Roman Catholics have traditionally taken good care of their flock and have rendered a great service in the education of both Christian and Muslim Arabs. The Maronite community, found predominantly in Haifa, Nazareth, Acre, and a few Galilean villages, has its roots in the Lebanon. It numbers less than six thousand and is fully indigenous in clergy and laity.

The Episcopal (Anglican) Church has always been referred to as the "Protestant" church of the land. In Israel it numbers a little over one thousand. Like the Latin Church, the Episcopal Church has an influence disproportionate to its size because of the number of institutions it had established prior to 1948. This number has dwindled considerably since then, and so, proportionately, has the church's influence. The Episcopal Church is fully indigenous, but a number of expatriate clergy are connected with special ministries in the diocese.

There are also a few hundred Armenians and Copts, and a smaller number of free-church groups, including the Southern Baptists, Brethren, Nazarenes, Church of Christ, and others. The Baptists are the most prominent and influential of these groups.

The Christian community, although reduced by 60 percent in size after 1948, fared better than the Muslims because of its organization around bishops and clergy, whether indigenous or expatriate.[11] Most of the numerous Christian institutions were administered by expatriate clergy or religious orders, dedicated people who worked tirelessly to offer aid to thousands of Palestinian refugees—including temporary shelter and housing at a time when hardly any facilities were available—with the help of relief agencies from abroad.

The presence of an expatriate hierarchy for the Roman, Greek, and Protestant churches often prevented the expropriation of church property by Israel. Thus, the expatriates were a blessing in disguise for the Christian community, which often resented the authority of ecclesiastical colonialism and its foreign hierarchy. The Christian community, therefore, was able in those crucial first years after the establishment of the State to safeguard the integrity of a sizable portion of its property. The government's apparent unwillingness to undertake more extensive expropriation of the Church's property has been interpreted by many as the result of its reluctance to take any action that might be viewed in Europe and America as directed against Christians.[12]

One of the most intriguing stories to emerge after the war of 1948 was the attempt of a few of the remaining leaders of the Episcopal Church in Israel to sell all its property to the government, and then to be helped by Israel to relocate and resettle as a community in Brazil. Fierce debates within the Church followed, in which proponents of the scheme were accused of collaboration with the authorities, and the proposal was vehemently rejected. The conspiracy was foiled by the loyalty and patriotism of the Church's members, and the Episcopal remnant, although frustrated and depressed, remained in its land.

The Christian community in Israel lived as a part of the Arab minority, under the system of control. With no Israeli Arab political party behind which to rally, many Christians as well as Muslims found the Communist party outspoken in expressing their grievances, venting their dissatisfaction, and demanding their rights. In 1965, after a period of internal strife between its Jewish and Arab constituents, the Communist Party in Israel (MAKI) split. The Arab splinter group (RAKAH) was organized under a Christian Arab triumvirate—two Greek Orthodox and one Episcopalian—who spoke not as Christians but as Communists.[13] The Communist party was the only outlet for any Israeli Arab, whether Christian, Muslim or Druze, who felt intensely about the justice of the Palestinian cause. Admittedly, some Israeli Arabs, including Christians, voted for Jewish parties that vied for Arab votes at election time.

During most of the first two decades of Israel's existence, its Christian churches remained quiescent, opting to stay out of politics. There were three main reasons for such an attitude. First, the Church was itself a victim of the tragedy of Palestine and was greatly demoralized after the 1948 war. Second, the leadership of many of the churches at the time was foreign and did not feel as deeply about the issues as the indigenous membership. Moreover, it did not want to endanger itself or its institutions. Some church leaders also maintained amiable relations with the authorities in order to solve such practical problems for their parishioners as securing work permits and reuniting families. The third and most important reason, however, was probably the severity with which the authorities reacted to any person or group that expressed dissident views. Such repression was facilitated by the fact of military rule, the efficient system of control, and the strict censorship that prevented the outside world from easily being made aware of the situation.

THE VOICE OF THE CHURCH

It was only during the late 1960s, during the period of awakening when the Arab community developed its new consciousness, that the voice of the Church was heard. Significantly, this voice came from the strongest and most indigenous church in Israel at the time, the Greek Catholic (or Melkite) Church.

Before his consecration as archbishop of the Greek Catholic Church in Israel, Joseph Raya had been a parish priest for over fifteen years in Alabama, where he was active in the civil rights movement. The archbishop espoused the cause of two evacuated Christian villages, Iqrit and Kufur Bir'im, situated near the Lebanese border in the north. The first village was predominantly Greek Catholic; the second, exclusively Maronite. In 1948, these two villages were occupied by the Israeli army and their inhabitants were forced to evacuate their homes. The villagers were told that a battle between the Israeli forces and the Arab armies was going to take place shortly and that, because of the proximity of these villages to the border and thus to the battle zone, it would be safer for them to evacuate temporarily. The villagers were assured that after two weeks they would be permitted to return to their homes; when they were not, they appealed their case to the Israeli Supreme Court, which ruled for their return. The military, however, still insisted on preventing this repatriation. In defiance of the law, the two villages were demolished by the army, one of them bulldozed on Christmas Eve in 1951.[14]

The archbishop's choice of this case was an excellent one because it had the support of the Supreme Court. In the early 1970s, he began agitating by nonviolent means for the return of the Christian villagers to their homes. He was supported by many Arabs and Jews, and a series of strikes, sit-ins, and protests ensued in 1972. But in spite of direct representation to the Israeli government, in-

cluding Prime Minister Golda Meir, the archbishop's efforts were
to no avail. Many Christian churches throughout Israel closed in
protest, and the archbishop publicly criticized the prime minister's
refusal to act as "persecution and crucifixion of my people."[15]
Nevertheless, the villagers were not permitted to return lest a prec-
edent be established for the repatriation of other Palestinian refugees.

On July 14, 1972, one Jewish journalist wrote in the Israeli daily
Yediot Aharonot:

> It is the duty of the Israeli leaders to explain to the public
> with clarity and courage a number of facts that have been
> submerged with the passage of time. The first of these is the
> fact that there is no Zionism, settlement, or Jewish State without
> eviction of the Arabs and expropriation of their lands.[16]

And in a 1974 letter to Prime Minister Meir, the archbishop pro-
tested the treatment of Christian Arabs in Israel:

> There is not enough justice in this country. There is neither
> democracy nor liberty. No end justifies injustice whether the
> end is to be the good of the state or the nation. If you base
> security on the denial of justice, there is no accumulation of
> money which will guarantee that security; not even an army
> as strong as the Romans will ensure it.[17]

Although the archbishop was a deeply committed person, humble
and highly motivated, he lacked the shrewdness and acumen of a
political leader. Beset by criticism from within his own denomination and by pressure from the authorities, he finally had to resign
his see and leave the country.

A quieter, though more forceful, Christian voice heard in the late
1970s was that of the United Christian Council in Israel (UCCI),
which is composed of predominantly Protestant bodies. The majority of the constituency of the Council are indigenous Episcopalians
and Baptists; the rest are expatriates. Although the UCCI does not
have a strong church base inside Israel, it is respected because its
expatriate members represent a large constituency abroad.

The UCCI has spoken out on behalf of Christians in Israel in opposition to that part of the proposed constitution for the State of Israel that dealt with human rights. Since most of the leadership of the council were born and raised in Western democracies, they rendered good service to the Christian community by frequently calling attention to the subtleties, intricacies, and innuendos of the document. At the same time, the work of the council has been hampered, even neutralized, in the last few years by the oversensitivity of some of its members, who are torn between what they believe is right and their fear of alienating the State of Israel. Many of them who hold deep-seated sympathy and allegiance to Israel are afraid that their criticism might be construed as disloyalty or treason, and could jeopardize their stay in the country. Consequently, some of the indigenous members have become disenchanted with the work of the council.

A few native-born Christian clergy in Israel have been expressing their concern for justice and peace to groups inside as well as outside of Israel. Such activity at times has created a certain tension within their own congregations. Some parishioners maintain that clergy should confine their activity to the pastoral and spiritual spheres of ministry. Others argue, along with the new cadre of educated clergy, that all of life is sacramental and that there should be no distinction between the sacred and the secular. The Church, they contend, should be involved in the daily life of people in all of its dimensions. Proponents of this holistic view are those indigenous clergy—whether Greek Catholic, Roman Catholic, Maronite, Episcopal, Baptist, or other—who have had mainly Western theological training. Some of the hierarchy of their churches have not been enthusiastic about their views, fearing that the Church might be hurt by the State. The reaction of the laity, especially the younger generation, to the political situation has expressed itself in three distinct ways: emigration, politics, and religion.

Since the 1960s, an increasing number of Christians have chosen to emigrate and establish permanent homes in Western countries. Most have settled in Canada and the United States, although a smaller number have gone to Europe and as far as Australia. More Christians would emigrate if permitted by the host countries, but immigration laws have become stiffer in Canada and the United States, the two countries most popular with Christian Israeli Arabs. The reasons usually given for emigration are to escape from the pressure and stress of politics; to secure a better future for one's children; to find better and more equal opportunities for vocational, professional, or business pursuits; and, above all, to live in dignity as human beings free from the shackles of discrimination. This phenomenon of emigration has deprived the Christian community in Israel of some of its ablest minds. Indeed, an alarming number of Christians have been emigrating to the West from other countries in the Middle East as well.

THE POLITICIZATION OF THE ARABS IN ISRAEL

Not all of those who have emigrated to the West have lost interest in what is going on back home. Some have sustained their political activity, while others have become even more active, given the Western climate of democracy and freedom. Some have been able to do more for the Palestinian cause since moving to the West than before their emigration.

Many Christian young people, especially those who are university educated, have become highly politicized. They are disenchanted with the Church, which they view as peripheral and isolated from the real issues of life. During his Iqrit and Kufur Birʿim campaign, Archbishop Raya influenced a great number of these young people. His unclear vision and strategy, however, was a drawback for them. This group still looks for viable avenues of political action and for political solutions. They generally support either the Democratic Front for Peace and Equality (DFPE), of which the Communist party is the chief component, or the Progressive List for Peace (PLP).

In spite of the general politicization of the Arabs in Israel, a new phenomenon has been observed since the beginning of the 1980s. Some of the Christian young people are not aligning themselves with any party but are again looking to the Church for answers to the political dilemma, as well as for the meaning of faith today. From this group has emerged a nascent community of young Charismatics. Although concerned about the political dilemma, their emphasis has been on spirituality and the life of prayer. Moreover, even some of those who have joined the DFPE or the PLP are not expressing as much animosity or bitterness toward the Church as one observed in the 1950s and 1960s. Many of them believe that the Church should play a role in justice and peacemaking.

SPEAKING THE TRUTH WITHOUT FEAR

The Christian Church in Israel needs to reach the politically active group that stands outside its door, while continuing to minister to those who stand inside it, so that their faith can mature in a holistic view of life. In order for the Church to do this, it must itself be strong and guided by a clear vision and strategy. Although Archbishop Raya's experiment failed, it demonstrated the important role that the Church can play in issues of justice and peace, thus making the Gospel of Christ meaningful to its people. Indeed, it has become increasingly important for Church leaders in all of Israel-Palestine to speak out. Many Christians look to their Church hierarchy to take the lead. They expect them to speak the truth without fear and to stand with the oppressed and the marginalized, even if they have to suffer for it. At the same time, Church members want their clergy to interpret current events from a Christian perspective. Christian men and women tell stories, relate experiences, and ask questions. The priests and pastors are expected to reply and to advise them in light of the Gospel. They must connect them to faith in a living God who cares about people and who indeed has something to say to both the oppressor and the oppressed.

At one and the same time, the Church hierarchy in Israel-Palestine is called upon to address both its own inner Church constituency and those outside it, whether living in the country or abroad. Only by doing so will Christians in Israel-Palestine see that the Church has finally fulfilled its God-given call to being relevant and prophetic.

Some readers might wonder: Why has the indigenous Church not spoken out before? Why has the Church not taken a more active role in working for justice? Why did the Church not emerge from the Arab-Israeli conflict stronger and more resilient? As I have suggested earlier, the answer lies largely in the subtlety and complexity of the political situation. The Church was not directly attacked as a church; had that happened, the Church undoubtedly would have emerged stronger. The Church was attacked as part of a national Palestinian entity. It was itself segmented by the war, as a result of which church members either fled or were displaced. Many churches lost most of their membership; others simply closed.[18] Church members were demoralized. The conflict, indeed, was political—it had to do with the usurpation of a country, with the expropriation of land, with refugees, with the denial of the political and human rights of an entire people. The Church suffered as its people suffered, not because of their faith, but because they were Palestinians. Thus, inadvertently, the Church was caught in the midst of the political forces and became a victim itself. The State of Israel, furthermore, tried to keep the Church on the periphery of political involvement so that it could exploit the Church's quiescence as an indication of its approval of the status quo. The Church was at the same time trying to regain its strength and sustain a ministry to its people, who were in dire need.

THE CHRISTIAN ZIONISTS

The predicament of the Church in Israel-Palestine has been compounded by the apparent ignorance, lack of balance, insensitivity, and one-sidedness of many Western Christians vis-à-vis the Palestinian conflict. As early as 1960, Howard A. Johnson, canon of the Cathedral of St. John the Divine in New York, made a quick visit to Anglican churches around the world and then wrote the book *Global Odyssey*. His visit to the diocese of Jordan, Lebanon, and Syria was only a few days in duration, but he wrote about the Church as if he were able to grasp the intricacies of its life and problems. He did not express a word of comfort or encouragement to the Church; on the contrary, his analysis was harsh and mostly erroneous. It certainly did not reflect the concern of a brother in Christ for a sister church of the Anglican communion. His criticisms of the indigenous Episcopal Church betrayed his greater sympathy for Israel, which he had visited in 1957 "as a guest of the government, at which time I was shown everything from Dan to Beersheba."[19] One telling example should suffice to show how he irresponsibly mixed theology with politics. Johnson attacked the Arabic edition of the revised *Book of Common Prayer* to expose a scandalous action by Arab Episcopalians. He must have thought that he was revealing to the whole world the underhanded way in which they reduced the number of Psalms in the prayer book from 150 to 100:

> I have no quarrel with that per se. In public worship fifty of them might well go out. But my curiosity was instantly aroused. What was the principle of selection? By what criterion did some go out and some stay in? I was not long in discovering. Deleted was every Psalm mentioning Israel![20]

On closer investigation, however, out of the one hundred Psalms that were retained in the Psalter, fifteen do mention Israel.[21] What is even more significant is that, of the fifty Psalms that were deleted, thirty do not mention Israel at all.[22] In light of the precarious life of Palestinian Christians in the Middle East, such erroneous statements only make the work of the Church more difficult.

Another example of the one-sidedness and naiveté with which the political situation is treated can be found in Paul van Buren's *Discerning the Way,* the prolegomenon of a projected four-volume "Theology of the Jewish-Christian Reality." In *Discerning the Way,* van Buren uses the term "Israel" so loosely that he does not distinguish between biblical Israel and the modern State of Israel. In one place he refers to God as fighting against the Arabs on the side of the Jews in 1948 as in the time of Joshua. In fact, modern Israel is, for him, the direct continuation of biblical Israel—he does not question the differences. Moreover, he writes without a hint of the complexities of the political dilemma and the possibility of injustice. By implication, he not only disassociates Israel from any injustices, but also gives it God's approval and blessing. Such actions might be expected from a rabid literalist, but seem very strange coming from a person like van Buren. In fact, he considers those Jews who acted in creating the State of Israel as themselves carrying out the act of God.

> If the Holocaust is a negative revelation of God's requirement of human responsibility, the founding of the state of Israel says the same thing in a positive form. Israel was founded not by divine intervention from heaven or the sending of the messiah, but by Jewish guns and Jewish effort against seemingly insuperable numerical and material odds. Had the early

pioneers, the fugitives from the Holocaust or the supporters of the project from the Diaspora waited upon a so-called act of God instead of daring to be the act of God, they would in all likelihood be waiting still, those who were still alive. This event which has begun to reorient the Church, this event of the founding of Israel and Jewish return to the Land, was one of humanly assumed responsibility for history, yes, for God's history with His people and their history with Him.

Although he states that for most Orthodox Jews the creation of the State of Israel seemed a departure from their tradition, van Buren goes on to say that

almost all Jews have come to accept the rightness of this Jewish effort to move the history of God with His people a step closer to the realization of God's promises. God's promises, we could say, have become increasingly seen to be promises of what shall be, but not promises of what God alone will do to bring about that which He has promised.[23]

Such naiveté betrays a real misunderstanding of God and of history. Does God act in a vacuum with Israel, as if there were no nations living around it? Does God act with total disregard for morality? About which God is van Buren writing? It appears at times that he has returned to the idea of a tribal God! Does God not care about injustice, the oppressed, and the vulnerable in society? Such questions appear to have relevance for van Buren if they are related to the existence of Jews who have been afflicted with great suffering, but not if they relate to those who have suffered at the hands of the Jewish people. This stance is paradoxically in contrast to van Buren's comments on Israel's injustices (presumably before the Exile): "injustice in Israel polluted the land, which would then 'vomit it forth.' "[24] It is ironic that van Buren is quicker to recognize ancient Israel's injustices of twenty-five hundred years ago than to perceive the State of Israel's injustices in his own day. A theology that does not grapple with present realities in their many dimensions and complexities will inevitably be condemned as too simplistic and irresponsible.[25]

As a Christian and as a Palestinian, it is difficult for me to read the second volume of van Buren's theology.[26] One feels that here is a Christian who has been entrapped by his own ideas. He seems to have an obsession with Israel as the sin and substance of the Jewish people. For him, to be critical of Zionism is to be anti-Jewish. "To be against Zion is to be against Israel. It was so in biblical times and it is so now."[27]

AN OMEN OF HATE

Another formidable group that has become loudly supportive of the State of Israel are the so-called Christian fundamentalists, one of whose leaders is Jerry Falwell, founder of the Moral Majority. These fundamentalists believe in the inerrancy of the Bible, and so their approach to it is very literalistic. They claim that "the strength of Christian Zionism is that it is based on confessional faith in God and His Word," that "Christian Zionism is only one aspect of following Jesus," and that "Christianity is by biblical nature 'Zionist.' "[28] This type of Christian Zionism has found expression since the early 1980s in the International Christian Embassy in Jerusalem, which is dedicated to the support of the State of Israel. Its total and unequivocal support blinds it to flagrant violations of Palestinians' human rights in the immoral and unjust practices of the State against the Palestinians. When a visitor asked one of the top leaders of the "embassy" to comment on the Israeli army's killings of many innocent Palestinians in the West Bank and on Gaza during the first few months of the *Intifada* of 1988, the very cold and matter-of-fact reply was that they would begin to comment when six million Palestinians had been killed. One is inclined to dismiss these insidious words as a slip of the tongue; otherwise, they would have to be judged as the utterings of an insane and irresponsible person who has not experienced the knowledge or the love of God—an omen of hate.

Fundamentalists see the creation of the State of Israel as the fulfillment of their eschatological hope for the future. It fits into their concept of the end of times and the Second Coming of Christ. Prophecy holds undue prominence in their belief and thinking, giving the impression that even God is entrapped in the prophetic utterings of the Bible, bound by them, unable to change or move away from what has already been decreed. Events must happen precisely as recorded—and as interpreted by the fundamentalists. Consequently, elaborate and fantastic schemes are predicted for the end of history.[29]

To the fundamentalists, God operates in bringing justice to the Jews. There is no justice here for the Palestinians; they must resign themselves to accept God's plan for history. The blatant injustice which Palestinians may feel is dismissed, justified as the hidden, inscrutable wisdom and mystery of the purpose of God. Some in the State of Israel may consider the fundamentalists useful friends politically, financially, and psychologically, but those who know something about their beliefs often abhor and reject them. Part of their biblical understanding of the last events in history is the annihilation of two-thirds of the Jewish people and the Christianization of those remaining.

Israel has been quick to exploit the support of van Buren, his like-minded colleagues, and the fundamentalists to its advantage. Many Muslims who do not differentiate between one brand of Christianity and another confuse Christian Zionism with the doctrines of the mainline Church, which further complicates the precarious position of Palestinian Christians.

A NEW GUILT

The theological naiveté of the fundamentalists is, happily, balanced by a few daring individuals and groups willing to speak out on behalf of justice and truth. In an address to the June 1981 Consultation of the Church and the Jewish People of the World Council of Churches in London, Krister Stendahl, chairman of the consultation at the time and former dean of Harvard Divinity School, reviewed the Christian-Jewish work of this century and the deeply guilt-ridden reaction of Christians to the Jews after 1940:

> I have increasingly the feeling as an observer of history that anything that human beings do out of guilt will not last and will come to haunt them and others at a later point. We did not really ask, neither theologically [nor] in other terms, the question that we should have asked, the healthier question: What is *right?* . . . Our guilt is enormous, but if one does

not go from that question on to the question about what is right, the action will not last, and the backlash will be severe. There is a lot of that backlash in the churches these days, partly in the form of a new guilt—the guilt for not having felt guilty sufficiently in relation to the Palestinians. There is the vicious circle of guilt out of which nothing lastingly good comes—not forgiveness, not renewal, not the seeking of rightness.[30]

Here was a Christian scholar, who had been active in Jewish-Christian dialogue for many years, showing the courage and integrity as a responsible Christian to expose the problem in its wholeness and complexity.

Another sobering word comes from Kenneth Cragg, an Anglican scholar who has looked at the concept of "chosenness" (the Jews as the chosen people of God) and the way it has been utterly abused by many pro-Israel Christians:

> The due Christian sense of being "children of Abraham" has critical duties in and with the State of Israel and that State's moral obligation to the Arab pain and cost of its creation. We must not be diverted by consideration of our biblical involvement in Jewry from the sure and steady assertion of there being in Christ "neither Jew nor Greek." For only in the strength of that final irrelevance of the distinction can we return rightly to its relative validity. "Male and female . . . Jew and Greek," the distinctions, indeed, persist. But we only have them rightly when we refuse to allow that the differences matter. And this works both ways. It commands our ultimate compassion; but it justifies no "chosennesses" to override moral realities.[31]

Such words are refreshing, indeed, since they are not pronounced in a spirit of prejudice or partisanship but express a mature and balanced reflection on pertinent issues—reflections that allow the mind of Christ to bear on the agonizing and complex situation of the Palestinian conflict.

BEYOND ZIONIST THEOLOGY:
TOWARD A JEWISH THEOLOGY OF LIBERATION

Similar reflections have been coming from another eminent theologian, Rosemary Radford Ruether, who in the past has shown the courage to expose the Christian roots of anti-Semitism.[32] Her work has been hailed as a "theological path-breaker, setting a whole new agenda for Christian theology for the next several decades."[33] *Faith and Fratricide* gained her great respect among the Jewish community as well. Ruether has shown equal courage by calling attention to the injustices of the State of Israel against the Palestinians. One of her many articles on this subject pointed to the Israeli confiscation of Arab land in order to build Jewish settlements on the West Bank:

> These stories of Palestinian farmers could be duplicated hundreds of times. The Arab Information Agency in East Jerusalem estimates that more than 500 Arab villages have been destroyed and their lands taken since 1948. . . . For many Americans, the problem of "peace in the Middle East" is seen primarily as a problem of "terrorists" and of the refusal of Arabs to live peacefully with Israel. The hidden story of Palestinian farmers presents a different perspective, of an Israel that does not wish to live in the same land with its Arab neighbors and that has steadily deprived villagers of their houses and lands."[34]

In another article, Ruether exposes the historical myths about an Israel often perceived as small and embattled. She maintains that Israel has systematically expanded its territory and has always been stronger than its Arab neighbors—the same Israel that continuously resists accepting the political rights of the Palestinians. She calls attention to the Israeli use of a form of cyanide tear gas that has caused the deaths of adults and infants during the Uprising of 1988. "The use of this gas constitutes a form of chemical warfare against the entire population. The gas was shipped to Israel from the United States in canisters dated 1988."[35]

Moreover, Ruether has been able to see through the facade of van Buren's Zionist theology. In reviewing his second volume of "A Theology of the Jewish Reality," she said that van Buren is "excessively preachy and self-righteous when addressing us 'gentiles,' who he is even exhorting to learn from the Jews how we might overcome our spiritual stupidity and hardness of heart. One has the uncomfortable feeling of reading an anti-Semite turned inside out." As to the way van Buren treats the Arabs and the Palestinians in his book, Ruether concludes that they are "hardly referred to at all, and when they are, it is only in the most hostile and contemptuous tones. They are regarded en masse as a people filled with baseless hatred against God's Beloved, the Jewish people, and the Jewish state."[36]

Similar courage has been exhibited by some churches, councils of churches, and other organizations that have produced position statements about the Arab-Israeli conflict. These documents, while not anti-Israel, have called attention to the possibility of peace in the Middle East. Although recognizing Israel's right to exist, they insist on the need to do justice to the Palestinians and give them their right to self-determination.[37]

It is not proper to end this discussion without calling attention to the voices of courageous Jews who have dared to speak out at the expense of being alienated from their own community. In his book *Toward a Jewish Theology of Liberation,* Marc Ellis discusses the life of the Jewish community between Holocaust and empowerment. The Holocaust represents tragedy and worthlessness, while Israel represents empowerment and redemption. He believes that with empowerment, the ethical side of Judaism has suffered. Holocaust theologians have redefined the notion of a practicing Jew from one who engages in ritual and observance of the Law to one who cherishes memory, survival, and empowerment. For Ellis this redefinition is not enough. As part of a Jewish theology of liberation he adds to that definition "a critical and efficacious pursuit of justice and peace."[38] On the Palestinian issue, Ellis is very clear:

> An ever-growing displaced Palestinian people challenges the integrity of the State of Israel. The desire to remain a victim is evidence of disease; yet to become a conqueror after having been a victim is a recipe for moral suicide. It is not too much to claim that the acquired values of the Jewish people, dis-

covered and hammered out over a history of suffering and struggle, are in danger of dissipation. In our liberation, our memory of slavery is in danger of being lost. This loss would allow us to forget what it means to be oppressed. Yet to forget one's own oppression is to open the possibility of becoming the oppressor.[39]

On another note, Ellis believes that a Jewish theology of liberation should continue to confront the issue of anti-Semitism, but he insists that it should not be used as a weapon to silence honest criticism.

The slogan "Never Again" too often becomes the rationale for refusing to trust and to risk. It also blinds us to the fact that we have fostered an anti-Semitism of our own by our treatment of the Palestinian and Arab peoples, who are, after all, Semitic people. It might just be that the real anti-Semitism of the day is found neither in the United Nations nor in the Jewish critique of Israel, but in the Jewish community, where images of the unwashed, the ignorant and the terrorist are repeated *ad nauseam*. And if the Palestinian people's refusal to accept occupation on the West Bank and Gaza is somehow seen as anti-Semitic, could we also say that Israel's refusal to recognize and negotiate with the Palestine Liberation Organization is equally anti-Semitic?[40]

And Ellis recognizes that a Jewish theology of liberation affirms empowerment, provided that it allows the empowerment of others:

The counterpart to Israel as an autonomous presence is Palestine, and a Jewish theology of liberation begins to speak of Israel and Palestine together. That Israel is a state has less to do with religious principles than with national organization of the modern world. The Palestinian people likewise deserve a state, and Israel ought to participate in its rebirth through recognition and material help if the Palestinians request it. A Jewish theology of liberation is unequivocal in this regard: the Palestinian people have been deeply wronged in the creation of Israel and in the occupation of territories. As we celebrate our empowerment, we must repent our transgressions and stop them immediately. If this is done today, perhaps a hundred years from now we can speak of a confederation of Israel and Palestine and how out of a tragic conflict a healing took place to the benefit of both communities.[41]

Another voice that Ellis cites is that of Roberta Strauss Feuerlicht, who considers the creation of the State of Israel a tragedy for the Jewish people, who, "having given the world the ethical imperative as well as the concept of an ideal state, created a state that seems neither ethical nor idealistic."[42] Feuerlicht states clearly that "the Zionists chose to create a state by superseding the indigenous population and culture of Palestine."[43] She describes in great detail the discrimination against the Sephardic Jews in Israel, as well as the injustices done to the Palestinians. She does not believe that Israel helped solve the problem of anti-Semitism. On the contrary, "Israel has become part of the problem, not the solution."[44] In her insistence on the ethical strength of Judaism, she concludes that Israel is not the Messiah for the Jews. Although created as a haven, it has turned on them, "corrupting and destroying them by its very success at making them a nation like all others." Then, in one of the superb observations that Ellis also quotes in his book, she says, "Judaism as an ideal is infinite; Judaism as a state is finite. Judaism survived centuries of persecution without a state; it must now learn how to survive despite a state."[45]

A NEW AGENDA FOR THE CHURCH
IN ISRAEL-PALESTINE

Attention should be given to these daring individuals whose understanding of ethical Judaism transcends any political allegiance. They (as well as such Western Christians as Krister Stendahl) are only prominent examples of those who, on the basis of their faith and knowledge of God, have taken a stand for justice. Although one feels grateful for their honesty and integrity, it is time for the voice of the indigenous Church of Israel-Palestine to be heard. The Church is, therefore, called to contextualize its faith and theology and address itself to those crucial issues that face it. The meaning of this contextualization is best expressed by Shoki Coe:

Contextuality, therefore, . . . is that critical assessment of what makes the context really significant in the light of the Missio Dei. It is the missiological discernment of the signs of the times, seeing where God is at work and calling us to participate in it. Thus, contextuality is more than just taking all contexts seriously but indiscriminately. It is conscientization of the contexts in the particular, historical moment, assessing the particularity of the context in the light of the mission of the Church as it is called to participate in the Missio Dei.[46]

Contextualization is, therefore, an ongoing process for the living Church as it moves through the rapid changes of time. It involves constant decontextualization and recontextualization, especially in a situation as volatile and war-torn as that of the Middle East.

Measured by this meaning and responsibility of contextualization, the Church in Israel-Palestine has hardly begun to contextualize. It must accept the political context as its challenge for a viable ministry to its own people, as well as to all others around it, including Jews and Muslims, and as its challenge to address that situation prophetically.

The prominent African theologian John Mbiti, reflecting on the Church in his homeland, said that "the Church in Africa is a Church without a theology and a Church without theological concerns."[47] The Church in Israel-Palestine may not as yet have a theology of its own to meet its contextual needs, but it certainly has deep theological concerns. In fact, the contextual concerns of the Church, although predominantly political in appearance, are deeply and ultimately theological in nature. These needs are perpetually frustrated by the increasing complexity of the political conflict.

Christians believe that the Incarnation is the divine form of contextualization. The duty of the Church in Israel-Palestine today is to take its own concrete and local context seriously. As Jesus recognized that his agenda included the preaching of the good news to the poor, the proclamation of release to the captives, the recovering of sight by the blind, the setting at liberty of those who are oppressed, and the proclamation of the acceptable year of the Lord, so should the Church.[48] It needs to incarnate itself in its context so that it can be the voice of the oppressed and the dehumanized. One is reminded of Frances Perkins (1882–1965), who tried in her own career to bring a Christian witness to bear on public policy. Perkins expressed her views on the role of the Church in the following way:

> The Church informs the conscience of the people; presents the moral implications of [their] choice; stimulates the strong defense of the dignity and with it the liberty and responsibility of the individual man in the course of collective action. The Church continues to present to the state the moral principles of restraint; of human rather than material consideration in its action; of respect for individual rights and differences and a sense that "the earth is the Lord's and the fullness thereof," and that officers of government are stewards.[49]

It is in this spirit that I have embarked on a Palestinian theology of liberation. I believe that the Church in Israel-Palestine has a unique role to play: to probe in depth the meaning of justice as it can be understood both biblically and theologically. To pursue peace with justice is the Church's highest calling in Israel-Palestine today, as well as its greatest challenge.

4

The Bible and Liberation:
A Palestinian Perspective

> The Spirit of the Lord is upon me, because he has
> anointed me to preach good news to the poor. He
> has sent me to proclaim release to the captives
> and recovering of sight to the blind, to set at lib-
> erty those who are oppressed, to proclaim the ac-
> ceptable year of the Lord.
>
> Luke 4:18–19

The purpose of this chapter is to explicate the major thrust of a
Palestinian theology of liberation. Since nothing of its kind has been
done before, I will attempt to lay the cornerstone for such a theology. It will not exhaust the subject; but I will try to raise the main
theological issues as I have come to see them as a Palestinian
Christian through my interaction with parishioners, colleagues, and
other Christians during the last twenty years of my ministry.

THE TWO MAJOR ISSUES

The first major issue, which stands above all others and lies at
the heart of the Palestinian problem, is justice. Since 1948 and the
creation of the State of Israel, Palestinians everywhere have been
talking about the injustice done to them—to young and old, educated and uneducated, rich and poor, male and female, religious

and secular, Muslim and Christian—all talk about the problem of justice. All of them remember what happened in 1948 and 1967, and they relate both the story of the loss of Palestine and their own stories of personal loss.

I have heard some Jews in Israel say that there is a great difference between the Palestinian and the Jewish claim to the land. The Palestinian's concern is focused on the loss of his house, his home, his business, and maybe his village. Injustice to him has to do with the fact that he was deprived of his own private property. The Jew's concern is said to be with the whole of the land, not with a particular spot.

My experience shows that such a distinction is a specious attempt on the part of some Jews to give a greater weight to their claim, a rationalization that only the ignorant or the prejudiced would accept. When Palestinians talk about injustice, they are talking about the tragedy of Palestine. When they tell their own story, it is told in order to illustrate vividly and to substantiate the extent of the injustice and the dehumanization to which the people of Palestine have been subjected; when Jews do not tell personal stories of how they lost their homes or villages in Palestine, it is because they did not have them.

Any theology of liberation must of necessity address the issue of justice. It is, after all, the major issue for Palestinians regardless of their religious affiliation.

For Palestinian Christians there is a second major issue that needs to be tackled in a theology of liberation: the Bible. The Bible is usually viewed as a source of strength, offering solutions and leading people to faith and salvation. Strangely—shockingly—however, the Bible has been used by some Western Christians and Jews in a way that has supported *in*justice rather than justice. Liberation theologians have seen the Bible as a dynamic source for their understanding of liberation, but if some parts of it are applied literally to our situation today the Bible appears to offer to the Palestinians slavery rather than freedom, injustice rather than justice, and death to their national and political life. Many good-hearted Christians have been confused or misled by certain biblical words and images that are normally used in public worship; words that have acquired new connotations since the establishment of the State of Israel. For example, when Christians recite the *Benedictus*, with its opening lines "Blessed be the Lord God of Israel, for he has visited and redeemed his people," [1] what does it mean for them today? Which Israel are they thinking of? What redemption? The eminent historian Arnold J. Toynbee comments:

Within my lifetime the mental associations of the name "Israel" have changed for those religious communities, the Jews and the Christians, in whose liturgies this name so often recurs. When, as a child, I used to take part, in church, in the singing of the Psalms, the name "Israel" did not signify, for me, any existing state on the face of the globe. No state of that name was in existence then. Neither did the name signify the ancient Kingdom of Israel that was liquidated in 722 B.C. by the Assyrians. The history of Ancient Israel was familiar to me. But the name, when I recited it in the liturgy, meant a religious community of devout worshippers of Ancient Israel's God—the One True God in the belief of present-day Jews, Christians, and Muslims. "Israel" signified "God's people," and we worshippers of God were living members of Israel, but members only conditionally. Our membership was conditional on our obeying God's commands and following His precepts as these had been declared by Him through the mouths of His Prophets.

This traditional spiritual connotation of the name "Israel" has been supplanted today by a political and military connotation. Today, if I go to church and try to join in the singing of the Psalms, I am pulled up short, with a jar, when the name "Israel" comes on to my lips. The name conjures up today a picture of a small, middle-Europe type state, with bickering political parties like all such states, with a rigid— and unsuccessful—foreign policy with respect to its neighbours and with constant appeal to the Jews of the world either to send them money or to come themselves. This picture has now effaced that one in our minds. It has effaced it, whoever we are: Jews or Christians, diaspora Jews or Israelis, believers or agnostics. The present-day political Israel has, for all of us, obliterated or, at least, adumbrated, the spiritual Israel of the Judeo-Christian tradition. This is surely a tragedy. [2]

If this has been true among Western Christians, it has been more painfully true of Palestinian and other Christians in the Middle East. The establishment of the State of Israel was a seismic tremor of enormous magnitude that has shaken the very foundation of their beliefs.[3] Since then, no Palestinian Christian theology can avoid tackling the issue of the Bible: How can the Bible, which has apparently become a part of the problem in the Arab-Israeli conflict, become a part of its solution? How can the Bible, which has been used to bring a curse to the national aspirations of a whole people, again offer them a blessing? How can the Bible, through which many have been led to salvation, be itself saved and redeemed?

These two concerns—justice and the Bible—will occupy most of our attention. Most of the other issues for a theology of liberation for Palestinian Christians, as we shall see, are derived from them. In fact, the two issues are very much interrelated. I will treat them in reverse order, beginning with the issue of the Bible; then in the next chapter, move to the issue of justice; and finally, consider the victims of injustice and the challenges that face them.

THE BIBLE: PROBLEM OR SOLUTION?

The Political Abuse of the Bible

For most Palestinian Christians, as for many other Arab Christians, their view of the Bible, especially the Hebrew Scriptures, or Old Testament,[4] has been adversely affected by the creation of the State of Israel. Many previously hidden problems suddenly surfaced. The God of the Bible, hitherto the God who saves and liberates, has come to be viewed by Palestinians as partial and discriminating. Before the creation of the State, the Old Testament was considered to be an essential part of Christian Scripture, pointing and witnessing to Jesus. Since the creation of the State, some Jewish and Christian interpreters have read the Old Testament largely as a Zionist text to such an extent that it has become almost repugnant to Palestinian Christians. As a result, the Old Testament has generally fallen into disuse among both clergy and laity, and the Church has been unable to come to terms with its ambiguities, questions, and paradoxes—especially with its direct application to the twentieth-century events in Palestine. The fundamental question

of many Christians, whether uttered or not, is: How can the Old
Testament be the Word of God in light of the Palestinian Christians' experience with its use to support Zionism?

Closely involved in the question of the Hebrew Scriptures is our
concept of God. With the exception of relatively few people within
the Christian communities in the Middle East, the existence of God
is not in doubt. What has been seriously questioned is the nature
and character of God. What is God really like? What is God's relation to the new State of Israel? Is God partial only to the Jews?
Is this a God of justice and peace? Such questions may appear on
the surface trite and their answers obvious. Nevertheless, they are
part of a battery of questions that many Christians, both in Israel-
Palestine and outside of it, are still debating. The focus of these
questions is the very person of God. God's character is at stake.
God's integrity has been questioned.

Generally speaking, the Church in Israel-Palestine has stood im-
potent and helpless before these questions. It is no wonder then that
there is widespread apathy among many Christians toward the Church.
The pervasive and crucial question for its leadership has been, and
still is: How can the Church, without rejecting any part of the Bible, adequately relate the core of the biblical message—its concept
of God—to Palestinians? The answer lies largely in the doing of
theology. The only bridge between the Bible and people is theology. It must be a theology that is biblically sound; a theology that
liberates; a theology that will contextualize and interpret while remaining faithful to the heart of the biblical message. Unless such a
theology is achieved, the human tendency will be to ignore and
neglect the undesired parts of the Bible.

Some Christians, clergy included, have found a way to deal with
the text through allegorization. Others use what I call spiritualiza-
tion. Although these and other methods can be helpful, they do not
meet the challenge of the political abuse of the Bible. One ob-
serves, too, that especially in this century in the West, biblical
scholarship has made real strides in the application of critical methods to the study of the Bible. These scientific tools can clarify many
ambiguities and help the student to get as close as possible to the
original text—its author, date, source, context, and so on. Unless
these methods are guided and informed by a larger theological un-

derstanding, however, they tend to leave the text dissected and to confuse rather than clarify matters of faith.

Generally speaking, all these methods do not throw light on whether or not the text is the Word of *God*. For Palestinian Christians, the core question that takes priority over all others is whether what is being read in the Bible is the Word of *God* to them and whether it reflects the nature, will, and purpose of *God* for them. In other words, is what is being read an authentic insight from God about who God is? Is it an authentic insight from God about persons or relationships or about human nature and history? Conversely, is what is being heard a reflection of authentic human understanding about God at that stage of development? Is it an authentic statement of humans about other human beings or about human nature at that stage of development? Or, to put it bluntly, is it basically a statement from humans put into the mouth of God, that has become confused as an authentic message from God to people? Do the words reflect an authentic and valid message from God to us today? What is eternally true in the Bible and what is conditioned? What is lasting and what is temporal? These are important questions for Palestinian Christians, whose answers will ultimately determine what God is or is not saying to them in the Bible.

The Central Biblical Hermeneutic

Palestinian Christians are looking for a hermeneutic[5] that will help them to identify the authentic Word of *God* in the Bible and to discern the true meaning of those biblical texts that Jewish Zionists and Christian fundamentalists cite to substantiate their subjective claims and prejudices.

The criterion that Palestinians are looking for must be both biblically and theologically sound, lest it in turn become a mere instrument to oppose Jewish and Christian Zionists and support subjective Palestinian claims and prejudices. The hermeneutic must ring true of a God whom we have come to know—unchanging in nature and character, dynamically constant rather than fickle and variable, responding to but not conditioned by time, space, or circumstances.

The canon of this hermeneutic for the Palestinian Christian is nothing less than Jesus Christ himself. For in Christ and through

Christ and because of Christ Christians have been given a revealed insight into God's nature and character. For the Christian, to talk about the knowledge of God is to talk about knowing God through Christ: this is the best source of the knowledge of God; this is the concept of God that has matured through the period of biblical history. For the Christian, it has found its fulfillment in Jesus Christ's understanding of the nature and character of God. This understanding of God was vindicated for us in the life, death, and resurrection of Jesus, whom we acclaim as the Christ, God incarnate. Jesus the Christ thus becomes—in himself and in his teaching—the true hermeneutic, the key to the understanding of the Bible, and beyond the Bible to the understanding of the action of God throughout history. In other words, the *Word* of God incarnate in Jesus the Christ interprets for us the *word* of God in the Bible.

To understand God, therefore, the Palestinian Christian, like every other Christian, begins with Christ and goes backward to the Old Testament and forward to the New Testament and beyond them. This becomes the major premise for the Christian.

Due to the human predicament of evil, however, one discovers that the use of this hermeneutic does not mean that all of our theological problems are solved automatically; but one can discover that the new hermeneutic (which after all is not new at all in the Church) is really liberating. The Bible for Palestinian Christians, then, can be retained in its entirety, while its contents would be judged by this hermeneutic and scrutinized by the mind of Christ.

To let the mind of Christ bear on situations and events is very important theologically. As C. H. Dodd explains:

Perhaps one of the most striking features of the early Christian movement was the re-appearance of a confidence that man can know God immediately. . . . Jesus Christ, with a confidence that to the timid traditionalism of His time appeared blasphemous, asserted that He knew the Father and was prepared to let others into that knowledge. He did so, not by handing down a new tradition about God, but by making others sharers in His own attitude to God. This is what Paul means by "having the mind of Christ." Having that mind, we do know God. It was this clear, unquestioning conviction that gave Paul his power as a missionary: but he expected it also in his converts. To them, too, "the word of knowledge" came "by the same Spirit." He prayed that God would give them a spirit of wisdom and revelation in the knowledge of Him. Such knowledge is, as Paul freely grants, only partial, but it is real, personal, undeniable knowledge. In friendship between men there is a mutual knowledge which is never complete or free from mystery: yet you can know with a certainty nothing could shake that your friend is "not the man to do such a thing," or that such and such a thing that you have heard is "just like him." You have a real knowledge which gives you a criterion. Such is the knowledge the Christian has of his Father.[6]

This criterion gives Christians great confidence, and informs their approach to the various problems that they encounter.

Some Practical Applications

The use of this "new" hermeneutic is accessible to all Christians, even to the simple of faith. It requires, however, a knowledge of the biblical records and demands the use of human reason—a reason that has been enlightened by the revelation of God in Christ. For humans have the capacity to grasp an understanding of God as it has developed and matured in biblical history through seemingly simple and unsophisticated stories, poetry, and historical events.[7] They can perceive the way God revealed himself to the men and women of the Old Testament, in spite of their human limitations, in light of the ultimate revelation in the Incarnation.

The constant application of this hermeneutic, therefore, is the best key for Christians to interpreting and understanding the biblical message. Furthermore, this theological understanding can determine the validity and authority of the Scriptures for the life of the Christian. It is grounded in the knowledge and love of God as revealed in the life, death, and resurrection of Jesus Christ. The revelation of God, God's nature, purpose, and will as revealed in Christ, becomes the criterion by which Christians can measure the validity and authority of the biblical message for their life.

When confronted with a difficult passage in the Bible or with a perplexing contemporary event one needs to ask such simple questions as: Is the way I am hearing this the way I have come to know God in Christ? Does this fit the picture I have of God that Jesus has revealed to me? Does it match the character of the God whom I have come to know through Christ? If it does, then that passage is valid and authoritative. If not, then I cannot accept its validity or authority.

This puts us in a quandary: Is all knowledge of God subjective? Does it not become an arbitrary matter of judgment depending on the prejudices of the individual? The danger is always there. But the risk is reduced if we faithfully allow ourselves to be enlightened by the New Testament's picture of God in Christ. Here there is for the Christian an objective knowledge which one cannot deny, in spite of certain human limitations. So, we do not approach the text with total subjectivity. The text of the New Testament provides us with a view of God—God's nature, character, and will. The subjective and the objective meet, and, guided by the Holy Spirit, we can let the mind of Christ bear on concrete events in history or concrete texts in the Bible; we can conclude whether God is pleased or displeased with such and such a thing by asking whether it does or does not fit God's character as we have come to know it in Christ. Liberation comes through the application and use of this hermeneutical key. Biblical texts and contemporary events or crises become an occasion for hearing and communicating the Word of God today. We do not need to force a text to yield a favorable explanation or to speak in such a way as to legitimate our own ideology or prejudice; we are free to open ourselves to hearing what God in Christ has to say to us through that text today.

It is possible to simplify this even further. So often Palestinian Christians are confronted with difficult existential situations: they are frustrated; they feel despair; they feel that God is against them. But the use of this hermeneutical key can help them understand how God is active in their situation and how God is speaking to them.

Things become clearer when we apply this hermeneutic to specific biblical texts. There are certain passages in the Old Testament whose theological presuppositions and even assertions need not be affirmed by the Christian today, because they reflect an early stage of human understanding of God's revelation that conflicts with the Christian's understanding of God as revealed in Jesus Christ. Although these passages need not impose particular doctrinal views or obligations on the contemporary Christian, they remain valuable pedagogically. Their value lies partially in their negative aspect: they clarify what God is not, as much as what God is. They offer the Christian a picture of God that contradicts the way God has come to be understood and known through Jesus Christ. Viewed from this perspective, the whole Bible is valuable, but not all of its parts have the same value and authority.[8] Every part of the Bible that brings people to an understanding of God's self-revelation in Christ has both authority and validity for the Christian. The Bible, therefore, remains the Word of God, "profitable for teaching, for reproof, for correction, and for training in righteousness"[9]; but it is continuously submitted to an authoritative concept, that is, the revelation of God in Christ.

To illustrate this point, one can look at the story of the fall of Jericho (Joshua, chapter 6), which includes God's injunction to "utterly destroy all in the city, both men and women, young and old, oxen, sheep, and asses, with the edge of the sword."[10] To this should be added the previous declaration of Joshua to the children of Israel, "The city and all that is within it shall be devoted to the Lord for destruction."[11] Is such a passage, which is attributed to God, consistent with how God is revealed in Jesus Christ? If not, we must say that it only reveals a human understanding of God's nature and purpose that was superseded or corrected by the revelation in Christ. In other words, such passages are revelatory of a stage of development of the human understanding of God that we must regard, in light of Christ's revelation, as inadequate and incomplete.

Another vivid illustration could be cited from the life of Elisha:

> He [Elisha] went up from there to Bethel; and while he was going up on the way, some small boys came out of the city and jeered at him, saying, "Go up, you baldhead!" And he turned around, and when he saw them, he cursed them in the name of the Lord. And two she-bears came out of the woods and tore forty-two of the boys.[12]

The problem that such a passage raises from a Christian perspective can be expressed by simply posing the following theological questions: What does this passage teach about God? Does it reflect an understanding of God's will that Christians can accept in light of their knowledge of God's revelation in Christ? If not, can it be valid and authoritative for their lives?

These and similar passages should always be read historically and contextually. In their *Sitz im Leben* they reflect a human understanding of God that is totally different from the God in Christ that Christians have experienced—a God of love, justice, and peace. For the Church in the Middle East, such passages can neither be authoritative nor valid for the Christian's understanding of God.

It is truly tragic when people invoke the details of certain Old Testament passages, transposing them into the twentieth century, and are intent on implementing their injunctions today. The Bible thus becomes a powerful weapon in the hands of a few staunch militants who are ready to act at the behest of their God to repress, kill, and murder their antagonists.

A case in point is the way some contemporary Jewish militants have debated the use of "genocide" to deal with the Arab problem. In 1984, Rabbi Moshe Segal—who was formerly aligned with Menachem Begin's terrorist underground, the Irgun—compared the Palestinian residents of the West Bank and Gaza to the Amalekites. One recalls the story of Amalek in 1 Samuel 15: King Saul is sent on a military campaign against the Amalekites in retaliation for their attack on the Israelites when they were journeying in the wilderness generations earlier after the exodus from Egypt. Saul is clearly, specifically, instructed by the prophet Samuel—at the command of God—to impose the *herem,* or ban, and to blot out the memory of Amalek from under the skies.[13]

> Now therefore hearken to the words of the Lord of hosts, "I will punish what Amalek did to Israel in opposing them on the way, when they came up out of Egypt. Now go and smite Amalek, and utterly destroy all that they have; do not spare them, but kill both man and woman, infant and suckling, ox and sheep, camel and ass."[14]

Rabbi Segal wrote, "One should have mercy on all creatures . . . but the treatment of Amalek—is different. The treatment of those who would steal our land—is different. The treatment of those who spill our blood—is different." [15]

How can a civilized person justify such statements? The rabbi is lifting material from the Hebrew Scripture that applied to a stage of Israelite development over three thousand years ago and using it in the twentieth century to incite the extermination of a whole people! Since he has labeled the Palestinians as "Amalek," they do not fall under the category of "all creatures" and therefore "mercy" does not apply to them. One can see the perverse logic behind the words, as he accuses the Palestinians of stealing "our land," and spilling "our blood." But in fact, it is the Israeli Jews who have been stealing land everywhere in Israel-Palestine and spilling Palestinian blood in the West Bank and Gaza. Obviously the rabbi's words make sense to the right-wing militants clutching a claim to the land that goes back thousands of years.

Rabbi Segal's case should not be seen as an isolated incident. A more respected scholar, Rabbi Israel Hess of Israel's Bar Ilan University, published an article, "The Genocide Ruling of the Torah," which also compared the Arabs to Amalek and stated bluntly that their extermination has been mandated by the Torah. [16]

Some Israeli liberals have been critical of such statements, recognizing that they are tantamount to inciting genocide, spelling doom and destruction to thousands of people. But the words of the militants reveal a primitive and tribal concept of God, a nationalist god who is more concerned with land than with human beings, with war than with peace. As Rabbi Meir Kahane (founder of the Jewish Defense League and a radical right-wing member of the Knesset, Israel's parliament) has often said, "Our God is a god of vengeance." [17] It is frightening to imagine what such inflammatory words can produce. Obviously, in light of our hermeneutical key, such concepts must be rejected. They are not worthy of the true God.

Such illustrations demonstrate the great care that needs to be exercised when one communicates the word and knowledge of God to people. For what is reported as the words and deeds of God in certain passages of the Bible is not at all the same thing as the authentic Word or the knowledge of God. God has indeed been revealed to us throughout history, but this revelation has been communicated through the human medium. Humans are not only limited by the scientific and historical knowledge of their time; they are equally, miserably, limited in their religious knowledge, that is, in their understanding and perception of God. For Christians, the normative picture of God has only been attained in Jesus Christ. The concern of the pastor-theologian is, therefore, how to help people to know God, to understand the Bible, and then to grow in their faith and love of God. This is not always easy given the complexity of the human predicament. Yet it is the challenge to all Christians who, with the help and guidance of the Holy Spirit, want to live their faith meaningfully and fruitfully.

Three Central Biblical Themes

With the use of this hermeneutic—interpreting the story of God's action in history in the light of our knowledge of God in Christ—the Bible can be reclaimed for Palestinian Christians. Without stretching it or forcing it, it can be contextualized so as to speak to people in their various conditions today. I have chosen three biblical themes from the Hebrew Scriptures, understood in the spirit of our hermenentical key, which I believe are helpful to Palestinian Christians as well as to others as part of their theology of liberation.

Naboth and the God of Justice (1 Kings 21)

Most theologies of liberation have used the story of the Exodus as their paradigm. But the way its message has been abused by both religious Zionists and Christian fundamentalists, who see in it a call for the physical return of the Jews to the land in this century, makes it difficult for Palestinians to appropriate at this time. This might surprise some people. Therefore let me briefly expand on it.

The events of the biblical Exodus from Egypt, read in light of an uncritically primitive concept of God, have been transposed by many Jewish religious Zionists and Christian fundamentalists into the twentieth century. This is theologically unacceptable from a Christian point of view. For the Jews who came to establish the State of Israel, their journey to Palestine was an exodus from the different nations where they had been living and a return to the promised land. Obviously, for them the imagery has connected the ancient past and the present. This uncritical transposition, however, makes the Palestinians appear to represent the old Canaanites who were in the land at the time and who *at God's command* needed to be dispossessed. The Exodus and the conquest of Canaan are, in the minds of many people, a unified and inseparable theme. For to need an exodus, one must have a promised land. To choose the motif of conquest of the promised land is to invite the need for the oppression, assimilation, control, or dispossession of the indigenous population. That is why it is difficult, in a Palestinian theology of liberation, to find the whole of the Exodus event meaningful. It will be reclaimed eventually when Palestinians enjoy their own exodus and return to their homeland. But my hope is that their exodus and return will not result in conquest, oppression, or dispossession. Certainly the concept of a God who wills such horrors is not acceptable. Instead of the wars and bloodshed of the biblical account, it is my hope that Palestinians will return to *share* the land of Israel-Palestine. This is the kind of return that is willed by the God whom we have come to see in the overall biblical revelation—a God of justice, mercy, and peace.

A more relevant theme is found in the story of Naboth and his vineyard, an ancient story with a modern ring to it. The death and dispossession of Naboth and his family has been reenacted thousands of times since the creation of the State of Israel. When reduced to its essence, it embodies the tragedy of Palestine as well as the suppression of the rights of the individual. But it is more than a story of tragedy, since at its heart stands a God who is a God of justice, the God who governs history, who has a long memory, and will not allow injustice to go unchecked forever.

Naboth (a name connected with the Arabic *nabata,* meaning "to sprout" or "to grow") owned land in Jezreel, not far from Beisan/Beth Shean.[18] As land he had inherited from his ancestors, it was very precious, even sacred, to him as in other Middle Eastern cultures.

Naboth's property adjoined the palace of King Ahab (869–850 B.C.) in Jezreel, his second capital. The king wanted to expand his estate and offered to buy Naboth's land. Naboth refused. It was not a question of money; the land was the family inheritance passed down from generation to generation and he would never part with it.

The king was upset and angry. He really wanted the land, but no amount of money could change Naboth's mind. Ahab's wife, Queen Jezebel, had the perfect solution. She plotted against Naboth in a conspiracy that involved the services of the "elders and nobles" of the city and the testimony of false witnesses.

Naboth was taken to court and accused of blasphemy and treason by cursing God and the king. With no one to defend him, Naboth was sentenced to death by stoning. Apparently his sons were killed as well.[19] Naboth's land was confiscated and annexed to that of the king.

The prophet Elijah was summoned by God to confront the king for his hideous crime. Their encounter took place in Naboth's vineyard, where Elijah announced divine judgment on the king and his wife. A few years later the king was killed in battle; about ten years after that, his wife died a very horrible death. Exact and strict justice was meted out as punishment for the crime.

The Naboth story provides a central biblical paradigm for a Palestinian theology of liberation. In applying this story, I would like to emphasize three points:

1. The story reveals God's uncompromising concern for *justice*. The land belonged to Naboth and his family. Because he was powerless and defenseless, he was victimized and his land expropriated. The powerful had the means with which to carry out their treacherous act. They had their agents. They could indict whomever they chose, dispose of them, and expropriate their land. Palestinians identify with the story of Naboth. Justice for them has been flouted. They feel liberated, however, when they recall that God is a living God with a long memory. God holds tenaciously to justice; as the apostle Paul wrote to the Christians in Galatia, "Do not be deceived; God is not mocked, for whatever a man sows, that he will also reap."[20]

2. Theologically speaking, the State of Israel has been guilty of the same misdeed as Ahab. Ahab knew that before God's law all people stood equal, including the king.[21] This was in contrast to the Canaanite view of things. Baal, the god of the Canaanites, tended to support the status quo, with the elite on top. So the king's rights and privileges could be extended arbitrarily to acquire whatever the monarch wished or desired. But Yahweh's ethical law, championed by the Prophets, operated impartially: every person's rights, property, and very life were under divine protection.[22] Whenever injustice occurred, God intervened to defend the poor, the weak, and the defenseless.

3. The last part of the story of Naboth demonstrates real retribution. Strict justice with no mercy was meted out, albeit after a considerable lapse of time. I do not wish to emphasize the consequence of Ahab's crime and the way he and his wife met their bitter ends. Indeed, as a Christian, and in light of our hermeneutical key, I do not advocate justice without mercy. I fully recognize that today, as in Naboth's time, many people still relish the exercise of strict justice—"an eye for an eye and a tooth for a tooth." As I will try to show later, I am repelled by such a formula, which only creates more injustice. I would plead for justice *with* mercy; not a dilution of justice, but of the use of justice in a dynamic and creative way for the achievement of peace in the land. Therefore, without emphasizing the epilogue of the story and without predicting the consequences of injustice, I want to insist on the basic theme of the justice of God that gives hope of liberation to the oppressed.

The Ecstatic Prophets—A Cautious Warning (1 Kings 22)

This episode is a sequel to the Ahab story and holds important lessons vis-à-vis the Israel-Palestine conflict.

Briefly, the story concerns a military campaign that King Ahab was planning against Aram (Syria). He enlisted the aid of his neighbor to the south, King Jehoshaphat, who was probably his vassal. As was customary in biblical times before important military decisions were made, the two kings looked for an oracle from God. Four hundred prophets were summoned who, with ecstatic frenzy, prophesied that the campaign against the Syrians would be successful and the king would be victorious. One prophet went so far as to dramatize the inevitable defeat of the Syrians. These nationalistic prophets agreed that the military objectives of King Ahab coincided perfectly with the will of God.

For some reason, Jehoshaphat was a bit uneasy and suspicious of the verdict, and he asked Ahab whether all the prophets had been consulted. Ahab explained that one had not, Micaiah ben Imlah: "I hate him, for he never prophesies good concerning me, but evil." [23]

Micaiah was duly summoned before the royal audience. When pressed to tell the truth and reveal an oracle from God, Micaiah prophesied doom for the campaign. Greatly angered, one of the ecstatic prophets struck Micaiah on the face, and King Ahab ordered Micaiah imprisoned for his negative oracle. The episode concludes with the vindication of Micaiah's prophecy: the campaign was a fiasco, and Ahab died in battle against the Syrians.

There are several warnings to be found in this story. By use of our hermeneutical key, they can bring a sense of liberation.

1. Often the powerful (leaders and governments) want to hear only what pleases them. They seek support for their policies and are not always concerned with the morality of their actions. They want the people to affirm, conform to, and legitimate what they are doing. Any criticism is considered damaging and negative; it must be suppressed.

2. There will always be yes-men and women, people who echo nationalistic feelings and are as much the slaves of the political establishment as were the four hundred ecstatic prophets. Instead of looking at events with an eye for justice, they see justice and truth only through the eyes of the state. Praised for what they are saying and doing, they are perceived as the real champions of the people and of the well-being of the nation. But they are not. They are false prophets, and believing them can only lead to disaster.

3. Those who view events with an eye for justice are disliked and often hated. It is not success and fame that attracts them, but morality. It is not the powerful arms of the state that impress them, but God's demand for justice. Narrow nationalistic utterances and slogans are not necessarily words from God; the yes-people are not always good for the state. Men and women who look for justice choose to be free. They choose to be critical even when isolated and silenced as a result. They rank justice above popularity.

Micaiah ben Imlah dared to stand against great odds, setting his voice against the voice of four hundred. He dared to speak the unpopular truth because he could see under the facade of Ahab's power an injustice that did not please God. And he was persecuted for it.

This warning is directed to all who, instead of fixing their eyes on justice, blindly support any state, especially one that has been guilty of injustice.

The Cry of a Refugee—Hope in God (Psalms 42, 43)

The third biblical theme that carries with it liberation and hope for the Palestinian Christian is found in Psalms 42 and 43.

From the perspective of a Palestinian, these two beautiful Psalms can be used as the real cry of a refugee. The Psalmist apparently has been forced out of his homeland. Living as a refugee in Jordan or Lebanon, he remembers happier times, his friends and neighbors, the worshipping congregations—especially the great feasts, when people celebrated together with excitement, with songs and praises to God. He reminisces about his own participation in these joyous festivities.

As he recalls the past, the Psalmist is aware of his painful present: expelled from his country, deprived of his own home, living with grief and despair, frustration and anguish . . . the turbulent waters and the stormy seas represent the troubles and disasters that he has experienced. His memories of Palestine are beautiful and exhilarating, but they make the present harder to bear. His only hope is in God. Trusting God is the only way to a better future; hope in God is the only medicine and cure for a depressed spirit. So he will not succumb to despair. God will vindicate his rights. God will come to his help and bring him salvation.

In Psalm 43, the Psalmist is praying for God's vindication of his rights, recognizing that injustice has been done, that he is dealing with ungodly, deceitful, and unjust people. He asks God to remove his troubles and restore him to his country. His joy and hope will remain in God.

For Palestinian Christians, these Psalms carry special significance:

1. God hears the cry of the oppressed. No matter where they are, God is not far from them. Those who have been wronged and dispossessed have God for their advocate. For Palestinian Christians this means specifically that in spite of the tragedy of Palestine, they should not lose their faith in God. Faith should not be abandoned. In the midst of a refugee life and in the heart of a life of exile, God is there with them. Faith should be a living relationship, helping them to confront God frankly, as the Psalmist did, with their frustrations, dilemmas, and even doubts.

2. Palestinians should live in trust and hope, grounded in faith in the living God of justice. People may fail us; leaders of nations may be silent in the face of injustice; the future of humanity may look grim; injustice may even seem to have the upper hand. In spite of it all, the Christian must maintain trust in God. God will act. Trust and hope are two liberating factors that are indispensable for

the Christian. Trust liberates us from the dark realities of the present. Hope brightens and liberates our future.

3. With faith, trust, and hope in God, the outcome, though not visible, is assured. Although the adversary may be ungodly, deceitful, and unjust, he or she will not have the final word. God will inevitably vindicate what is right and just.

A THEOLOGY THAT CONFRONTS NATIONALISM

Scholars can identify a number of important themes that run through the Bible—polytheism versus monotheism, promise and fulfillment, law and grace, sin and forgiveness, faith and works, to mention only a few. Another of the pairs of themes is universalism and particularism—whether God is *in*clusive or *ex*clusive in divine love for human beings. The Bible is a record of the dynamic, sometimes severe, tension between nationalist and universalist conceptions of the deity. For Palestinian Christians, this theme is one of the most fundamental theological issues, since it is directly related to the concept of God. This is why it demands attention in a Palestian theology of liberation.

The tension between the inclusive and the exclusive concepts of God permeates the entire Bible. The two are dynamically related, always influencing and affecting one another. Indeed, it is difficult to point to a specific date when the inclusive view of the sovereignty of God began to take hold in the minds of some of the characters in the Hebrew Scripture. John Ferguson maintains that the seed of universalism lay in the covenant itself:

> God was not indissolubly linked with Israel. If Israel ceased to exist, he did not cease to exist. His relation to Israel was covenanted, not organic. If Israel was defeated, that was due to the Lord's withdrawal of support; he was not defeated. This further meant that what he was to Israel he could be to all people. The covenant bore within it the seeds of universalism.[24]

Certainly by the eighth century B.C. Amos was able to express a universalist concept of God quite clearly:

"Are you not like the Ethiopians to me, O people of Israel?" says the Lord. "Did I not bring up Israel from the land of Egypt, and the Syrians from Kir?"[25]

This universalist concept began to crystallize during the experience of the Exile after 587 B.C. This does not mean, however, that one can detect a definite and unswerving line of progression in the maturing knowledge of God. There was still a continual tension between the old, more pervasive idea of God's exclusiveness, which involved a special and unique relationship to Israel, and the newer, emerging view of God's inclusiveness. These were not two defined and distinguishable camps, with all of those who espoused a universalist and inclusive view on the one side and those who rejected it on the other. The same prophet could be the author of both views, affirming both, swerving from one to the other; or else, as so often happened, later redactors might have made sure that the prophet's view was balanced by including the other view. Such a prophet as Second Isaiah could, in spite of his great, universalist concept of God, still at times express a narrow, nationalist outlook.[26]

The tension between the two views never disappeared. G. Ernest Wright has written that the Old Testament comes to an end without a definite solution to the problem of salvation.[27] The same could be said about the tension between the universalist and nationalist concepts of God. In fact, as the biblical period drew to a close, the tension had reached climactic proportions but was not to be resolved within the pages of the Old Testament. Its resolution lay beyond the biblical period.

It is possible to detect three distinct streams of tradition flowing from the Hebrew Scriptures, those that were nationalist, Torah-oriented, and prophetic in their emphasis. Each reflected an understanding of God that differed from the other two. These streams of tradition spanning and flowing from the whole of the Old Testament literature (and even some parts of the New Testament) are interspersed in the Bible with a dynamic tension between them. Let us examine how the three streams of tradition emerged from the Old Testament and left their indelible imprint on history.

The source of inspiration for the nationalist tradition came largely from those books of the Bible that are commonly referred to as the earlier, or former, prophets: Joshua, Judges, 1 and 2 Samuel, and

1 and 2 Kings. These books are characterized by their favorable reporting of the use of force to achieve the Israelites' national goals. The later proponents of this tradition believed that the Jews had a special, privileged relationship with God. Yahweh was their God in a unique sense: they recalled God's mighty acts in the past and were determined to realize the same acts in the present. The past had become idealized and they believed that it could be reclaimed. They refused to accept the reality of their relative weakness vis-à-vis the great power of the day, Rome.

Their faith was in the God of Israel and the Lord of Hosts. If God had become lethargic, he could be stirred through their own activity. This was a purely nationalistic and militaristic approach, aimed at regaining Jewish independence. Illustrated by the Maccabean revolt in the second century B.C., it also appeared in the rise of the Zealots and their revolts in A.D. 66 and 132. The Zealots were fighting for the cause of God as they conceived him to be. They strongly believed that God would inevitably intervene on their behalf and come to their aid:

> The basic principle of the Zealots as enunciated by its founder, Judas of Galilee, was that of the absolute sovereignty of Yahweh over Israel. Which meant accepting no human being, especially one who was a heathen, as Lord, and the refusal to have any of the resources of Yahweh's Holy Land as tribute to a foreign ruler who claimed such lordship. Resistance inevitably involved suffering; but the Zealot was ready to take up his cross and die a martyr's death in the belief that his sacrifice would not be in vain and that God would ultimately intervene to save Israel.[28]

This obviously was a very narrow concept of God. The Zealots were blinded and totally obsessed by this view. They succeeded in attracting and swaying the loyalty of many Jews and temporarily gaining the upper hand over Rome, but eventually they led their nation to destruction and plunged themselves into the abyss of oblivion after 135.

The source of inspiration for the Torah-oriented tradition was received from the books of the Law and from its observance. The

major adherents of this tradition were the Pharisees.[29] They were
the offspring of the second-century B.C. Hasidim, some of whom
had joined Judah the Maccabee in the revolt against the Greeks.
When Demetrius Soter seized the throne of Syria in 162 B.C. and
offered the Jews religious freedom, the Hasidim withdrew their
support from Judah and were satisfied to make their peace with the
Hellenizers so long as they could worship God and observe the
Torah.[30] The destruction of the temple in A.D. 70 and the final
collapse of the Zealots in 135 were undeniable proof of the bank-
ruptcy of the military option. It was left to the Pharisees to make
Judaism Torah-centered. Any prophetic, eschatological, or apocalyptic writing that would attempt to compute the date of the mes-
sianic redemption of Israel was discouraged: "May the curse of
heaven fall upon those who calculate the date of the advent of the
Messiah and thus create political and social unrest among the people." Religious belief rather than political power began to be the
cement that held Jewish society together, especially in the diaspora.[31] The redemption of Israel lay entirely in God's hands. When
that happened, it would be by spiritual, divine intervention and by
"no human hand."[32]

Much credit for this transformation goes to Rabbi Jochanan ben
Zakkai, who was acclaimed as the savior of Judaism.[33] In A.D. 68,
ben Zakkai escaped from Jerusalem in a coffin and, having received
permission from Vespasian, he set up a small Jewish academy of
learning at Javneh, south of Tel Aviv. Ben Zakkai argues that "un-
disturbed religious practice, and in particular the study of the Torah, were decisively more important than the achievement or main-
tenance of political independence."[34]

The main source of inspiration for the Pharisees and their descendants was the Torah. Its laws were interpreted and its traditions
developed. This gradually gave birth to Rabbinic Judaism, which
produced the Talmud and the Mishnah. In spite of the presence of
a maturing concept of God, Rabbinic Judaism exhibited a tendency
toward legalism and isolation, especially with regard to an often
hostile European Christianity. Its concept of God at times betrayed
exclusivity. With the emancipation from ghetto life in Europe and
the influence of the Enlightenment, some Jews, especially in Germany, began to stress the universalist character of Judaism.[35] The

epitome of this was the emergence of Reform Judaism, which considered the core of Judaism to be its code of ethics, morality, and justice.[36]

The third stream is that of the prophetic tradition. It is called prophetic since its most profound inspiration was drawn from the great prophets of the Hebrew Scriptures.[37] The word prophetic, therefore, is used because it best describes the ethos of this tradition with its deep, profound, and mature understanding of God.

The later prophets were able to produce profound truths about the universal and inclusive nature of God, although these insights are set within a massive quantity of material that is narrow, nationalist, and exclusive. Nor are such perceptions restricted to the writings of the later prophets; they shine through the other parts of the Hebrew Scriptures, though sometimes dimly, in the context of human prejudices and national interest. Second Isaiah could express a quite nationalist view in 45:22–23, and yet still see God as the savior of the whole world:

> Turn to me and be saved,
>   all the ends of the earth!
>   For I am God, and there is no other.
> To me every knee shall bow,
>   every tongue shall swear.[38]

Undoubtedly, the book of Jonah is one of the strongest voices against an exclusive view of God. Johah was ready to accept God's mercy as long as it applied to himself and no one else. In fact, he was ready to choose death rather than acknowledge God's mercy for others.[39] The message of the book of Jonah is a powerful one, having to do with God's mercy on Israel's staunchest enemy, the Assyrians. The best illustrations for the inclusive nature of God, however, are those given by the prophets, who saw God as a God of justice and righteousness who demands ethical living of all nations. So Amos pronounced God's judgment on Moab for atrocities committed not against Israel, but against Edom.[40]

Some scholars have even suggested that the development of apocalyptic literature in the Hebrew Scriptures reflects a growing understanding of God. John Shae says that "Apocalypse is the leap beyond nationalism" and that apocalyptic language is the result of a "thirst for totality." God is no longer concerned about only one people, but about all people.[41]

A proponent of this prophetic tradition was Jesus, and after him the Church, although it often strayed from his message. Jesus drew on the prophets and stood in their tradition. Though Jesus was also a product of an age that was greatly influenced by apocalyptic literature, he stressed God's activity in history, thus emphasizing again the great prophetic tradition. Jesus refused the Zealots' understanding of God.[42] Likewise, he was critical of the legalistic concept of God held by some of the Pharisees, and he tried repeatedly to draw their attention to the essence of the prophetic tradition:

> Woe to you, scribes and Pharisees, hypocrites! for you tithe mint and dill and cummin, and have neglected the weightier matters of the law, justice and mercy and faith; these you ought to have done, without neglecting the others.[43]

In Jesus' day the concept of the Kingdom of God had acquired an eschatological and apocalyptic meaning. Jesus used this concept but often gave it a very concrete and historical meaning. In the preaching of John the Baptist, for instance, it is possible that John was expecting an apocalyptic figure to follow him, whose "winnowing fork is in his hand, and he will clear his threshing floor and gather his wheat into the granary, but the chaff he will burn with unquenchable fire."[44] To the question of John's disciples, "Are you he who is to come or shall we look for another?" Jesus answered, "The blind receive their sight and the lame walk, lepers are cleansed and the deaf hear, and the dead are raised up, and the poor have good news preached to them."[45] In other words, Jesus was affirming history and God's activity within history. The rule of God was present in power and in history in the ministry of Jesus. This again represents a return to the prophetic tradition:

> The Kingdom of God is for Jesus clearly both present and future. This presence of the rule of God in power negates apocalyptic suspicion of, and even hostility toward, historical activity. It bends eschatological imagery away from the present usage—apocalypticalism—to its earlier rootage—prophetic understanding.[46]

To stand in the great prophetic tradition was to recognize the prophets' maturing understanding of God. Jesus represents the continuing link with the prophetic tradition. It is true that in the prophetic material the inclusiveness of God was expressed sporadically. In the New Testament, however, it received a consistent and persistent intensification amid the prevailing nationalistic and legalistic concepts of the times, including those of Jesus' disciples themselves. Jesus' concept of God clashed with the views of many of his contemporaries, changing and shattering some, while alienating others and incurring their intense hostility.[47] To change people's exclusive concept of God proved to be one of the most difficult revolutions to effect. Even Jesus' closest companions could not be converted easily to this new concept, nor were they able to comprehend its real impact on them and on the Church. The New Testament is full of eloquent illustrations of this revolution that Jesus introduced in the concept of God. Indeed, the whole of the New Testament could be seen as a witness to the God who "so loved the *world*" that he sent Jesus Christ to die for it.[48]

Matthew, for example, intended that the genealogy of Jesus should express the universalist character of God. Jesus' ancestors, therefore, include foreign women—a Canaanite, a Moabite, and a Hittite.[49] Moreover, the first visitors to pay homage to the Christ Child were non-Jewish wise men.[50] Similarly, the only land that could provide safety for the Messiah was not the land of Israel but the foreign land of Egypt.[51] The first two healing miracles of Jesus that Matthew records are those of a Jewish leper and the servant of a Roman centurion. They are reported with no distinction between Jew and Gentile, as if this were the way it had to be. In fact, Jesus praises the faith of the Roman, adding, "Not even in Israel have I found such faith. . . . Many will come from east and west and sit at table with Abraham, Isaac, and Jacob in the Kingdom of heaven."[52] Even the story of the healing of the daughter of the Syro-Phoenician woman, which some have used to point to the bigotry of Jesus and his exclusive outlook, in reality supports his inclusive character. Some commentators in exegeting this text have suggested that Jesus may have assumed the position of the Jewish people, or perhaps some of his disciples toward the Gentiles, whom they generally regarded as "dogs," only to repudiate it and declare that the kingdom of God was open to all people.[53] Even if this interpretation is not totally accepted, the daughter was healed, and that is what reflects the real character of Jesus.

According to Luke, the inclusive nature of God was expressed by Jesus at the outset of his ministry. In the synagogue in Nazareth, Jesus read from the prophet Isaiah. After appropriating the words to himself, Jesus is reported to have said:

> There were many widows in Israel in the days of Elijah . . .
> and Elijah was sent to none of them but only to Zarephath,
> in the land of Sidon. . . . And there were many lepers in
> Israel in the time of the prophet Elisha; and none of them was
> cleansed, but only Naaman the Syrian.[54]

These were inflammatory words that resulted in Jesus' expulsion from his home town.

Jesus' ministry to the Samaritans in Sychar expresses his universalist concept of God.[55] In another place, he healed ten lepers, one of whom was a Samaritan. The Samaritan was the only one to express gratitude, thus reflecting a greater spiritual perception than the nine other (Jewish) lepers.[56] Similarly, the parable of the Good Samaritan expresses the profound love of neighbor that set the despised Samaritan apart from the priest and the Levite.[57]

It was not easy for the early disciples to break away from traditional exclusive and nationalist concepts. Even after the Resurrection, they showed an incomplete understanding of the inclusive nature of God. "Lord, will you at this time restore the Kingdom to Israel?"[58] The whole book of Acts seems, from one perspective, to be an answer to this question that shatters its nationalist implications and moves the Gospel from the heart of Jewish Jerusalem to the heart of pagan Rome.[59]

Paul in his epistles likewise repeatedly emphasized God's inclusive nature.

> For in Christ Jesus you are all sons of God, through faith.
> . . . There is neither Jew nor Greek, there is neither slave
> nor free, there is neither male nor female; for you are all one
> in Christ Jesus. And if you are Christ's, then you are Abraham's offspring, heirs according to promise.[60]

The author of Ephesians calls the inclusiveness of God a mystery that he received through revelation, thus pointing attention to its great significance:

> The mystery was made known to me by revelation, . . . the mystery of Christ, which was not made known to the sons of men in other generations as it has now been revealed to his holy apostles and prophets by the Spirit; that is, how the Gentiles are fellow heirs, members of the same body, and partakers of the promise in Christ Jesus through the gospel.[61]

The writer of the Gospel of John can boldly declare in his prologue, as if constructing a new genesis for the world:

> To all who received him, who believed in his name, he gave power to become children of God; who were born, not of blood nor of the will of the flesh, nor of the will of man, but of God.[62]

This inclusive understanding of God, which breaks through the pages of so many books of the Old Testament, is shared with that tradition by Christianity. It had found its profound culmination in Jesus' understanding of God, and then continued in the early Church right down to the present. A Palestinian theology of liberation stands in the authentic biblical tradition and affirms the inclusive character and nature of God.

A THEOLOGY OF THE GOD OF JUSTICE AND ZIONISM

The third stream of the prophetic tradition has been discussed in this study not only for the sake of Palestinian Christians, but for Western Christians and for Jews as well. Most Jews would not accept the validity of our perception of the New Testament as continuation of the prophetic tradition; that I understand. In order to address them, one would need to use their Bible (the Christian's Old Testament) and its development in the Talmud. However, as I have already indicated, since the source of the three traditions—the nationalist, the Torah-centered, and the prophetic—is the Old Testament, that is, the Hebrew Scriptures, I hope I may at least ask to be heard by them.

What is quite clear from a Palestinian Christian point of view, and in light of the above analysis, is that the emergence of the Zionist movement in the twentieth century is a retrogression of the Jewish community into the history of its very distant past, with its most elementary and primitive forms of the concept of God.[63] Zionism has succeeded in reanimating the nationalist tradition within Judaism. Its inspiration has been drawn not from the profound thoughts of the Hebrew Scriptures but from those portions that betray a narrow and exclusive concept of a tribal god.[64] Consequently, the finely worded Declaration of Independence of the State of Israel is no more than a mask behind which these retrogressive ideas hide:

> [The State of Israel] will be based on the principles of liberty, justice and peace as conceived by the Prophets of Israel; will uphold the full social and political equality of all its citizens, without distinction of religion, race, or sex . . .[65]

Although this declaration is not considered legally binding, it nevertheless represents a great ideal. From the point of view of the Palestinians in their experience with the State of Israel, this ideal, which was "envisioned by the prophets of Israel," has never been adequately realized.

Furthermore, although the Zionist movement at its inception was not basically religious,[66] it has used religion to its advantage and has emerged (especially after the 1967 war) with a definitely religious character.[67] Certainly the most vociferous exponents of Zionism today are the religious militants, people dedicated to the creation of what they call Greater Israel. "If we can't have a Greater Israel, then we don't want peace."[68] This same militancy was expressed in June 1967 by Chief Rabbi Nissim, leader of Israel's Sephardic Jews. When asked about Israeli withdrawal from the territories occupied by conquest during the 1967 war, he replied, "It is forbidden by the Torah for all Jews, including the Israeli Government, to return even one inch of the territory of Eretz Israel now in our hands."[69] The support by the Jewish Orthodox religious establishment of Israeli government policies is itself an indication of how far the Jewish religion has been influenced by the Zionist ideal and nationalist tradition. This has been done at the expense of the prophetic tradition and by the suppression of the higher tenets of Judaistic faith and of the God who was portrayed by the prophets as the God of righteousness. In writing on "Judaism in Israel" in *Religion in the Middle East*, Norman Bentwich mentioned the need for Orthodox Jews to modify the *halakha* in order to adapt it to present-day life in Israel. Then he added,

> One grave defect of the *halakha* is the discrimination against the Gentile in the Jewish law. The failure of the rabbinate and the religious political parties to oppose the reprisal policy of the government against Arab guerillas may be due in part to their acceptance of two standards of conduct, to the Jews and to Gentiles.[70]

From my perspective as a Palestinian Christian, Zionism is a step backward in the development of Judaism. What the Jewish community had finally and unequivocally rejected in the second century A.D., with the defeat of the Zealots, many Jews have accepted again eighteen hundred years later. This has been done at the expense and even the weakening of the higher principles and demands of the Jewish religion. Ethical Judaism, with its universalist outlook, has been swamped by the resurgence of a racially exclusive concept of a people and their god.[71]

The tragedy of the State of Israel today is that it has locked itself up and entrapped its people in an impasse from which there is no escape so long as it espouses this exclusivist understanding of God.

Ironically, Israel today is in precisely the same position as the Palestinians in 1947. The Palestinians refused the partition of Palestine, insisting that the whole of Palestine was theirs. Unfortunately, they lost even the part they then still had. On the other hand, the Jews, who were eager to accept only their part, eventually gained the whole. At the end of the 1980s, the positions have been reversed. Many Palestinians, who once had the whole land, are willing today to compromise and settle for a part, while many Jews, out of a religious understanding of God's exclusive claim for the land, are not willing to give up a part and share it with the Palestinians. Will they, too, eventually lose the whole?

Transcending the Zionist Claim to the Land

Since 1967, the issue of the land has become so central in the conflict between Israel and the Palestinians that it is mandatory to tackle it as an important issue in a Palestinian theology of liberation.

Both Jews and Palestinians claim indisputable right to the same piece of land—Palestine. The Palestinians base their claim on the observed facts of history: they have lived in the land for many centuries. It is quite probable that the ancestors of some have lived in the land from time immemorial. The land was never at any one time inhabited by one homogeneous population; the Bible as well as history attest to this. The Hebrew Scriptures themselves record that many ancient peoples—including the Hittites, the Amorites, the Canaanites, the Perizzites, the Hivites, the Jebusites, the Geshurites, Maacathites,[72] and the Philistines—lived in the land before the ancient Hebrew tribes joined them. The land was conquered and occupied. Great kingdoms came and went—the Assyrians, Babylonians, Persians, Greeks, and Romans. Populations moved and shifted. Many people mixed and assimilated to form the population of Palestine in the early centuries of our era.

With the Arab Islamic conquest of Palestine in the seventh century, almost all of those who were living in the land (mostly Christians and some Jews) gradually became Arabized in language and culture. They were joined by an increasing number of Arab Muslims who settled in the land. Consequently the indigenous population of Palestine, although of different religious backgrounds, has lived in the land continuously for at least the last thirteen hundred years. Over time, the country witnessed shifting movements of tribes, clans, and families, but basically the indigenous inhabitants remained in the land.

The Jews, on the other hand, would claim that the land was given to them by God in the promise to Abraham over three thousand years ago.[73] They occupied the land with the conquest of Canaan (c. 1250–1200 B.C.). While living in the land they set up first a united kingdom and then two separate kingdoms in the north and south of the country. The northern state was destroyed in 722 B.C. by the Assyrians, the southern in 587 B.C. by the Babylonians. Yet they continued to live in the land in lesser or greater numbers.

Although only small and scattered Jewish communities have lived on the land since the third century A.D., the majority of Jews (who lived outside the land in the diaspora, praying for "next year, in Jerusalem") never forgot it, and some of them returned in the twentieth century and established the State of Israel in 1948.

Furthermore, Western anti-Semitism, culminating in the atrocities of the Holocaust in the early 1940s, helped speed up the process of Jewish immigration to Palestine and heightened the urgency of creating a Jewish homeland.

Most Palestinians do not deny the evils of anti-Semitism or the vileness of the Holocaust; but they feel that the solution of the "Jewish problem"—a Western phenomenon that had little or nothing to do with their home, Palestine—was achieved at their expense, by their loss of Palestine. Palestinians would argue, furthermore, that if people in different lands based their claims to territory on divine promises or conquests, our world would be a shambles; we would face major demographic shifts, social chaos, and personal injustices no less severe than those that Palestinians themselves experienced at the hands of the Jews in 1948 and 1967.

I have tried thus far to record the basic positions of the Israeli Jews and the Palestinians. It is easy to observe the unreconciled claims of the two groups, especially when seen from each proponent's vantage point.

The Problem of the Land—Two Proposals

In the past, many people attempted to find viable explanations for the problem of the land. Three basic views have been suggested.

1. The promise of the land to Abraham and his descendants after him included both of his sons, Ishmael and Isaac. Since, it is claimed, the Jews are the descendants of the younger son, Isaac, and the Arabs of the older son, Ishmael, they should share the land.

2. Before the coming of the Zionists and the establishment of the State of Israel, the descendants of Abraham were already living in the land. The inhabitants of Palestine, whether Muslims, Jews, or Christians, are monotheists with a strong link to Abraham. The memory of these people, their traditions, their beliefs, and even their racial ancestry make them see themselves as Abraham's chil-

dren. Abraham is their ancestor, whether physically or spiritually.

3. Most Zionists who came from Eastern Europe were not Semites at all and probably do not share blood lineage with the biblical Israelites.[74] They are more recent converts to Judaism. The Semitic Arabs are, surely, more entitled to the land than are these Eastern European Zionists who, from a Palestinian viewpoint, are considered twentieth-century colonizers.

This is only a sample of the kind of theorizing that has been put forth. Although they are interesting and make for lively discussion, I have never found these theories helpful in seeking a solution, and I disagree with some of their basic assumptions. The existential situation that confronts us as Palestinians is the presence on the land of Palestine of a strong and powerful group of people, many of them fanatic, who refuse to share it with its historic inhabitants. Some of them are willing to go to any extreme to implement their own understanding and interpretation of the biblical promises to the land and, without any scruples, to deny the rights, evict, and even dispose of the indigenous population.

Without claiming total objectivity, I would like, as a Palestinian Christian, and in light of the hermeneutical key that I have already suggested, to look at the issue of the land both biblically and theologically. This is not intended to be a detailed study; such scholars as W. D. Davies have already produced books on the subject.[75] My aim here is to be concise and focused. I would like to propose two views of my own.

The Earth Is the Lord's

It is clear in the Hebrew Scriptures that the land of Canaan really belongs to God. In the Hexateuch[76] the land invariably is referred to as the "Land of Canaan." In Joshua 24:8 it is called the land of the Amorites. Interestingly, the phrase "land of Israel" (*Eretz Yisrael*) does not appear until 1 Samuel 13:19. It seldom appears in the Hebrew Scriptures, occurring only six times in all.[77] It is very clear that the reason for this is that the land belongs to God. God is its owner.

In Leviticus 25:23, the divine claim to the land is so strongly emphasized that the Israelites are regarded as strangers and foreigners themselves:

The land shall not be sold in perpetuity, for the land is mine;
for you are strangers and sojourners with me.

Thus, the division of the land into different lots for the tribes of
Israel, the cultic statements about the harvest, and the commandment that the land should keep a Sabbath to the Lord need to be
understood in light of God's ownership of the land.[78]

Consequently, since the land belongs to God, and the Israelites
were only stewards of it, God "had imposed on the land—indeed
upon nature—a sacred order or pattern or law, the violation of which
produced a dissolution, a return to chaotic disorder and formless-
ness."[79] This is the sanction for the command

You shall not defile the land in which you live, in the midst
of which I dwell.[80]

In Jeremiah it becomes clear that defilement of the land has actually
taken place:

. . . when you came in you defiled *my* land and made *my*
heritage an abomination.[81]

Again:

And I will doubly recompense their iniquity and their sin,
because they have polluted *my* land with the carcasses of their
detestable idols, and have filled *my* inheritance with their
abominations.[82]

Those who want to live on the land, therefore, must obey the
owner of the land. Disobedience to God defiles the land, violates
its sacred character, and incurs the unequivocal loss of the land; it
could even lead to utter destruction:

When you beget children and children's children, and have
grown old in the land, if you act corruptly by making a graven
image in the form of anything, and by doing what is evil in
the sight of the Lord your God, so as to provoke my anger, I
call heaven and earth to witness against you this day, that

you will soon utterly perish from the land which you are going over the Jordan to possess; you will not live long upon it, but will be utterly destroyed.[83]

W. D. Davies maintains that the land when defiled would thrust the inhabitants out because of its holiness. "The implication is that it is not even the Torah that lends the land holiness. The land was already characterized by holiness before Israel brought the Torah: it was already holy in Canaanite days because Yahweh owned it and dwelt in the midst of it."[84]

In light of the contemporary conflict over the land, and the often-heard fallacy that the Jews came to a country that was a wasteland—and that it is they who developed it, built it, and made the desert bloom—Joshua 24:13 has a modern ring to it:

I gave you a land on which you had not labored, and cities which you had not built, and you dwell therein; you eat the fruit of vineyards, and oliveyards which you did not plant.[85]

For our purpose, the basic point to keep in mind is the insistence—so prominent in the Bible—that the land really belonged to God. So one can conclude that 3000 years ago the Israelites, in their own context at the time and their own understanding of God at that stage of history, accepted even then the basic fact that the land was really God's.

One can go on to say that as a result of the development of the knowledge of God in the Old Testament, God is gradually perceived as not only the God of Israel but indeed the God of the whole world:

The earth is the Lord's and the fullness thereof, the world and those who dwell therein.[86]

This concept becomes clearer as we move to exilic and post-exilic times:

Thus says the Lord,
who created the heavens (he is God!),
who formed the earth and made it (he established it;

he did not create it a chaos, he formed it to be inhabited!):
"I am the Lord, and there is no other."[87]

In the literature of the post-exilic period, there is undeniable re-location of interest from the land to human issues.[88] Some scholars would even point out that the book of Ruth reflects a universal dimension in post-exilic Judaism, in which lands other than Judah are accorded great significance.[89] We have already seen how the whole history of Pharisaism reflects a concentration on the Torah rather than on political control of the land.[90]

To summarize: as their concept of God matured, people began to understand that God's concern was not limited or even focused on one particular land but on all lands. Davies insists that "at no point should the doctrine of the promise of the land be separated from that of Yahweh as creator of the universe."[91] In other words, our understanding of God today obliges us to conclude that the God who was perceived by the Israelites as the God who owned "the land of Canaan" is none other than the God whom we have come to know as the God who owns the whole world:

> For the Lord is a great God,
> and a great King above all gods.
> In his hand are the depths of the earth;
> the heights of the mountains are his also.
> The sea is his, for he made it;
> for his hands formed the dry land.[92]

The land that God has chosen at one particular time in history for one particular people is now perceived as a paradigm, a model, for God's concern for every people and every land. As God commanded the Israelites to obey God's laws in their life in the land, so God demands the same from all peoples in their lands. God's unequivocal demand that the Israelites not defile or pollute the land with injustice, lest the land thrust them out, becomes a warning to all governments and to the peoples of every land. God requires every human being to live according to the divine standard of righteousness.

The particular has become universal. The blessing of God's concern for one people is universalized to encompass every people and

every land. Consequently, every nation can say about its own country, "this is God's land, God's country, this is a part of God's
world. This is the Lord's land and the Lord demands a life of
righteousness and justice in our land."

Such a blessing obviously does not exclude the Jews or the modern State of Israel. Neither does it justify their invoking an ancient
promise—one that betrays a very exclusive and limited knowledge
of God in one stage of human development—in order to justify
their uprooting an entire people and expropriating their land in the
twentieth century. To cling only to the understanding of God in
those limited and exclusive passages is to be untrue to the overall
biblical heritage.

The tragedy of many Zionists today is that they have locked
themselves into this nationalist concept of God. They are trapped
in it and they will be freed only if they discard their primitive image of God for a more universal one.

The Concept of God

My second proposal is closely linked to the first. From the point
of view of a Palestinian theology of liberation, the whole issue of
the land must center on a theological discussion of the nature of
God: who God is and what God is like. Does God's character change?
If human nature in its sinfulness remains what it has been all along,
would it not follow that God's character and nature do not change?
Indeed, God does not change. God was not bad yesterday and good
today! God's character or nature of goodness, love, mercy, righteousness, and justice is totally consistent.

The biblical heritage offers ample evidence of how people's understanding of God and of the land had to be shattered. Early in
their history, the Israelites thought that God was confined within
the borders of the land, that God did not operate outside it. It was
difficult for them to conceive of praying to God in a strange land,
outside what they thought of as God's homeland. This narrow concept of God persisted in spite of the strong words of Amos, who
expressed a broad conception of God. Indeed, for Amos God was
active outside the land. God had intimate knowledge of and grave
concern for what was going on in the neighboring countries—Da-
mascus, Gaza, Tyre, Edom, Ammon, and Moab, as well as Judah
and Israel.[93] The land-bound concept of God was finally shattered

by the Babylonian captivity. There, the Israelites had to learn that God was not confined to "their" land.

In fact, some of the great events—if not the most important ones—in the ancient Israelites' history took place outside the boundaries of the land. The Exodus, the giving of the Torah, the making of God's covenant, all took place outside the land. The greatest prophet of Judaism, Moses, never set foot in the land. The great Babylonian Talmud was compiled outside the land. Among the greatest prophets were those like Second Isaiah of the Exile, who prophesied outside the land. Jeremiah finished his ministry in Egypt; Ezekiel finished his in Babylon. One can go on and on to show from the biblical material how often people's understanding of God had been limited, narrow, and wrong. In the beginning it was tribal and provincial. It took them hundreds of years to realize that God is the God of the whole world—not simply the greatest God among other gods, and not exclusively *their* God, but the only true God, the God of the whole world. Throughout their history the people vacillated between a narrower and a broader image of God, between attributing to God an exclusive or inclusive character. Indeed, as I have previously shown, one can point to different strands within the biblical material that emphasize the nationalist or the universalist perception of God.

I have no doubt that the universalist understanding of God—developed in spite of the resistance that it encountered—is the truer concept. I say this not because it suits my purpose as a Palestinian, but because it is the only worthy concept of God—the true God. It fits the nature of God, the God who is the God of all, inclusive in nature, just in all ways. One cannot deny the existence of the nationalist strand within the Hebrew Scriptures, but one can point to the development of a strong universalist trend reflected in the work of Second Isaiah and the book of Jonah, to give only two examples.

Obsession with the land has had disastrous consequences for the Jews at different times in their ancient history. For it is not the land that carries a blessing to the people, but faithfulness to the God of justice, righteousness, and mercy. It is true that the land of Israel-Palestine has been singled out as host to great events in history, but I do not believe that it is intrinsically more holy than other lands. If God has done great things here, God has done great things everywhere. If God loves this land and its peoples, that is a sign—a sacrament—that God loves each and every land and its peoples. The whole Earth is the Lord's. This is all God's world. The whole world should be holy. It is all sacramental. When God commanded Moses to take off his shoes because he was standing on holy ground, it was in Sinai and not in Canaan *(Eretz Yisrael)*.[94] I return to my insistence that, theologically speaking, what is at stake today in the political conflict over the land of the West Bank and Gaza is nothing less than the way we understand the nature of God.

History teaches us that whoever concentrates heart and mind on the land will be cursed and vomited out of the land. This is what happened to the Crusaders, Christians who fell into this trap. The land can, however, *become* holy to those who put their trust in the God of the whole universe, whose nature does not change—a God of justice for all, who desires goodness and mercy for all people living in this and every land.

Kenneth Bailey, who has been working on the interpretation of the prophetic literature for many years, tells us that the great exilic prophet whom we call Second Isaiah made the remarkable discovery that the promise of God to the people after the Exile was not about land and nationhood but about the outpouring of God's Spirit on the people:

> For I will pour water on the thirsty land,
>   and streams on the dry ground;
> I will pour my Spirit upon your descendants,
>   and my blessing on your offspring.
> They shall spring up like grass amid waters,
>   like willows by flowing streams.[95]

Isaiah's great theological breakthrough lies in his realization that God's promise of outpouring the Spirit of God on the people is essentially more important than the possession of the land. The relationship with God did not depend on being in the land. God without the land is infinitely more important than the land without God. With God's Spirit poured on the people, they can be the carriers of God's blessing and become God's witnesses everywhere. That is why the great prophets were never hesitant or reluctant to warn the people that they could lose the land.

What I am trying to say in the present situation is this: if the

State of Israel clings to its obsession with real estate, it will only heap destruction on itself and on all the people living in the land. The blessing will only come when Israel transcends the narrow concept of a nationalist God and embraces the more universal image of God. For its own survival, Israel and Jewry must recognize that God is the God of the whole universe, who lives and cares for all people, the God who desires justice and mercy. The salvation of the Jews in Israel and the Palestinians in Palestine right here and now lies in acknowledging the truth of Micah's words:

> He has showed you, O man, what is good. And what does the Lord require of you? To act justly and love mercy and to walk humbly with your God [6:8].

"This Property Belongs to God"—The Significance of the Land for Palestinian Christians

One of the most beautiful customs that a visitor can observe among Arabs in the Middle East is the way they give recognition to God's ownership of the land. When people build their houses, many of them ask the builder to engrave on a stone in bold Arabic one of two phrases that will usually appear above the front door of the house: either *Almulk lillah,* which means "property belongs to God," or *Hatha min fudli Rubbi,* "this house has been built as a result of the beneficence of my Lord."

Having conceded that all of life and all land belong ultimately to God, Palestinian Christians, like all other Palestinians, cherish the land and are loyal to it because it is the land of their birth and the land of their ancestors. It is their homeland, *watan.*

Those of us who have been born and brought up in Israel-Palestine recognize that it is indeed a privilege to have been born in the land that has witnessed some of the greatest events in history. The land is sacred to the three monotheistic religions—Judaism, Islam, and Christianity. Each in its own way, and using its own vocabulary of faith, must express the significance of the land to its adherents and to the millions who choose to visit it.

As part of a theology of liberation for Palestinians, I would like to call attention to the significance of the land for its Christian population, especially at a time when the presence of indigenous Christians is rapidly dwindling because of emigration. There are three significant things that define and inspire Palestinian Christians' devotion to the land:

The Land of Palestine Hosted the Great Event of the Incarnation

> Jesus was born in Bethlehem, grew up in Nazareth, was baptized in the Jordan River, lived most of his life in the Galilee, was crucified, died, and was buried in Jerusalem. Jesus Christ's resurrection took place in Jerusalem. Therefore, the first witnesses to the Resurrection were Palestinians; the Church was born in Palestine as the early disciples and followers of Jesus were Palestinians. In Jerusalem on the day of Pentecost the Holy Spirit was poured out, the Gospel of the living Christ was first proclaimed in Jerusalem, and from Jerusalem his witnesses went out to the ends of the earth.

The Palestinian Christians of today are the descendants of those early Christians, yet this is no cause for *hubris*. With a humility that befits their Lord, they accept it as a privilege that carries with it a responsibility for service. Palestinian Christians of today are the present generation of that great cloud of witnesses to Jesus who came before them, and who will, God willing, come after them until Christ comes again. They and their ancestors have maintained a living witness to Jesus and his Resurrection from the beginning of the Church, and they should see themselves dynamically continuing such a witness in the land, witnesses to the Resurrection.

The Witness of Our Land to Scripture

A seminal biblical scholar of the nineteenth century, when visiting Palestine in 1860–61, called it a "a fifth Gospel". He saw a "striking agreement of the texts with the places, the marvelous harmony of the Gospel ideal with the country."[96] The direct personal knowledge and experience of the land of the Bible can supplement the accounts of the Gospels by enriching and deepening the faith and devotion of the believer.

In his *Catechetical Lectures,* St. Cyril of Jerusalem (c. 304–386) considered the various places of Palestine as bearing a true witness to Christ. Such sites as the Jordan River, the Sea of Galilee, and the Mount of Olives were for him an eloquent witness to Jesus Christ.[97] What was true for St. Cyril, the archbishop of Jerusalem in the fourth century, is still true today in the experience of countless pilgrims. Palestine is a fifth Gospel to them. Indeed, the faith of the pilgrim can come alive through visiting the holy sites, from being where Jesus had been, and walking where he had walked. It is, however, equally important for Christian pilgrims to meet the living stones of the land—the Christians. To visit the holy sites is a very moving experience for many; meeting the "holy" people can be a very rewarding and enriching experience for both. Visiting museums can give a person an important sense and appreciation for the past; but to visit the churches of the land, to worship with the indigenous Christians, and to meet them personally can give the pilgrim both a sense of appreciation for the present and an invaluable experience and insight into the life of the living and pulsating Christian communities of the land, who with their ancestors before them have borne a continuing witness to Christ for the last two thousand years.

Indigenous Christians who are privileged to live in Israel-Palestine today have a responsibility to Christian pilgrims from all over the world—to make their pilgrimage a revitalizing experience of their faith. Their responsibility and privilege is to be host to their brothers and sisters from abroad.

Jesus Christ, Prince of Peace

Christians believe that the message of the only truly authentic peace first resounded from the hills of Bethlehem:

> Glory to God in the highest,
> and on earth peace
> among men [and women] with whom he is pleased![98]

Palestinian Christians, therefore, recognize their responsibility as peacemakers. As will be made clear in chapter 6, they should be actively involved in the work of justice, peace, and reconciliation, calling into remembrance the words of Jesus,

> Blessed are the peacemakers,
> for they shall be called sons [and daughters] of God.[99]

5

A Palestinian Cry
for Justice and Compassion

He has showed you, O man, what is good; and
what does the Lord require of you but to do justice, and to love kindness, and to walk humbly
with your God?

Micah 6:8

JUSTICE MISUSED

The most basic and crucial issue of the Israel-Palestine conflict
is that of justice. The word itself has been overused and misused in
our day. Everybody is looking for justice for his/her cause, nation,
or self, but what they really mean by justice is often uncertain.
More important, how can justice be justice for some when it is
perceived as injustice to others? It is, therefore, important to begin
with a definition of the word "justice."

Aristotle defined justice as refraining from *pleonexia,* that is, from
gaining some advantage for oneself by seizing what belongs to another—property, reward, office; or by denying a person that which
is his or her due—the fulfillment of a promise, the repayment of a
debt, or the showing of proper respect, for example.[1] *Webster's
New World Dictionary* defines justice as "1. the quality of being
righteous. 2. impartiality; fairness. 3. the quality of being right or
correct."[2]

It is interesting that Aristotle's definition of justice is framed in the negative ("refraining from"), while *Webster's* approach is more positive ("the quality of being"). One can say that justice has two dimensions: the positive and the negative, the inner and the outer, the being and the doing. It is a quality that a person should possess—being righteous and fair. It is also a relationship that a person must maintain—not gaining advantage by taking what belongs to others. Each dimension is important; each can be seen as a natural extension of the other. The inner quality produces the outer relational aspect of a just living with other people.

The crisis of justice in the Israel-Palestine conflict has been exacerbated by what has become, since the uprising of December 1987, a crisis of justice within the Jewish community itself, both inside and outside the country, and by a crisis in the way Israeli Jews have been perceived by others. In fact, the great enigma is how can the Jewish people who experienced such suffering and dehumanization at the hands of the Nazis, turn around and inflict so much suffering and dehumanization on others? Why should the price of Jewish empowerment after the Holocaust in the creation of the State of Israel be the oppression and misery of the Palestinians?

It is a great tragedy of human nature that people too easily forget what it was like to be powerless and oppressed. They remember their suffering—constantly remind the world of it—but it does not seem to affect for good the way they themselves exercise power over another people. Their mistreatment and oppression of the powerless within their power seems to be a basic denial of their past suffering, a stark unfaithfulness to their own past.[3]

That is why I have deliberately chosen to stay as much as possible within biblical parameters in this study: to invoke the prophetic tradition of the Hebrew Scriptures, in order to make it clear that the Jewish people have such a good, meaningful biblical tradition to which they can turn. It is part of the genius of the Bible that it preserved a record both of the good and of the bad. Some things were touched and changed here and there by later redactors; but basically there was a genuine effort to present people and events as they were.

Taking the old dictum of Moses, "I have set before you life and death, blessing and curse; therefore choose life, that you and your descendants may live,"[4] I want to apply the same principle to the issue of justice. In the world today, the possibility of doing justice or injustice is there before all of us. The powerful have the choice of either living and acting justly or of living and acting unjustly. That is why I have insisted that in its highest points of inspiration and understanding of God, the Old Testament presents God as One, the Creator of the world, active in history; the God of righteousness, justice, and mercy. Abraham Heschel said that righteousness is "God's stake in human history"—when the prophets spoke, they did not speak in the name of the moral law but for the God of justice.[5] Righteousness "is the heart of God, the core of his being; and no one knows him who does not know justice."[6]

In the Hebrew Scriptures, God is called the God of justice.[7] Justice is God's measuring line and righteousness is God's plumb line.[8] Justice is inherent in God's essence and identified with all God's ways:

> The Rock, his work is perfect;
>   for all his ways are justice.
> A God of faithfulness and without iniquity,
>   just and right is he.[9]

God's justice, righteousness, and kindness are extended to all people on the Earth. Human beings should pride themselves in knowing this righteous God:

Let not the wise man glory in his wisdom, let not the mighty man glory in his might, let not the rich man glory in his riches; but let him who glories glory in this, that he understands and knows me, that I am the Lord who practice steadfast love, justice, and righteousness in the earth; for in these things I delight, says the Lord.[10]

God's justice extends beyond the limits of one nation to encompass the whole world:

> But the Lord sits enthroned for ever,
>   he has established his throne for judgment;
> and he judges the world with righteousness,
>   he judges the people with equity.

> The Lord is a stronghold for the oppressed, a
> stronghold in times of trouble.[11]

It is not only humans who should glory in such a God; God himself is exalted in justice:

> But the Lord of hosts is exalted in justice,
> and the Holy God shows himself holy in
> righteousness.[12]

The Prophets stressed justice and righteousness over sacrifice. Deeds of injustice negated people's worship:

> Even though you offer me your burnt offerings and
> cereal offerings,
> I will not accept them,
> and the peace offerings of your fatted beasts
> I will not look upon. . . .
> But let justice roll down like waters,
> and righteousness like an everflowing stream.[13]

For the prophets, morality and religion were inseparable. The unity between them derived from the very nature of the Creator-God, a God with explicit expectations:

> Thus says the Lord:
> "Keep justice, and do righteousness . . .
> Blessed is the man who does this,
> and the son of man who holds it fast."[14]

All those who stand in the prophetic tradition recognize that these verses express a profound knowledge of the nature, will, and expectations of God.

It is no longer the history of a particular group of people (Israel) but all peoples, the kingdoms of the world. . . . No one group . . . can claim God, for God is the movement of justice among all groups and classes. The reality of God does not exclusively belong to a particular people precisely because it belongs to all peoples. . . . God is shaking free of chauvinism, refusing to allow any group to own him and tame him and turn him into a household god. God, as the painful experience of most religions attests, is preeminently faithful to himself (Justice). The fidelity of God does not mean that any one people will be favored but that the offer of justice will never disappear from human reality. . . . What God has elected beyond all else is not one nation but the just living of all nations.[15]

This vision of God becomes the biblical and theological basis for approaching problems of justice in the world—God desiring and demanding of all nations that they live justly. It is on this basis that I want to go on to examine the relationship of justice to other areas of life in the State of Israel vis-à-vis the Palestinians. The Palestinians' experience is that Israel has trampled their rights. Although one can think of many different areas where this has been done, I have chosen to highlight just two: law and power.

WHEN JUSTICE IMPLIES INJUSTICE

For many people, justice has come to mean an impartially administered system of settling grievances under law. Law, however, can hold many ambiguities. In the Palestinian experience with the State of Israel there are two ambiguities, one concerning those who established the law and the other concerning how the law is administered.

Law is established by the people in power. It is they who enact legislation creating new laws. Problems arise here because such laws tend to favor one segment of the population—those in power—over another. Paul Tillich expressed this well:

The justice of a system of laws is inseparably tied to justice as conceived by the ruling group, and this justice expresses both principles of right and wrong and principles by which the ruling group affirms and sustains and defends its own power. The spirit of a law inseparably unites the spirit of justice and the spirit of the powers in control, and this means that its justice implies injustice.[16]

Important laws are enacted to serve the good and the welfare of the ruling group. What is good for them becomes law. This is the classic utilitarian view of justice. The good is defined independently from the right; and the right is defined as that which maximizes the good.[17] In the case of the State of Israel, this means that the value judgment that determines the good is the value judgment of the Israeli Jews. The good for them is judged without reference to what is right. The good for the powerful becomes right, and, therefore, law. Because of this apparent utilitarian ambiguity, the Palestinians look upon some of the laws that govern their lives in Israel, the West Bank, and Gaza with deep apprehension.[18]

Such ambiguities seem insurmountable when many of the laws of the country are discriminatory and unjust toward the indigenous people of the land. In today's world there is a designated remedy to deal with all discriminations and unjust law. The laws of the land should conform to international law.[19] International law—a body of principles imposing limitations on the use of national power—is established by agreement among a community of nations. Transcending individual national interests, it represents an expression and a record of what the international community at its best moments of humanity recognizes to be just and fair to all. Ideally, the laws of all nations should be in harmony with international law.[20]

The second ambiguity is found in the way the law is executed and administered. This is solely dependent on the attitude of those in power who render judgments, who—like those who establish the laws—cannot totally escape certain amounts of subjectivity, bias, and self-interest: "Each of their judgments expresses not only the meaning of the law, not only its spirit, but also the spirit of the judge, including all the dimensions which belong to him as a person."[21]

A glance at the situation of the law on the West Bank and in Gaza reveals the inherent ambiguities and the oppression to which the Palestinians are subjected. The system of law that operates here is a hodgepodge of Ottoman, British, Jordanian, and Israeli civil and military law. Israeli military courts have jurisdiction over the Palestinian population, who are not permitted to appeal their rulings. Palestinians on the West Bank and in Gaza live within the bounds of no less than twelve hundred orders issued by the military governor since 1967. By 1988, more than fifty percent of the Palestinians' land had been expropriated by means of legislation enacted by the military government in flagrant violation of international law pertaining to occupied lands. All judges in the military courts are Israeli soldiers, some of whom are not legally qualified.[22] Palestinians have been able to take some cases to the Supreme Court of Justice in Jerusalem, but the results have not been encouraging. "The reason for this lies primarily in a series of self-imposed restrictions which the Court placed on its proclaimed role which permitted it to avoid dealing with many of the thornier issues raised by the occupation."[23] Some of these issues include the refusal of the Court to apply the Fourth Geneva Convention; the limited scrutiny of claims of "security purposes"; the use of quasi-judicial bodies as substitutes for courts; psychological barriers; the expenses involved in resorting to the Supreme Court; and the inaccessibility of the Supreme Court to West Bank lawyers.[24] It is the experience of Palestinians that the Supreme Court has yielded to the authority of the military government in the West Bank and Gaza. Thus the Supreme Court has been tacitly involved in the violation of the human and political rights of the Palestinians.[25]

Because of these ambiguities, which Palestinians believe constitute real threats, they have appealed from the beginning to the international community, that is, to the United Nations and to international law. Yet even here, one meets with certain real ambiguities. International law is useless and ineffectual unless it is respected and enforced. It must "be applied consistently in order to promote the objectivity and uniformity associated with law."[26] In the Israel-Palestine conflict, there has been more recourse to force and violence than to international law. It has even been suggested by some that international law has not yet been tried in any seriousness to resolve the Middle East conflict.[27] The following examples are presented to clarify this important point.

It was stated in Israel's Declaration of Independence on May 14, 1948, that the dual legal bases for the State's establishment were the Balfour Declaration of November 2, 1917[28], and the United Nations General Assembly Palestine Partition Resolution of 1947.[29] In *Palestine and International Law*, Henry Cattan has shown by careful legal analysis that neither the Balfour Declaration nor the Palestine Partition Resolution are valid ground for such action under international law.[30] Even if one concedes to Israel the validity of the two documents in international law, one has to go on to recognize that Israel has not fulfilled the provisions for the protection of human rights that are stipulated in them. The Balfour Declaration specifically provided that "nothing shall be done which may prejudice the civil and religious rights of existing non-Jewish communities in Palestine." And the Partition Resolution guarantees "to all persons equal and non-discriminatory rights in civil, political, economic and religious matters and the enjoyment of human rights and fundamental freedoms, including freedom of religion, language, speech and publication, education, assembly and association." [Part I, Section B (10)(d)]

In the Geneva Civilian Convention of 1949—in whose adoption the government of Israel was one of the leaders—Article 49(6) provides that "the occupying Power shall not deport or transfer parts of its own civilian population into the territory it occupies." Article 49(1) prohibits individual or mass "forcible transfers" and "deportations" of civilians from occupied territory.[31] Even if one disregards the violations of these principles during the creation of the State of Israel as stemming from its immaturity, how can one justify the repeated violations since 1967 in the Golan Heights, Gaza, and the West Bank, including East Jerusalem? On November 26, 1973, by a vote of 109 to 0, the Special Political Committee of the United Nations General Assembly passed a resolution that confirmed the applicability of all four of the Geneva Conventions of 1949 to the Middle East conflict and to all the occupied territories.[32] The position in international law is clear, but unenforceable.

On December 8, 1979, the General Assembly of the United Nations, by more than the two-thirds vote required for important questions, decided that the people of Palestine are entitled to self-determination:

Bearing in mind the principle of equal rights and self-determination of peoples enshrined in Articles 1 and 55 of the Charter of the United Nations and more recently reaffirmed in the Declaration on Principles of International Law Concerning Friendly Relations and Cooperation Among Nations [the United Nations General Assembly], recognizes that the people of Palestine are entitled to equal rights and self-determination, in accordance with the Charter of the United Nations.[33]

Since Israel refuses to grant self-determination to the Palestinians, they remain living in their own country under the rule of an occupier's unjust law that is gradually stripping away most of their rights to their land and country.

These examples express clearly, though briefly, the ambiguities in the relationship between justice and law that exist in Israel-Palestine because of the unwillingness of the State of Israel to abide by international law and to grant to the Palestinians the same measure of justice that it has demanded and claimed for itself.

Yet in spite of all of these ambiguities, international law remains a very significant factor that could play a decisive role in achieving justice and peace in the Middle East if Israel were willing to submit to it. This would require a passionate dedication to justice for all people, even for one's enemies, which, I am sorry to say, Israel has not so far shown.

THEOLOGICAL DILEMMAS OF POWER AND JUSTICE

Power, like law, is a force closely related to justice; it is meant to enhance the establishment of justice in the world, but it is all too often abused. The blessing that law and power should bestow on people can easily be turned into a curse in situations of conflict. My intention is to point out the theological dilemmas of power in the State of Israel.

By power I simply mean the ability of a person or a group to initiate action, to bring about change, and to try to achieve a desired end. There are different types of power. The most obvious in the world today are military, political, and economic power. Theologically, God, who is the God of justice, is also the God of power and might. In God, justice and power are harmonized completely as God's justice and love. God, the source of all power, gives power to humans in order to fulfill the divine purpose of justice and peace in the world. Power is, therefore, entrusted by God to people; but like all other trusts, it can either be used responsibly or abused terribly. It can carry with it a blessing or it can become a curse. Such consequences are not inherent in power itself but in the sinful human condition that puts power to responsible or irresponsible use. Power can be used to maintain justice, peace, and order in society; or power can destroy it all. At its worst, power can be a "poison which blinds the eyes of moral insight and lames the will of moral purpose."[34]

Power is very closely linked with justice, so much so that the one may easily be confused with the other. This is illustrated daily by the frequent claims of the powerful—often heads of governments—that their power is justly gained and used to support justice.

The possession of power by humans does not necessarily create or guarantee justice. Only God's power necessarily creates justice. Moreover, justice itself is inherently powerful. Since contrary to all appearances, this world is ultimately governed by justice. God, in whom justice and power are one, would not allow it otherwise.

What is true of God's exercise of justice and power, however, is certainly not true of human beings. It is very easy for power to corrupt, intoxicate, and deceive us. The prophet Micah addresses one such situation. Speaking to the elite of Judah's society, who had come to see their power as giving them the right to act as they desired. The source of their dreams is opportunity created by their power. Might has become their right.[35]

> Woe to those who devise wickedness
>   and work evil upon their beds!
> When the morning dawns, they perform it,
>   because it is in the power of their hand.
> They covet fields, and seize them;
>   and houses, and take them away;
> they oppress a man and his house,
>   a man and his inheritance.[36]

The words of Micah seem remarkably relevant to the Israel-Palestine conflict, where the powerful Zionists have been able to carry out, with exact precision, what Micah was warning his audience against doing. Power somehow intoxicates those who wield it and clouds their sense of right and wrong so that they can justify and rationalize their wicked actions. Under the guise of "national security" or of "national interest," all kinds of injustice can be committed. A pertinent warning is found in the wisdom literature that addresses such a tendency in humans: "Do not withhold good from those who have a right to it, because it lies in your power to do so."[37] Power can have an intoxicating effect on people. On the one hand, I am sure that Israeli Jews would readily agree that justice is much better for them than injustice; on the other hand, once they come to a position of power, their sense of justice becomes clouded. As Coote puts it, "What is better for us in our powerlessness is not necessarily better for others when we are powerful."[38]

Such dilemmas and paradoxes underlie the frequent coups d'etat in many countries. One political regime topples another in order to redress injustice, only to become guilty itself of similar or even greater injustices and abuses of power. The two forces of justice and power that are meant to complement one another have become in Israel enemies opposing each other and creating a vicious circle of violence and suffering for thousands of Palestinians.[39]

It is part of the tragedy of the human predicament that justice between people is not usually given but almost always has to be exacted. The powerful refuse to render justice, and power has to be challenged by power rather than by moral or rational persuasion.[40] Even this dubious process becomes less and less effective in a world where power is so unevenly distributed. If there is no power to match the strength of the evildoers and redress the wrong they do, injustice tends to be perpetuated and intensified.

This balance of power against power also has its dilemmas in the world today. It can be used by each of the two superpowers, the United States and the Soviet Union, to deter the other from attacking; but it does not prevent either of them from feeding internecine conflicts among smaller nations in the process, creating in them many opportunities for aggression and injustice. This can be done both directly and indirectly.[41] The balance of power and a degree of peace are maintained between the giant powers, while smaller and weaker countries are ravaged and destroyed and millions of people suffer and die.[42]

In order to understand the extent of the dilemmas between power and justice, it is essential to highlight the deceptions of power. Two of these are directly related to the conflict in the Middle East.

The first is what Reinhold Niebuhr has called "the limitation of the human mind and imagination, the inability of human beings to transcend their own interests."[43] Human nature is such that, while it is conceivable for persons to consider the rights and needs of their families, relatives, and friends, "there are definite limits in the capacity of ordinary mortals which makes it impossible for them to grant to others what they claim for themselves."[44] Power becomes a strong weapon for personal or national gain without any consideration for the rights of others; self-interest or national interest blind reason and logic. This is epitomized in the Israel-Palestine conflict. Many western Jews have been in the vanguard of the struggle for human rights in the United States and Europe, and they have claimed that their commitment stems from the rich heritage of Judaism and is rooted in the ethical teachings of the prophets. Paradoxically, many of them have lacked the capacity to discern acts of injustice by the State of Israel. Once the injustices are mentioned, they feel threatened and become defensive. They are quick to rationalize and justify those unjust actions that they would have readily condemned had they been done by any party other than the State of Israel.[45]

One common rationalization is to point out the great achievements of the State of Israel in raising the educational and economic standards of its Arab citizens and of those in the occupied territories. "The Arabs have never had it so good" is the usual claim. Israel's generosity and benevolence are supposed to be adequate compensation for any inconvenience or injustice that the Arabs may feel. But as the common saying goes, "a slave with a full belly is still a slave"; people who have suffered from injustice look for justice rather than for a higher standard of living.

"REASON'S INSISTENCE ON CONSISTENCY"

It is part of the deception of power that repressive governments are deluded into believing that through benevolence they can lay the right foundation for harmonious relations with the people they rule. Such governments cannot see that what people really need is not benevolence but a sense of justice. A sense of justice, as Niebuhr has said, is "the product of the mind and not of the heart. It is the result of reason's insistence upon consistency."[46] However, the ability of reason to be consistent is hindered by the intoxication and deception of power. It is far easier for repressive governments and military regimes to resort to philanthropy than to justice. Sympathy and philanthropy in such cases are part of the exhibition of hypocrisy. The guiding factor is basically the self-interest or national interest of the powerful and their unwillingness to render justice to others when it conflicts with their own self or national interest.

It is even more frighteningly true that a country's national interest—and the power of people in control who want to pursue their unjust and selfish ambitions—can become so strong that neither democracy nor religion can temper it. Napoleon was successful in so exploiting the democratic sentiment in France as to create a tyranny that bathed Europe in blood: it is truly shocking that "the dream of equality, liberty, and fraternity of the French Revolution could turn so quickly into the nighmare of Napoleonic imperialism."[47] A classic illustration of the abuse of religious sentiment is U.S. President William McKinley's (1897–1901) explanation to a group of clergy of how he arrived at his decision to occupy the Philippines:

> I walked the floor of the White House night after night until midnight; and I am not ashamed to tell you gentlemen that I went on my knees and prayed to Almighty God for light and guidance more than one night. And one night it came to me this way—that there was nothing left for us to do but to take them all, and to educate the Filipinos, and uplift and civilize and Christianize them, and by God's grace do the very best we could for them, as our fellowmen for whom Christ also died. And then I went to bed and went to sleep and slept soundly.[48]

The epitome of deception is further observed when those in power pursue an absolute goal: "In religion [absolutism] permits absurdities and in politics cruelties."[49] The Israel-Palestine conflict offers a case in point from the Jewish as well as from the Palestinian side. The absolute ideal for many Zionists is the achievement of Greater Israel.[50] At the same time, for many Palestinians the absolute ideal is the regaining of the whole of Palestine.[51] Such an absolute cannot be achieved except by the use of force, and this gamble for the attainment of the absolute would put the lives of millions of people at risk. Justice has no place in such a gamble; military power would inevitably take over; and the consequence would be unbearable tyrannies and cruelties. When the absolute becomes the end, no questions are raised about the means, as long as they achieve the end.[52] Some people might argue that such extremism can be checked only by the development of rationality and the growth of religiously inspired good will.[53] The situation in Israel, which, since 1967, is heavily supported by religious zeal, does not validate such a theory. The pursuit of the absolute goal negates the possibility of bringing this fanaticism under the dominion of reason or conscience. Force and coercion are the only instruments that can achieve the ideal. In such cases justice is victimized by power and sacrificed on the altar of force.

The second area, very similar to the first, has to do with the deception of power that arises when humans' desire for a life of security is transmuted into subjugating and controling others as the only conceivable way of achieving that security. Niebuhr has said that ''man unlike other creatures is gifted and cursed with an imagination which extends his appetite beyond the requirements of subsistence.''[54] In nature one can observe that animals kill only when they are hungry and fight or run only when they are in danger, but the human impulse for self-preservation can be so easily transmuted into a desire for aggrandizement that the will to live becomes transmuted into the will to power:

> ''Fear may easily lead to courage and the necessity of consolidating the triumph won by courage may justify new fears. . . . Power, once attained, places the individual or the group in a position of perilous eminence so that security is possible only by the extension of power.''[55]

This point is very relevant to the Israel-Palestine conflict and can best be illustrated by the existence of the State of Israel itself. The will to live for the Jewish people, after centuries of dispersion and suffering, has found expression in the creation of the State of Israel. Such a phenomenon can be attributed to the human instinct for survival. This survival instinct, however, is prone to develop imperialistic ambitions. Its armors of defense become its armors of aggression, thus leading to expansion. Its will to live becomes its will to power. The human spirit holds a curious mixture of the fear of extinction and the love of power. Once power is attained, the individual or group find themselves in a sensitive position, when they are tempted to believe that their security can be maintained only by the extension of their power. This is translated into the acquisition of new territory and the subjugation of its inhabitants. Subsequently, temporary peace might be achieved; however, it is always an uneasy and shaky peace, because it is an unjust peace. Power apparently sacrifices justice in order to achieve peace and then destroys it.[56] Peace has not been attained by a rational or moral adjustment of rights, but by the force of the more powerful party. Peace would, therefore, last until those who are weak become powerful enough to challenge that force. "The same power that prompts the fear that prevents immediate action, also creates the mounting hatred which guarantees ultimate rebellion."[57] Therefore, the danger of an impending conflict looms continuously ahead.

THE PARADOX OF POWER

In summary, it is important to emphasize again the theological dimension of the deception of power and its delusional effects. There is a natural tendency to link justice and power together. The two are united in God, but not in humans. In God, power and justice are founded in goodness and love; power is always directed to the establishment of justice and peace among people. Power and justice are not grounded in the inherent goodness and justice of humans but in their propensity toward sin and evil. Instead of using power to establish and maintain justice and peace, power is easily transmuted into self-aggrandizement and the oppression of others. In other words, people who have power and wield it whenever they choose usually confuse themselves with God. Theologically speaking, this becomes the greatest menace in the abuse of power. It is idolatry in its starkest form, and human beings can too easily fall prey to it.

The ambiguity, deception, and corruption of power must be exposed because power becomes a god that is worshipped and obeyed. The demands of power escalate daily. The occupying party has to increase its coercive power in order to maintain control. The god of power increases its demands and eventually heaps destruction on

its user. It is the duty of the Christian not only to call attention to
this basic danger but to expose its underlying fallacies:

> No resistance to power is possible while the sanctioning lies,
> which justify that power, are accepted as valid. While that
> first and chief line of defense is unbroken there can be no
> revolt. Before any injustice, any abuse or oppression can be
> resisted, the lie upon which [it] is founded must be clearly
> recognized for what it is.[58]

Finally, one can observe in history many abortive attempts to
achieve justice and peace by the use of power. They have failed,
either because of the complete elimination of force or because of
an undue reliance upon it.[59] The paradox of power is that it is both
an essential component in achieving and sustaining justice and peace
and, at the same time, a menace that continually threatens to destroy them. Thus, it is almost impossible for people and governments to bring all power under their control. People lack the moral
strength that is "sufficiently potent to destroy the effects of the
poison of power upon character."[60] Realizing such dangers, the
challenge in the Middle East, once justice is achieved for the Palestinians, is to maintain justice in such a way that power is used as
infrequently and as nonviolently as possible, thus preventing the
destruction of millions and the inevitable negation of whatever justice and peace has been achieved.

A THEOLOGY FOR THE VICTIMS OF INJUSTICE

The concept of God as inclusive in character and just in all ways
becomes clearer when one considers the recipients of God's justice.
Throughout the Hebrew Scriptures and the New Testament, God
shows special concern for the underprivileged, the disadvantaged,
and the vulnerable. This attribute of God, as concerned for the welfare of the weak, is not peculiar to one section of the biblical literature but is characteristic of the Pentateuch, the Prophets, the
Writings, and the New Testament.[61]

At least four groups of people receive specific mention as the
objects of God's special concern—widows, orphans, the poor, and
strangers (sojourners or aliens).[62] They constitute the powerless in

society. The widows have no husbands, the orphans have no fathers, the poor have no money, the strangers have no relatives or roots in the land. These people become the focus of the divine compassion because they are so easily exploited. Consequently, the Bible has special provisions for their protection: for example, the leftover sheaves in the field, the gleanings in the olive orchards and the vineyards, and the tithe every three years belong to them.[63] Moreover, they should be treated righteously in judgment.[64] Because they have no human protector, God intercedes; because no one else pleads their cause, God will be their advocate:

> Do not rob the poor, because he is poor,
>   or crush the afflicted at the gate;
> for the Lord will plead their cause
>   and despoil of life those who despoil them.[65]

These groups represent the oppressed. So divine protection and concern were extended to all who suffer from injustice or oppression:

> Woe to those who decree iniquitous decrees,
>   and the writers who keep writing oppression,
> to turn aside the needy from justice
>   and to rob the poor of my people of their right,
> that widows may be their spoil,
>   and that they may make the fatherless their
>   prey![66]

The Prophets not only pronounced God's sentence of condemnation against the oppressors; they also promised that God would vindicate the oppressed. Amos called the oppressed from the start, a priori, the righteous.[67] God would be the savior of the oppressed:

> From the heavens thou didst utter judgment;
>   the earth feared and was still,
> when God arose to establish judgment
>   to save all the oppressed of the earth.[68]

In discussing God and justice in the book of Amos, Robert Coote lays down four theological premises that are basic to Amos's pronouncement against the powerful people of his day who were responsible for the injustice in society. First, God is "an agent who stands beyond the world who acts in the world." Second, "this agent acts according to justice."[69] Justice for Amos meant salvation for the powerless and the oppressed. In his view the Israelites should have known this, since they had experienced injustice and had received God's justice.[70] Third, "the one who acts in the world chooses justice ahead of life." God chooses "life for the powerless before life for the powerful," and "those who take life from the powerless will lose their own lives." Finally, "the one who acts in the world tilts the balance of power by giving leverage to human beings to make God's justice known."[71]

The Bible expresses a divine partiality toward the powerless and the oppressed of the world. In the words of Karl Barth,

> God always takes His stand unconditionally and passionately on this side and on this side alone: against the lofty and on behalf of the lowly; against those who already enjoy right and privilege and on behalf of those who are denied it and deprived of it.[72]

Similarly, John Bennett has written:

> God's love for all persons implies a strategic concentration on the victims of society, on the weak, the exploited, the neglected persons who are a large majority of the human race.[73]

What Barth has called "unconditional stand," and Bennett "strategic concentration," Reinhold Niebuhr terms candidly a "bias in favor":

> Justice was not equal justice but a bias in favor of the poor. Justice always leaned toward mercy for the widows and the orphans.[74]

In working out his *Theory of Justice,* John Rawls recognized two major principles for justice. The first has to do with equal liberty for all. The second affirms that people usually live in social and economic inequalities, but these inequalities "are to be arranged so that they are . . . to the greatest benefit of the least advantaged."[75] This theory is based on the biblical principle that God shows concern for the poor and the victims of injustice and oppression.

This divine concentration and apparent bias toward the powerless and the oppressed is a strong incentive for God's children to take active responsibility on behalf of all the vulnerable people of the world. Barth is again helpful in this regard. The human being is summoned

> to espouse the cause of those who suffer wrong. Why? Because in them it is manifested to him what he himself is in the sight of God; because the living, gracious, merciful action of God towards him consists in the fact that God Himself in His own righteousness procures right for him, the poor and wretched, because he and all men stand in the presence of God as those for whom right can be procured only by God Himself.[76]

This discussion shows from the Palestinian Christian perspective where God stands regarding oppression. The oppressed are not necessarily more righteous than their oppressors—God's rescue of the Israelites from Egypt stemmed not from their goodness but from God's justice and mercy.[77] This is helpful to Palestinian Christians not only for its educational value, reminding them that they cannot claim justice and mercy from God as a just reward, but also because it allows them to reaffirm their faith in a God who is just and righteous and who takes an "unconditional" stand on the side of the powerless and the oppressed. This affirmation of faith carries with it both comfort and hope.

Yet to help people affirm their faith in a just and righteous God is only half of the biblical task. Powerful rulers, in this case the leaders of the State of Israel and above all those who count themselves religiously observant, ought to take note of the biblical truth that God's principal concern is for the victims of injustice. Once this biblical and theological idea is understood, it should produce political responsibility.

Every person who is grasped by this truth about God wants to

live in this faith. They know "that the right, that every real claim
which one man has against another or others, enjoys the special
protection of the God of grace. As surely as he himself lives by the
grace of God he cannot evade this claim. He cannot avoid the question of human rights. He can only will and affirm a state which is
based on justice." [78]

THE WAY OF NONVIOLENCE

Most Palestinians, whether Muslim or Christian, have a strong
faith in God. So the assurance that God takes a stand beside the
oppressed and the victims of injustice is a source of hope and comfort to them. Hope in the midst of injustice and oppression, however, can produce passivity, and it can be frustrated. Real hope in
the God of justice should be an active and dynamic hope, inviting
people to become co-laborers with God. A theology of hope for the
Palestinians stems from the concept of a God who stands beside the
oppressed and with whom the oppressed work for a better day and
confront their oppressors with their sin. Hope becomes an incentive
for the Church's leaders to be actively involved with the victims of
injustice against their powerful oppressors. In order to do this the
Church needs to be cognizant of its Christian tradition regarding
resistance to violence.

The fundamental Christian attitude toward conflict and war familiar to the Christians in the Middle East is that of Jesus—the way
of nonviolence. It is very difficult to study the life of Jesus in the
Gospels and not conclude that nonviolence was his philosophy. This
is substantiated in the Sermon on the Mount. [79] For Eastern Christians, this is their tradition, their Gospel milieu, their heritage.

Christians in the East have also, however, been exposed to Western Christian attitudes to war and conflict, and have suffered unjustly as a result. The Crusades were "holy wars" fought by the
Western church, not in response to injustice but in defense of the
Christian faith—a Western expression of the Christian faith drawn
largely from the Old Testament. The Crusades left a bitter legacy
for the Eastern Christians, who paid a heavy price in successive
centuries because they shared with the Crusaders the title "Christian."

Western Christians developed another attitude toward war after the Constantinianization of Christianity in the fourth century—the "just-war" theory. The object of the just war is to vindicate justice and restore peace; it is a war that the state can lawfully wage (while observing certain rules).

Although these views have appeared within the Church in various configurations at different times in history, the just-war theory, subject to a number of developments and modifications, has found favor most often.[80] Yet the only way of life that really makes sense to Eastern Christians is the way of Jesus. To begin with, Eastern Christians, including Palestinian Christians, still live in a pre-Constantinian world. They constitute a minority in the various countries of the Middle East. They have to live their faith and witness, at times daily, in difficult situations. They have to continue to be both salt and light in their communities.[81] While they are not isolated from their fellow citizens who belong to other, more dominant, religious faiths, their frame of reference is the teaching and life of Jesus—in this context, the way of nonviolence.

Having said that, I do not want to leave the impression that the Christians of the East have always been practicing pacifists. Far from it. They have lived for centuries in violent societies, subjected to fierce assaults from both neighbors and governments. At times, out of desperation, they have resorted to force to protect and defend themselves, but on the whole this has proved counterproductive, resulting in the massacre of thousands.[82] Their harsh experience has reinforced the validity for them of Jesus' way, so I still maintain that Eastern Christians are brought up to understand that the way of Jesus is the way of love and peace. Some of them might debate this heatedly. They might wish to reject it. They might consider it defeatist and weak in light of the growing institutionalized violence around them. But they know that the way of Jesus is not the way of war but of peace.

I have always believed that the Church in Israel-Palestine can play a powerful role in promoting justice and peace through active nonviolent means. I believe that the authorities have done in the past and continue to do all they can to keep the Church politically dormant because they realize the potential power of the Church in Western circles. The authorities try to control the hierarchy, whether by giving them certain privileges or by subjecting them to subtle forms of blackmail, in order to keep them silent and marginalized.

An example of this is what happened at the height of the *Intifada* in January 1988, when the heads of the Christian communities in Jerusalem decided to express their solidarity with the Palestinians who were resisting occupation. The heads of the churches said, in part:

> The recent painful events in our Land which have resulted in so many victims, both killed and wounded, are a clear indication of the grievous suffering of our people on the West Bank and in the Gaza Strip. They are also a visible expression of our people's aspirations to achieve their legal rights and the realization of their hopes.
>
> We, the Heads of the Christian Communities in Jerusalem, would like to express in all honesty and clarity that we take our stand with truth and justice against all forms of injustice and oppression. We stand with the suffering and the oppressed, we stand with the refugees and the deported, with the distressed and the victims of injustice, we stand with those who mourn and are bereaved, with the hungry and the poor. In accordance with the Word of God through the prophet Isaiah, chapter 1, verse 17:
>
> > "Learn to do good; seek justice, correct oppression;
> > defend the fatherless, plead for the widow."
>
> We call upon the faithful to pray and to labor for justice and peace for all the people of our area.[83]

These words were not particularly strong, but they were very clear. Some Israeli Jews and even Arabs expressed themselves in the newspapers in much stronger language. But when the statement of the heads of the Christian communities was circulated to all the East Jerusalem Arabic newspapers, the Israeli censor prevented its publication. It was a clear recognition that the State saw the potency of such a joint statement by the churches.

The challenge for the Palestinian Christian, indeed, for all Palestinians, is that of nonviolent resistance. This cannot be said, however, without certain important qualifications, so that it will not be interpreted as naive and simplistic. Since the establishment of the State of Israel in 1948, and more pronouncedly after the occupation of the West Bank and Gaza in 1967, the Palestinians have faced one of the toughest armies in the world. Since the *Intifada* of December 1987, Palestinians have been subjected to both State violence and violence from fanatical religious settlers. The State of Israel lives in a state of paranoia. Any resistance to the State, even the most nonviolent resistance, is interpreted as undermining the security of the State. It is destroying itself because of its morbid fear of peace. The State of Israel is at its best in times of war, not in times of peace. The Israeli soldier is well trained to confront the "enemy" at war. His war machine is one of the best in the world. But he is utterly helpless when facing nonviolent resistance. That is why the basic Israeli reaction to it has been to rationalize the *Intifada* as an act of war in order to legitimate the killings and beatings of so many innocent civilians. As a result of so much State violence, the talk of nonviolence seems to many Palestinians totally irrational.

Yet, the experience of black people of South Africa is very similar in this regard. The *Kairos Document* states unequivocally:

The problem for the church here is the way the word "violence" is being used in the propaganda of the State. The State and the media have chosen to call violence what some people do in the townships as they struggle for their liberation, i.e., throwing stones, burning cars and buildings, and sometimes killing collaborators. But this *excludes* the structural, institutional, and unrepentant violence of the State and especially the oppressive and naked violence of the police and army. These things are not counted as violence. And even when they are acknowledged to be "excessive," they are called "misconduct" or even "atrocities" but never "violence." Thus, the phrase "violence in the townships" comes to mean what the young people are doing and not what the police are doing or what apartheid in general is doing to people. If one calls for non-violence in such circumstances one appears to be criticizing the resistance of the people while justifying or at least overlooking the violence of the police and the State.[84]

Christians in South Africa were asking questions that it is equally pertinent for Christians in Israel-Palestine to ask:

Is it legitimate, especially in our circumstances, to use the same word "violence" in a blanket condemnation to cover the ruthless and repressive activities of the State and the desperate attempts of the people to defend themselves? Do such abstractions and generalizations not confuse the issue? How can acts of oppression, injustice, and domination be equated with acts of resistance and self-defense? Would it be legitimate to describe both the physical force used by a rapist and the physical force used by a woman trying to resist the rapist as violence? It is simply not true to say that every possible use of physical force is violence and that no matter what the circumstances may be it is never permissible.[85]

The experience of the Church in South Africa is important because it is shared by many Christians in Israel-Palestine. They find it difficult to be nonviolent in a context that breeds so much State violence every day and brings dehumanization, deportation, and all kinds of injustice to the Palestinians, who have every right to be free.

In spite of it all, I still believe that the Christian should choose at every confrontation the nonviolent path—the way of Jesus. Unfortunately, many people find themselves unable to do so. And the Church must continue to press forward, condemning the violence of the state and impressing on its people the need to follow the way of nonviolence.

Nonviolence is dreaded by the Israelis because it reminds them of their situation before their empowerment, appealing to their memory of their own powerlessness and awakening their consciences to deal with those now in their power more justly. If it does not awaken Israeli consciences, I hope and pray that it will help raise the consciousness of many people in the West, both Jews and non-Jews, to what is happening in Israel-Palestine, and provoke an outcry that results in putting pressure on Israel to stop its death-wish policies and to adopt policies that will give Jews and Palestinians a life of peace in the land both love so dearly.

JUSTICE ALONE IS NOT ENOUGH

As Palestinian Christians continue to emphasize that God is a God of justice, that righteousness and justice are the foundations of

God's throne,[86] and that nonviolence is the way to resist occupation, it should be clear that in a theological understanding of God justice does not stand alone. John Shae can rightly say that justice "is the heart of God, the core of his being."[87] Karl Barth, on the other hand, can very well say that "God's very being is mercy."[88] It should be clearly understood that these divine attributes are not independent of one another, nor are they contradictory. Humans, depending on what they are discussing about God, tend to emphasize one attribute over another to prove a point. God's attributes, however, do not exist as separate components that are only loosely joined together. They are inextricably united and harmonized within the One Being of God. God's justice cannot be separated from God's peace and love and mercy. There are no dichotomies in the person of God; the dichotomies lie in humans. Unless we humans are extremely careful, we tend to talk about the justice of God without keeping in mind that God's being is also righteousness, mercy, love, and peace. All of these are an indivisible whole in God's nature.

Since, as a result of the Fall, the dichotomies lie within the fragmentation of the human being, people have a propensity to talk about justice in a strict sense, especially when they have fallen prey to injustice. The symbol of justice has become a blindfolded virgin carrying a scale in one hand and a sword in the other, rendering impartially to each person his or her due. In other words, justice is invoked as a totally uninvolved, independent, objective standard.

Legally speaking, such a concept might satisfy human demands for justice, but it would leave much to be desired because there is a sense in which blind, impersonal, and exacting justice can easily become injustice. If strict justice were left to operate by itself, the line that separates it from injustice would be very thin indeed. It is, of course, quite understandable that humans who have been wronged usually demand that absolute justice be done. Absolute justice not only restores their rights but also has a way of condemning and humiliating the wrongdoer. Yet so often such an outcome leaves the persons, the human family, or the nation involved fragmented and lost. What we need in the Israel-Palestine conflict is a way in which justice can be exercised so that the ultimate result would be peace and reconciliation between and within each people and not the fragmentation and destruction of either or both. Our problem is that, while such positive results are innately natural in God, they are alien in unredeemed humans.

Justice, mercy, and peace find total harmony and unity in God. In humans they are conceived as individual and separate characteristics that seldom join in harmony. If and when they do join, they are easily corrupted, abused, and again separated from each other. So humans tend to exercise justice without mercy, and the outcome is cruelty. Conversely, when mercy is extended without justice, it is naive and tantamount to a license for greater injustice. Similarly, justice without peace tends to fragment and destroy a society. Peace without justice is always shaky and uneasy and never permanent.

For Christians, a taste of restored wholeness and harmony, both within themselves and in their relationships with others, has been experienced in the agony, death, and resurrection of Christ. It is in this complete event that a person can see, at one and the same time, the justice, the righteousness, and the mercy of God. The parable of the unforgiving servant expresses it beautifully:

Therefore the kingdom of heaven may be compared to a king who wished to settle accounts with his servants. When he began the reckoning, one was brought to him who owed him ten thousand talents; and as he could not pay, his lord ordered him to be sold, with his wife and children and all that he had, and payment to be made. So the servant fell on his knees, imploring him, "Lord, have patience with me, and I will pay you everything." And out of pity for him the lord of that servant released him and forgave him the debt. But that same servant, as he went out, came upon one of his fellow servants who owed him a hundred denarii; and seizing him by the throat he said, "Pay what you owe." So his fellow servant fell down and besought him, "Have patience with me, and I will pay you." He refused and went and put him in prison till he should pay the debt. When his fellow servants saw what had taken place, they were greatly distressed, and they went and reported to their lord all that had taken place. Then his lord summoned him and said to him, "You wicked servant! I forgave you all that debt because you besought me; and should not you have had mercy on your fellow servant, as I had mercy on you?" And in anger his lord delivered him to the jailers, till he should pay all his debt. So also my heavenly Father will do to every one of you, if you do not forgive your brother from your heart.[89]

Strict justice requires the servant to pay his debt to his master. Because he was unable to pay, the debt was written off and his master had to absorb the loss of the large loan. This is mercy. For the master to confront his servant, who refused to forgive his own colleague, is righteousness. To bear the consequences of being unmerciful is judgment.

This analogy, as with all analogies, is not perfect, but it does illustrate the interplay of justice, righteousness, judgment, and mercy in humans. In other words, the demands of justice are absolute, because God is both the absolute God and the God of justice. What happened in the agony, death, and Resurrection of Christ far exceeds what humans are capable of doing. God's demand for justice, righteousness, and judgment received its satisfaction on the cross. For God to meet and fulfill the demands of justice basically means that God is faithful to God, that God is authentically God. If the cross therefore expresses this fidelity of the God of justice, then the Resurrection expresses the fidelity of the God of mercy, grace, and love to God. The Resurrection, therefore, is the absolutely unexpected surprise of God, the breaking of all molds.[90] Moreover, it is an expression of the total unity and harmony of the being of God, that is, God's justice and mercy, righteousness and grace, and so on. God is able, at one and the same time, to act both justly and mercifully. God can absorb the demands of God's justice and righteousness and still emerge as the God of mercy and love. God emerges from the cross unfragmented. God is still God in unity and harmony. God in essence is still saying that the demands of justice will not disappear from the world. At the same time, God still affirms that there will always be mercy, peace, and love.

To summarize: if we are to approach justice from a biblical standpoint, it is essential to establish first of all that God who is the God of justice demands the exercise of this justice in the world. There can be no circumventing this fact, no shortcuts to justice. It has been the experience of salvation history that God ultimately does not allow justice to be trampled upon, although for awhile it might appear that injustice has the upper hand.[91] Injustice will not go on forever unchecked. The oppressed and those who suffer injustice have an advocate: God. Justice must be established. Christians are called to acknowledge and proclaim this basic truth. They must go on to affirm that God's justice, as understood and seen in Christ, is never "blind" and is always exercised with mercy and grace. It is only when justice is ultimately defined by both mercy and peace, and when it has an inherent bias toward the underprivileged, that there is hope in the resolution of any conflict. This fact is painful for those who wish that justice would be fully and strictly satisfied, but it is the only way that promises reconciliation and peace. The search for strict justice, with its overtones of retaliation, can all too easily lower people to the level of the inhuman or even the subhuman; while the exercise of mercy and reconciliation can lift them up to the level of the genuinely human and even to the divine.

RIGHTEOUSNESS LINKED WITH MERCY

Biblically speaking, one cannot talk about justice without referring to righteousness. Both concepts are similar in meaning and are often used as parallels in the Bible. Usually, however, the word *mishpat* (root, *shafat*) is translated "justice," and *tsedek* (root, *tsadak*), "righteousness." The difference between them becomes conspicuous when one considers that the noun from *shafat* is *shofet*, meaning a judge; while the noun from *tsadak* is *tsadik*, which means a righteous or pious person. In Arabic the cognate word of *tsedek* is *sidq*, "truthfulness." From the same Arabic root, *sadiq* means friend, that is, "one who speaks the truth to you;" *siddiq* is a pious person, a person who lives in truthfulness before God;[92] and *sadaqah* is almsgiving, which is considered rewarding for the giver. Deuteronomy 24:12–13 carries a similar meaning:

> You shall not sleep in his pledge; when the sun goes down, you shall restore to him the pledge that he may sleep in his cloak and bless you; and it shall be righteousness to you before the Lord your God.

In this sense, righteousness goes beyond justice. It carries the meaning of kindness, compassion, and mercy:

Hear my prayer, O Lord. . . .
answer me, in thy righteousness *[tsedakah]!*
Enter not into judgment *[mishpat]* with thy
servant. . . .[93]

He will judge the world with righteousness,
and the peoples with equity.[94]

To talk about the righteousness of God, therefore, means to talk about God's compassion and mercy. In fact, God's concern for justice grows out of compassion and mercy. Injustice is condemned biblically not because the law has been broken, but because a merciful God is flouted and people are hurt:

He who oppresses a poor man insults his Maker, but he who is kind to the needy honors him.[95]

You shall not afflict any widow or orphan. If you do afflict them, and they cry out to me, I will surely hear their cry. . . . If he cries to me, I will hear, for I am compassionate.[96]

This aspect of God's compassion is best illustrated in the story of Cain and Abel.[97] Cain was condemned after he killed his brother Abel, not because he broke a law, but because his brother's blood was crying out of the ground. A human being had been hurt and God had become his advocate.[98] According to the demands of strict justice, Cain should have been killed. Instead, he is spared by the compassion of God and even protected.[99]

When God asks people to live righteously, it is meant that they should live according to God's standards of justice and compassion. The tragedy of the human predicament is that justice is mostly understood in terms of something to be exacted from another, while mercy is usually understood in terms of something we ask for ourselves. Jonah expected mercy for himself and destruction for the Ninevites. He preferred to die rather than to acknowledge that God's loving will and purpose included mercy for others. This loving purpose for others is stated clearly in the words of Amos: "Are not you Israelites like Cushites to me? Says the Lord. Did I not bring Israel up from Egypt, the Philistines from Caphtor, and the Aramaeans from Kir?"[100] Robert Coote has convincingly argued that the Cushites in this passage are not the Ethiopians, as commonly believed,[101] but the Assyrians, and the Babylonians[102]—the deadliest enemies of Israel and Judah. Thus the compassion of God is extended to all people.

To live justly is, therefore, to live righteously. To live righteously is to live compassionately in the midst of the complexities of social and political life, seeking God's loving will and purpose for our neighbors as well as for ourselves. Such a living implies a true understanding of the common humanity of all people and of God's justice and mercy as extended to all:

> Compassion is the way into the lives of others to understand their claims and shape our social and political institutions to respond to them. This sense of solidarity is grounded in the valuation of life. [Justice is stressed because life,] every life, is valuable. We do not struggle for a more just society for the sake of justice but as a way of valuing what we have received. Justice in the last analysis is an act of respect.[103]

THE UNFLINCHING PURSUIT OF PEACE

The Middle East has known little peace throughout its history. The twentieth century is no exception. People hardly know how to think of peace without thinking of war. Peace has come to mean only the absence of war and, ironically, the time in which governments prepare for the next war. As Nietzsche said (in another context), "You shall love peace as a means to new wars—and short peace rather than long! Let your peace be victory!"[104] Every war in the Middle East has increased the old injustice and created new injustices. Every military conflict has demonstrated the interplay and deception of power, the flaunting of international law, and the victimizing of thousands of people. Both Jews and Palestinians yearn for genuine and lasting peace. The Palestinians seek peace with justice, while the Israeli Jews want peace with security. The common denominator is peace, yet peace seems to be far off. Because of the demands of "strict" justice on the one hand and those of security on the other, peace has become a victim. The cry is constantly for peace but there is no peace. How can there be peace if there is no recognition of injustice done? How can there ever be security if justice is not exercised? The situation is similar to that in the time of Jeremiah, when there was a great argument over peace. Jeremiah had warned the people of impending destruction. His reasons were very simple: there was nothing but wickedness, violence, injustice, and oppression in Judah.[105] Moreover, the official prophets had added insult to injury by comforting the people and by calling the absence of peace, peace:

> They have healed the wound of my people lightly,
>> saying, ''Peace, peace,''
> when there is no peace.[106]

The extent of the depravity of the people was evident in the perpetuation of injustice and oppression that had made them hardened and calloused. It is not only that they had been living in the delusion of peace, but that they had become insensitive to the injustice they were committing:

> Were they ashamed when they committed abomination?
> No, they were not at all ashamed;
> they did not know how to blush.[107]

The prophets were clear about what makes for peace. Their words were very pertinent to the social, economic and political life of the people, and especially to the ruling elite:

> seek justice,
>> correct oppression;
> defend the fatherless
>> plead for the widow.[108]

Jeremiah addresses King Jehoiakim and contrasts him with his father:

> Did not your father eat and drink and do justice and
>> righteousness?
> then it was well with him.
> He judged the cause of the poor and needy;
>> then it was well.

> Is not this to know me?
>   says the Lord.[109]

By preaching social justice the prophets emphasized that peace refers to the totality of life, that peace is a holistic concept that has to do with life lived in its wholeness. To live in God's peace requires of us that we live justly and righteously because God is just and righteous.

The word for peace in both Arabic *(salam)* and Hebrew *(shalom)* has the same etymological root and the same breadth of meaning: wholeness, health, safety, and security. It refers to a peace experienced and lived out in the everyday historical situation of life. Peace is understood in relationship. It can be a fruit of something, or it can be a basis or cause that leads to something else. It is either a prerequisite or a by-product. Many biblical passages reveal the pertinence of peace and its relationships to the Israel-Palestine conflict—peace linked with justice, peace linked with truth, and peace linked with security.

Isaiah, for example, sees peace as the fruit of justice.

> Then justice will dwell in the wilderness
>   and righteousness abide in the fruitful field.
> And the effect of righteousness will be peace,
>   and the result of righteousness, quietness and trust
>   forever.[110]

The link between justice and peace is fundamental in the Old Testament. Again and again the prophets condemned any false peace that was based on oppression. "There is no peace," says the Lord "for the wicked."[111] Justice first, then peace: this is the order. Dom Helder Camara, the former Roman Catholic archbishop of Olinda and Recife in Brazil, has said,

> There is no doubt that Christ came to bring peace to men. But not the peace of stagnant swamps, not peace based on injustice, not peace that is the opposite of development. In such cases, Christ himself proclaimed that he had come to bring strife and sword.[112]

Robert McAfee Brown has written in the same vein: "We need to measure our world and the imperative for peacemaking, with an eye to justice. Whatever is unjust threatens peace. Whatever fosters justice is an act of peacemaking." [113] This point cannot be over-emphasized in the Israel-Palestine conflict. Unless the government of Israel and its supporters recognize that justice must of necessity precede peace, the prospects for peace will always remain dim. One recalls the words of Pope John XXIII: "If you want peace, work for justice." In the encyclical *Pacem in Terris,* Pope John outlined the full range of what he saw as preconditions for peace. These included provision for and protection of human rights; the just ordering of relations within and between the nations; and an international order that would protect the world from war. This immense task faces all people of goodwill. It is

a most exalted task, for it is a task of bringing about true peace in the order established by God—an order founded on truth, built according to justice, vivified and integrated by charity, and put into practice in freedom. [114]

Peace is linked with truth. In Zechariah, the exhortation of the Lord to the people has been "love truth and peace." [115] In Israel-Palestine one of the major factors contributing to the perpetuation of the conflict has been the use of falsehood and lies. It has been said that "in time of war, the first casualty is truth." [116] The experience of both Palestinians and Israelis is that truth has suffered, not only during war, but just as much if not even more when governments and political leaders were preparing for war. The truth has seldom been told. Falsehood and calumny have flourished, and falsehood and calumny breed war, not peace. As Thomas Merton put it,

Peace demands the most heroic labor and the most difficult sacrifice. It demands greater heroism than war. It demands greater fidelity to the truth and a much more perfect purity of conscience. [117]

Peace is prerequisite to security and safety. As King Hezekiah says for himself, "there will be peace and security in my days." [118]

This is a strong reminder that ultimately neither the stockpiling of sophisticated armaments nor an extension of territory are an adequate guarantee or a viable substitute for peace. They are illusory. The best borders are peaceful borders, and the best security lies in a truly peaceful relationship between neighbors.

The earthiness of peace can be discerned from its simple, agrarian depiction in the Bible. It is a way upon which people can walk:

> The way of peace they know not,
>   and there is no justice in their paths;
> they have made their roads crooked,
>   no one who goes in them knows peace.[119]

Peace is a seed which a person can sow: "there shall be a sowing of peace."[120] It can be sought and pursued: "Depart from evil, and do good; seek peace, and pursue it."[121] It is even within the possibility and capability of people to make peace. On its makers the highest of all honors will be conferred: "Blessed are the peacemakers for they shall be called sons [and daughters] of God."[122]

The Talmud likewise emphasizes peace. John Ferguson even says that "seek peace and pursue it" had become a central tenet of later Judaism.[123] The rabbinic exposition saw peace as part of God's original purpose for humanity. That was why God initially created a single individual. All humankind is thus essentially one.[124]

One of the most astonishing affirmations in the Talmud makes peace take precedence over the greatest of all commandments, namely, to believe in the oneness and uniqueness of God: "Great is peace, because if the Jews were to practice idolatry, and peace prevailed among them at the same time, God would say, 'I cannot punish them, because peace prevails among them.' "[125] In the Talmud Abraham's trained soldiers become scholars.[126] Jacob's sword and bow are treated as metaphors for prayer and supplication.[127] David is remembered as a poet, musician, and scholar rather than as a soldier and ruler.[128]

Almost all the references drawn out of the Hebrew Scriptures deal with *shalom* as a social concept. In fact, as Gerhard von Rad has observed, "we are struck by the fact that there is no specific text in which it denotes the specifically spiritual attitude of inward peace. . . . We are forced to say that in its most common use *shalom* is an emphatically social concept."[129]

Things are not much different when we come to the New Testament. It is hard to find one New Testament reference in which peace is primarily an inward reality.[130]

Above all, peace means reconciliation. The peace that Jesus brings breaks down the barriers of hostility and alienation between humans and God and between humans and each other.[131] Thus, the author of the letter to the Ephesians reminds his readers that Jesus Christ is himself the condition for, and the possibility of, positive interaction between people.

> For he is our peace, who has made us both one, and has broken down the dividing wall of hostility, by abolishing in his flesh the law of commandments and ordinances, that he might create in himself one new man in place of the two, so making peace, and might reconcile us both to God in one body through the cross, thereby bringing the hostility to an end. And, he came and preached peace to you who were far off and peace to those who were near; for through him we both have access in one Spirit to the Father.[132]

THE CROSS OF PEACE

The cross expresses the costliness of peace. Christians understand this well when they experience reconciliation with God through Christ, who is "our peace." It is this experience of reconciliation that creates the commitment in the believer, not just to live peaceably with one's neighbor, but also to *be* a peacemaker, like Jesus, to risk all to *make* peace. That is why Jesus calls peacemaking the work of the child of God. As God is the supreme Giver of peace, God's children show themselves to be truly God's sons and daughters when they are active peacemakers. At the same time, Christians become involved in the work of peacemaking without illusions. They embark on it with trepidation, fear, and trembling.

There is an intellectual content to peace. It is not a simple venture. It involves diligent and disciplined action. It cannot dispense with objective knowledge of the past and present. It cannot take injustice lightly, or simply brush aside differences. Peacemaking has to be a dynamic process, a process in which conflicts are not avoided, but are harnessed to construct the building of a better society for all the people involved.

Peacemaking is a costly and difficult task because of the immensity and intensity of evil and human brokenness in the world. It is, therefore, a complex process, and if peace is to be genuine and effective it must be multidimensional so that it can embrace the different interlocking problems of conflict. Peacemaking can be nothing less than the daily experience of the cross in all its agony and pain, but also, thank God, with all its promise of new life.

Christians are called to be the agents of peace in the world—not out of personal or national interest or security, but because of the responsibility that stems from their new nature in Christ.[133] This is the same as being "children of God."[134] At the same time, Christians recognize that peace ultimately has an eschatological dimension. While humans must strive to have "peace on earth,"[135] peace is too elusive to be fully attained in the world. The vision of total peace and harmony lies at the consummation of history.[136] Peacemakers, however, are called to try to make the eschatological vision of peace inform their work of peacemaking, to try to make that vision, at least in part, a present reality so that it will exert a powerful formative influence on every real historical situation of conflict. As J. Edward Barrett has said, "The universal realization of peace is currently not an immediate possibility. But the relative and proximate increase of peace is in every moment a very realistic possibility."[137]

6

Blessed Are the Peacemakers: The Prophetic and Peacemaking Imperatives of the Church

> Blessed are the peacemakers, for they shall be called sons of God.
>
> Matthew 5:9

How can the Church in Israel-Palestine, given its unique history and heritage, relate its ministry contextually amid the existing political crisis? What should be its role? How and to what extent can the church become involved? In essence, how can we translate into practice our Palestinian Christian theology of liberation? These are the most relevant and pertinent questions that need to be addressed.

THE DUAL IMPERATIVE

It is my strong conviction that in response to the conflict, the Church in Israel-Palestine is called to a two-dimensional ministry, a prophetic and a peacemaking one. These roles constitute a dual imperative for the Church, and should be the focus of its strategy today.

The prophetic imperative directs that the Church should dare to analyze and interpret events theologically. It should discern carefully the signs of the time and allow the mind of Christ to bear upon them. The prophetic imperative arises out of the Church's conviction that the active promotion of justice is not outside its purview and competence. Justice belongs to God, not to governments and politicians. The Church, therefore, would assume its God-given prophetic role.

With the peacemaking imperative, the Church recognizes that it is called by God to be a catalyst of peace and reconciliation. By its very nature in Christ, the Church is a peacemaking community in its own context of life. This is its servant role in the world.

Its Basis

The Church in Israel-Palestine is a composite, a rich mosaic bringing together Orthodoxy, Catholicism, and Protestantism. For centuries, the differences have been emphasized by the hierarchy, and the faithful have been confused and separated, although they were all originally Eastern Christians and go back to the same roots. For some of the hierarchy, the past still carries with it pain and grievances. For most Arab Christians, however, the emphasis is no longer on denominational affiliation, but on their common faith. The denominations, while reflecting the divisions and disunity of the Church, can also be seen as a rich heritage, a living variety of expressions of the Church in the world. Indeed, the Church should continue to work for greater unity, but it can accept its different traditions as parts that together make up a complete whole.

In the Middle East, such an understanding of the Church is still far off, but by the grace of God we are moving in that direction. Moreover, the presence of the Middle East Council of Churches, which brings together almost all of the Christians of the Middle East, is helping its member churches to grow together into greater understanding, respect, and cooperation.

The dual imperative of the Church in Israel-Palestine would help the different churches to concentrate on a common plan of action rather than focusing their attention on internal differences. It would emphasize the positive rather than the negative aspects of the situation.

One hopes also that in spite of the historic sensitivities, the churches in Israel-Palestine would agree that the biblical and theological basis for the prophetic and peacemaking strategy of the church today is threefold: God's continuous action and involvement in history; God's love for the whole world; and God's concern for justice, mercy, and peace in the world.

Its Theological Implications

The dual imperative consists of three strategic and concrete theological implications for the ministry of the Church. These comprise the underlying substance of the Church's strategy and are based on a theological understanding of justice and peace as expounded in Chapter 5. These implications are like three bright torches that must remain lit and lifted up by the Church in society.

The first implication of the dual imperative is the importance for the Church to keep alive among the people a concept of God that is both biblically and theologically based—God universal and inclusive in nature, the God of justice, love, and peace. The Church should proclaim its concept of God, as it has come to know God through Christ, to all people in society, including Muslims and Jews. This should be done unashamedly and uncompromisingly. The Church should insist on what God is really like—not in a spirit of superiority or condescension, but in humility and love. The Church must be conscious of its own failure in not living up to the responsibility of the knowledge of God that it has been given. It has not attained perfection, but still seeks a deeper understanding of God in Christ. It is not so much the Church that possesses the truth; rather, the truth in Christ has possessed the Church.

The second theological implication of the dual imperative for the Church is the exposition of truth. This carries a double responsibility, both for exposing and interpreting truth. To speak the truth is synonymous with speaking the Word of God prophetically. It is allowing the God of truth to shed light on events. When that happens, the hypocrisy and self-deception of individuals and governments is exposed. At the same time, to know and live by the truth offers freedom and liberation.[1] For the Church to keep the facts known and the truth exposed is to call attention to the pervasiveness of sin, evil, and injustice, and to call people to repentance and change.

This is a very difficult task, but it is an integral part of the prophetic imperative. It does not mean that the Church has specific answers to complicated political problems. What it means is that the Church has a sense of justice and is always ready to cry out against injustice and to encourage and promote justice and peace. A good illustration of this kind of Christian action took place at the height of the United States involvement in Vietnam in the late 1960s. A group of concerned Americans met with Henry Kissinger, who was, at the time, the chief architect of United States policy.

> The conversation became heated. Kissinger asked them how would you get the boys out of Vietnam? William Sloane Coffin, minister of Riverside Church, N.Y. *[sic]*, then chaplain at Yale University and prominent in antiwar protest, responded, "Mr. Kissinger, our job is to proclaim that, 'justice must roll down like waters, and righteousness like a mighty stream.' Your job, Mr. Kissinger, is to work out the details of the irrigation system." [2]

To speak the truth is to transcend both self and national interests and to give allegiance to God. The truth spoken and exposed passionately and sincerely for the good of people has a way of penetrating the toughest barriers and always evoking a response. Reactions against it may vary from conspiracies to silence and suppress it to attempts to control and bridle it.[3] Truth, even crucified and buried, still has a way of rising forth out of the grave, reasserting itself and challenging people to repentance and change.

The third theological implication of the dual imperative is for the Church to keep lifting high the banner of peace. This means constantly challenging the credibility of war and violence. It also means keeping alive a concept of peace that it is possible to attain if people are willing to accept a change in their war mentality. This concept of peace should be informed by a vision of peace.[4] A vision of peace must be sustained by the Church and should keep challenging people, calling them to the realistic possibility of peace based on justice—a justice not lacking in mercy.[5]

> Where there is a deep, simple, all embracing love of man, of the created world of living and inanimate things, then there will be respect for life, for freedom, for truth, for justice, and there will be humble love of God. But where there is no love of man, no love of life, then make all the laws you want, all the edicts and treaties, issue all the anathemas, set up all the safeguards and inspections, fill the air with spying satellites, and hang cameras on the moon. As long as you see your fellowman as a being essentially to be feared, mistrusted, hated, and destroyed there cannot be peace on earth.[6]

Its Strategy

It is important for all the churches in Israel-Palestine to adopt the dual imperative as a valid basis for their strategy of action. Specifically and concretely, this requires two things: first, bringing the churches to act together, and then actually adopting the dual imperative, and second, establishing a concrete organization, a center for peacemaking.

In order for the prophetic and peacemaking ministry to have the greatest impact on the country, it must be the joint work of all the churches in Israel-Palestine. This effort can begin only when it is recognized that the dual imperative is the responsibility of all the Christian churches in the land. There are two steps to take in carrying out this strategy.

A New Knowledge of God

The initial contact would be made with the hierarchy of the historic churches. The bishops must be approached first. Their position and prestige are invaluable to the effort, and they need always to be kept informed and consulted. This, however, is a delicate task, as many patriarchs and bishops tend to be conservative, and oversensitive to traditional attitudes and the status quo, and this can hinder progress.[7] Nevertheless, they should not be bypassed. Should the patriarchs and bishops be willing to commit themselves and their flocks to the prophetic and peacemaking ministry, it would be a miraculous feat of the Holy Spirit, having great consequences for the ministry of the Church.

Simultaneously, as contacts with the hierarchy of the churches are initiated, indigenous members should be made aware that this campaign for a peacemaking ministry is under way. The door should be open for all Christians, both clergy and laity, to participate. This ecumenism at the grass roots of the Church must be carried out wisely, so as not to antagonize the hierarchy of the churches. Generally, it is an easier task to involve the laity, since in many churches they are further advanced in ecumenism than their leaders. The process of changing people's war mentality to one of peace will not, however, be easy. It will be a slow and difficult task, because peace has always been viewed as the result of war. People need to undergo a new conversion experience to become peacemakers. In the words of the Preamble to the Constitution of the United Nations Educational, Scientific, and Cultural Organization (UNESCO), "Since war begins in the minds of men, it is in the minds of men that the defences of peace must be constructed."[8] Not only the mind but the whole being of the person must be converted to a new knowledge of God. So the movement for peacemaking will have to be based on a well-organized educational program through the churches and the Christian schools, one that employs the best and most up-to-date methods to reach ordinary people, children as well as adults, and the sophisticated elite.[9]

Involving the whole Church in the work of the dual imperative is a good way to promote Christian unity, a fact as significant as the work of peacemaking itself. Working for peace makes the churches focus on a common Christian concern. One hopes it will lead them to avoid ecclesiological controversies and intrigues and to concentrate on a positive Christian witness that stresses the importance of peace and reconciliation. This would be the joint response of the Church to the words of Christ: "Blessed are the peacemakers, for they shall be called sons of God."[10]

The hierarchy of the historical churches should be assured that the work of peacemaking does not mean that the Church is on its way to becoming a political party with a political agenda. Neither does it mean that the church is going to identify unconditionally with one side against another or espouse one cause over another. Rather, the Church has opted for involvement in the society and the nation. It takes the Incarnation seriously, choosing to be the conscience of the nation—or at least informing that conscience. If and when the Church takes sides, it must stand on the side of the poor, the weak, the oppressed, and the persecuted.[11]

From Quiescence to Dynamism

The ministry of the dual imperative would enhance the work of Christian unity, provide a positive channeling of the energy of the various churches, and facilitate wider, healthier communication among them all. It would testify to the Christians' faith in their Lord, lending credibility to the Church's presence in society. It would move the Church from a peripheral position in the life of the nation to one of greater involvement and centrality: from quiescence to dynamism.

In light of past history, the ministry of the dual imperative will undoubtedly be difficult for the churches in Israel-Palestine to achieve. The fragmentation of the Body of Christ because of doctrinal and theological differences as well as historical and political events has hindered the Church's witness to and dialogue with Muslims and Jews. Denominational divisions have bred suspicion and distrust among Christians. Their internecine conflicts have often been exploited by the ruling powers and tended to strengthen the rulers' control of the people.

Another major difficulty has been and still is the Christians' minority status, which is reflected in their entire attitude and mentality. They have been able, by the grace of God, to preserve their faith in spite of centuries of oppression that have drained their vitality.[12] They have survived with less rights than the majority around them possessed. They have lived in fear of the strange phenomenon of Levantinism.[13] They have been careful not to become overly involved lest they antagonize their neighbors and rulers and bring upon themselves further suffering.[14]

Any involvement of the Church in the dual imperative, therefore, is likely to be discouraged by the ruling powers and misunderstood at times by both Muslims and Jews. In spite of the risks, however, the ministry of the dual imperative has the potential of transforming the Church from a mere presence in the land to a purposeful and dynamic witness.

A Place for Peace

The second action of the basic strategy should be the creation of a Center for Peacemaking in Israel-Palestine. The purpose of the Center would be to translate the dual imperative into a concrete organizational, operational, and programmatic ministry of the Church.

Ideally, such a center should be set up by the joint effort of all the churches in Israel-Palestine. Considered an extension of the churches' existing ministry, it should be both morally and financially supported by them.[15] If this venture fails, the Center should, though regrettably, be set up by as many denominations as are willing to participate. At the same time, it should unswervingly pursue its efforts to include the other Christian churches. I believe that the establishment of the Center is the greatest calling of the Church in Israel-Palestine and should receive the highest priority.[16]

The rationale and foundation of the Center for Peacemaking should be the three theological implications of the dual imperative: the concept of God, who God is and what God expects of people; the exposition of facts and truth and their interpretation in light of the concept and knowledge of God; and the active promotion of justice and peace, in the belief that peace is possible and that it is more basic than war.[17] The thrust of the ministry of the Center should focus on the following points:

—The Center should never fail to remind people of a sense of justice.

—The Center should constantly carry on a theological contextualization of issues.

—The Center should look to the United Nations as the best forum for establishing criteria that can determine and adjudicate justice and resolve conflicting claims.

—The Center should itself provide a forum for communication and reciprocity so that differing views can be discussed and conflicts become creative when faced and mediated in an atmosphere of concern for justice and peace.

—The Center should monitor the development or deterioration of events, championing human rights, denouncing the arms race and the threat of nuclear arms.

The Center should be both multidimensional and comprehensive in its ministry and outreach. In the nascent phase of its development, it is natural to focus its work among the Christian population, using Church facilities to conduct workshops and seminars; but gradually the Center must reach Muslims and Jews, religious and laity, educated and uneducated, young and old. The work of the Center should be included in people's worship, supported and upheld by prayer groups throughout the country whose composition cuts across denominational barriers. Through its publications, the Center should address itself to the leadership of the country and sustain a challenge for peace. It should go beyond the immediate area of conflict to reach people abroad, especially in the West. This outreach should aim at de-stereotyping Western images of the people of the Middle East, de-Zionizing the Bible, and de-mythologizing the State of Israel. The support of Western Christians is invaluable in the struggle for justice and peace. They can encourage their governments to act evenhandedly in the pursuit of a peace based on justice.[18]

In addition, the Church should be farsighted in its projection of the future work of the Center for Peacemaking. The vicious circle of violence in the Israel-Palestine conflict is on the increase. Hatred and antagonism are accelerating at a phenomenal pace, bred by mutual acts of hostility and the intransigence of Israel. There is currently no internal machinery for peacemaking. Ultimately, there must be a resolution of this conflict, either one imposed as a result of much bloodshed and violence, or one created as a result of peaceful negotiations and pressure from the superpowers. Peace will not come automatically; it will be a slow and painful task. And beyond peace is the harder road that leads to reconciliation. Peace and reconciliation must be constructed out of the ravages of war, hatred, and animosity—the personal no less than the international—especially since "history lives with a special intensity in the consciousness of Middle Eastern peoples."[19] The Center for Peacemaking must, by the grace of God, become a place where peace and reconciliation are constructed—a place whose credibility for peacemaking becomes recognized, respected, and sought by all people.

THE CHURCH, THE CROSS, AND THE DUAL IMPERATIVE

War is being made every day in the Middle East, producing destruction and devastation. War breeds only more war, and the consequences of war are long-lasting hatred and animosity. Unless there is an internal process for peacemaking, then what is being planted in Israel-Palestine will be sown and reaped for many generations to come.[20] People who are immersed in a conflict find it almost impossible to become peacemakers themselves; most people in Israel-Palestine are drawn in, exhausted by warmaking. This applies to Christians as much as to Muslims and Jews. I believe that it is important for the Church, in light of its knowledge of God in Christ, to transcend the conflict and play a unique role in peacemaking.

The Muslims, who constitute the majority of the population of the Middle East, consider Palestine an integral part of the Islamic lands, whose population was predominantly Muslim until 1948 when Palestine was appropriated by the Zionists. Muslims consider Zionism and Israel a new form of Western colonialism imposed on their territory, which must be resisted. As Muslims have ultimately prevailed against the nineteenth- and twentieth-century colonialists, most of them believe that in the long run they will prevail against the State of Israel, this foreign Western body in the heart of the Arab East.[21] Such a view is not alien to the basic concept of *jihad* that Muslims espouse. The word means not only "holy war" but "striving" as well. There is a *jihad* of preaching and persuasion, as well as a *jihad* of perseverance and endurance. With the rise of Islamic militancy, it is less likely that Islamic leaders could play a radical peacemaking role without jeopardizing themselves, unless that role is in line with Islamic principles.[22]

The Jews, whose prophetic tradition and long history of suffering qualify them to play a peacemaking role, have acquired a new image since the creation of the State of Israel in 1948. By espousing the nationalistic tradition of Zionism, they have relinquished the role of the servant that they had claimed for centuries, becoming oppressors and warmakers themselves. This has been a revolutionary change from the long-held belief that Jews have a vocation for suffering.[23] Many rabbis had taught that Jews should accept suffering rather than inflict it as a means of changing the world. A rabbinic dictum was, "Be of the persecuted rather than of the persecutors."[24] And Scholem Asch cried, "God be thanked, that the nations have not given my people the opportunity to commit against others the crimes which have been committed against it."[25] Yet with the creation of the State of Israel, Menachem Begin could boastfully declare,

We fight, therefore we are.

Out of blood, fire, tears and ashes, a new specimen of human being was born, a specimen completely unknown to the world for over eighteen hundred years—the fighting Jew![26]

In contrast to both Judaism and Islam, Christianity in Israel-Palestine exists as a minority. Christians live their lives in a pre-Constantinian context. The object of much persecution, they have endured faithfully throughout the centuries, sustaining their faith tenaciously against great odds. Even now, when many Muslims and Jews are living in a spirit of militant triumphalism, the Church continues to live in the shadow of the cross. Therefore, in contrast to both Judaism and Islam, and in spite of the good in each of them, Christianity has a special foundation which lends itself to the work of peace and reconciliation. At the heart of the Christian faith is the cross and the Resurrection of Christ, and this gives the Church a special insight into peace and reconciliation with God and with humans. For the Church to follow in the footsteps of its Lord Jesus Christ it must walk the way of the cross. The *via dolorosa* is not a burden but a joy, joy in doing Christ's work of peace and reconciliation in the world. It is the Church's vocation to spend and be spent in love and service to the world that God has so loved and for which Christ died.

The Church lives in the power of the cross. Its strength comes from its crucified and living Lord. It is enlivened by the Holy Spirit. This power enables the Church to overcome its physical and psychological weakness as a minority and transcend any bitterness or hostility resulting from the political conflict, in order to assume the role of the servant and, for Christ's sake, to become the agent and instrument of both peace and reconciliation.

To be the Body of Christ requires an openness to the Spirit, an awareness of historic opportunity, a radical understanding of life within the Kingdom of God both present and becoming. It is a vision of unity expressed first and most powerfully in the sacrament of communion through which the incarnate Christ is revealed to the community and the community becomes that Body of Christ in service to the world.[27]

7

A Dream of Peace:
One Palestinian's Vision

Where there is no vision,
the people perish.

Proverbs 29:18 (KJV)

We have come to view the Palestine dispute as insoluble. We
have come to accept the political impasse as everlasting. Although
rays of hope flicker from time to time, despair has become our
companion in the land, the norm of our lives. It has been, on the
whole, a dark winter of occupation and oppression. When will the
spring of justice and peace come to Israel-Palestine?

Many people—presidents, prime ministers, politicians, officials
and nonofficials of various professions—have tirelessly proposed
solutions. Some, having favored one side, arrived at conclusions
wholly unacceptable to the other side. Even those who genuinely
tried to be balanced and fair could not escape the accusation of
being biased.

My own vision of a solution will, on the surface, look like other
futile attempts and, like the others, may well be discarded. But I
have decided to offer it nevertheless, as a vision, a dream. It might
be new to some, and not so new to others. It comes from a person
who is not a politician and who can never be one. A person who is
at heart a priest and a pastor. A person who has a strong faith in a
God of justice and love. A person who tries by the grace of God to

be honest and truthful. A person who strongly believes that politicians do not have a monopoly on issues of justice and peace. I would, therefore, like to believe that I speak prophetically, from the foundation of my faith in God, on issues of justice and peace in the world. I consider this part of my calling.

The following vision is, therefore, not haphazard, not an idea that has come to me on the spur of the moment. It has been growing in me for many years. It took me all these years to accept the unacceptable: a Jewish state on part of "our" Palestine. As a boy, remembering my family's harsh exile from Beisan, and later, as a person of faith and a clergyman, my own struggles with hate, anger, and humiliation were not easy. But these feelings had to be challenged continuously by the demands of love and forgiveness. At the same time, I knew without a doubt that injustice is sinful and evil; that it is an outrage against God; and that it is my duty to cry out against it. It has taken me years to accept the establishment of the State of Israel and its need—although not its right—to exist. I now feel that I want it to stay, because I believe that the elimination of Israel would mean greater injustice to millions of innocent people who know no home except Israel.

The journey of faith in my inner soul continues. I have come to believe that any genuine solution offered should pass the test of these two sayings of Jesus Christ:

So whatever you wish that men would do to you, do so to them; for this is the law and the prophets.[1]

You shall love your neighbor as yourself.[2]

In other words, any proposed solution involving Israel should be an offer I would accept for my own people, the Palestinians. Every proposal should be weighed carefully so that each side can recognize it as good and just to both. Otherwise, the proposal would have no credibility.

This is the basis from which I have worked. I offer the proposal in its unpretentious simplicity. Even if rejected, I hope it will still reflect the spirit of an imaginative solution that is vitally needed in the Middle East.

As I have indicated, I do not represent a political party. I am not a member of any political party. I will never be one. I am a member of the Church, and I speak as a Christian from the position of faith. I speak as a person who believes in the inescapability of justice and the indispensability of peace.

THE MAJOR PREMISE:
A LAND FOR PALESTINIANS AND JEWS

The issue of Palestine has come to resemble a syllogism to me. It all really depends on the major premise. If one's major premise is "Palestine belongs to the Jews," the minor premise "the Palestinians have no right to it" will have to follow logically. If you reverse it by saying "Palestine is the land of the Palestinians," the Jews will have to go.

The key to the solution is found in a clear and emphatic major premise that both the Israeli Jews and the Palestinian Arabs must accept. If they do not—and unless the community of nations by some miraculous feat can convince the two sides to accept it—there will always be conflict and bloodshed. At this point in the 1980s, it is Israel that needs convincing; the pressure on Israel to accept a political solution must come from both the American Jewish community and the United States government.

The major premise is simply this: *Palestine is a country for both the Jews and the Palestinians.* There is no other viable, just option that can be adopted. Any change in the delicate balance of the major premise will risk the lives of millions.

Contrary to what some people may feel—and this will come as a shock to many others—the PLO has always proposed the ideal solution for Palestine: one united and democratic state for all Palestinians and Jews. Interestingly, the United States, which prides itself on being the champion of democracy, has never accepted this proposal.

I still believe that this solution is feasible. It is the best and the easiest to implement. And it can very well be the minor premise in the syllogism. However, in line with the biblical injunctions above, I would have to agree, with Israel, to reject it. Israel insists above all on being a Jewish state. As a part of a democratic, binational Palestine, the Jews would eventually become a minority in the country. Furthermore, many Jews so distrust the Palestinians that they would not wish to consign their future to them. So in spite of all of its attractiveness, the idea of a binational state must be discarded.

The preservation of Israel as a Jewish state is important not only to Israeli Jews but to Jews all over the world. I believe that we must honor their wish and accept it. In fact, the Palestinians should eventually guarantee the survival of Israel by accepting it as a Jewish state. They are the only ones who can do it. If, for any reason, the State of Israel disappears, it should not be the result of a military act, but the result of the Jews' own decision to leave Israel. For it is quite conceivable that, fifty or one hundred years from now, life in the Middle East could, for one reason or another, become unbearable to some Jewish Israelis. They might choose to leave for the West (indeed, many have already done so) or for other countries in the Middle East where life is less taxing and more relaxed. That should be their own decision. But there will always be that faithful remnant of the Jews who will live in Israel-Palestine, close to their Holy Places. As an observer of history, I feel that the historic memory of the Jews for the land is much stronger than their actual roots there. When times became rough, many of them left the land for easier lives in more secure countries. In fact, although it is a *mitzvah,* a religious duty, for a Jew to live in the land, most of the Jews, some of whom are religious, have chosen not to do so. Be that as it may, the land will always be treasured in their historic memory.

Having said this, I want to make it clear that I am not suggesting some future solution along demographic lines. I am merely saying that we should put aside the idea of one democratic Palestine and insist on preserving the Jewish character of Israel so as to alleviate the insecurity of the Jewish people.

THE MINOR PREMISE: A PALESTINIAN STATE

The only other minor premise that one can deduce in the syllogism is the establishment of a Palestinian state alongside the State of Israel. There is *no* other alternative offering *real* justice, and a good measure of peace and stability, for our area. Such a nation, as the PLO has long insisted, should be established in the eastern part of Palestine (the West Bank) and in Gaza as a state that is free, independent, and democratic, and where all those who live in it, regardless of their religious affiliation, will be first-class citizens. And I believe that the Palestinians are capable of making that dream come true.

As a Palestinian, I recognize that the solution of two states in Palestine is what the Jewish settlers wanted in the first place, before 1948, and that the Palestinians rejected it. Now, it is what the Palestinians have come to accept, while the Israeli Jews have repeatedly rejected it.

The Palestinians' acceptance of their own state on one part of the land should not be seen as a sign of weakness or resignation. The *Intifada* of 1988 has given the Palestinians a sense of power and effectiveness. Those who have lived in Israel, either as Israeli Arabs since 1948 or as Palestinians on the West Bank and in Gaza since 1967, have become more realistic in their demands and aspirations. They are willing to accept the reality of a Jewish state.

It is Israel that has become intransigent. The reversal of roles is at once fascinating and tragic. Israel has so barricaded itself in fear of the Palestinians that it will be difficult to remove the fortifications and live in peace with its neighbors. Israel also used its fear of the Palestinians to keep the world on its side, supporting and defending, keeping the money flowing into the country. So the Palestinians, and Arabs in general, were labeled as inhuman, bloodthirsty terrorists who wanted to drive the Jews into the sea. Since the *Intifada,* however, the world has come to recognize this falsification of the Palestinian image. The Palestinians are now seen realistically: a people made up of men, women, and children who know how to cry when beaten by the Israeli army, who hurt when their bones are crushed, and who lament their beloved who have been killed for no reason except their resistance to occupation and their struggle for freedom and dignity. The image of the Palestinian has changed, and it is now Israel's image that is tarnished, Israel and its few staunch friends who are left to live with the phobia of the Palestinians that Israel has created.

It is for the security and well-being of Israel that a Palestinian state should be established. In fact, it would be appropriate for Israel itself to make such a proposition. This is the kind of leadership that Israel needs if it is to survive at all. But the creation of a Palestinian state should be only the first step in a dynamic process of peace and reconciliation. For the resolution of the conflict will not happen suddenly, at the moment a Palestinian state comes into existence. The work of reconciliation can only then begin, when Jews and Palestinians meet each other on equal footing and not as oppressor and oppressed. There will be much work to be done to deal constructively with the damage that the Israeli Jews have inflicted on the Palestinians, as well as with the fear of the Palestinian Arabs that has haunted the Jews.

NEW ATTITUDES: FOUNDATIONS FOR PEACE

Before the process of peacemaking can begin, a change in attitude of Israeli Jews and Palestinians toward one another is necessary. They need to face each other with candor, to create the new attitudes that will be the foundation for peace and stability in the region.

For Palestinians: Acknowledging the Holocaust

The Palestinians need to become really conscious of and sensitive to the horror of the Holocaust, Nazi Germany's attempt to exterminate the Jews. Granted, the Holocaust was not a Middle Eastern phenomenon, and the Palestinians had nothing to do with it; nevertheless, we need to understand the extent of the trauma for the Jews. Our need to be educated in this matter is similar to that of the Eastern Jews, the Sephardim, for whom the Holocaust was also not part of their frame of reference. Admittedly, we as Palestinians have refused to accept, much less internalize, the horrible tragedy of the Holocaust. We have resisted even acknowledging it, believing that we have been subjected to our own holocaust at the hands of the Jews. Many Palestinians have doubted that the Holocaust even occurred; they could not believe that those who suffered so much could turn around and inflict so much suffering on the Palestinians. We have also refused to admit or acknowledge its uniqueness, pointing to the attempt to destroy the Assyrian and Armenian Christians in this century.[3]

Be that as it may, a new attitude is expected of us vis-à-vis the Holocaust. We must understand the importance and significance of the Holocaust to the Jews, while insisting that the Jews understand the importance and significance of the tragedy of Palestine for the Palestinians. The new attitude would make us Palestinians face Israel quite candidly and state that the only justification that the Palestinians will accept for the creation of a Jewish state in Palestine is the Holocaust. It was the Holocaust and only the Holocaust that necessitated the creation of a home for the Jews. Some Western countries did not open their doors to the Jews, and the Zionist leadership at the time was glad about this because it really wanted all the Jews to go to Palestine! The Palestinians, as hosts, have to come to accept giving the Jews the best part of Palestine (western Palestine), not because they had any right to it, not because of the Balfour Declaration,[4] and not even because of anti-Semitism, but because of the Holocaust.

Evan M. Wilson, former United States consul general in Jerusalem, has written, "The creation of a Jewish state in Palestine . . . against the wishes of the majority (two-thirds) of the inhabitants of the country was a mistake. . . ."[5] Many people agree with this sentiment. But as Wilson says, "this is not the issue today."[6] We must evaluate the past truthfully, but we must go beyond it.

As to the problem of anti-Semitism, I have come to accept it as an evil directed against the Jews in a special way. Although one can point to a lot of racism, prejudice, and discrimination that still exists in the world today in one form or another, the Jews have endured in their historic experience the longest continuous manifestation of this racism because of their wide dispersion among different nations. It is more prevalent in Jewish history because the Jews, more than many nations, have recorded and catalogued their history. But as I have mentioned earlier, other groups, no less than the Jews, have been subjected to racism and discrimination. It has been the sad lot of many, though not all, minorities. Be that as it may, the presence of anti-Semitism is not, in my own judgment, a sufficient reason to uproot another people, usurp their land, and create a new state. It is not a principle that should be applied every time racism or anti-Semitism appears. My observation is that even in a place as democratic and free as the United States, one can find a great measure of anti-Semitism, not to mention racism, prejudice, and discrimination against other minorities. In spite of this, I do not see American blacks emigrating in hordes to Africa. Neither do I see American Jews flocking to Israel. America is their home, and they will stay in it and fight both racism and anti-Semitism.

The Palestinians can, therefore, look the Jews in the eye and say that the only justification that they can accept today for the presence of Israel is the Holocaust. And with a new, magnanimous attitude they should say to the Jews, we will accept you and share the land with you. You have suffered for so long. Come share our land. This is God's land. We will live in it together as brothers and sisters.

This new attitude is not communicated in a spirit of triumphalism or superiority. It does not even have to be uttered verbally; but it should reflect the new attitude of the Palestinians to the Jews.

For Jews: "You Have Been Wronged"

The new attitude of the Israeli Jews toward the Palestinians should be simply this: We are sorry that we came to you with arrogance and a feeling of superiority. We came with good and not so good reasons. But we are now here in the land. Forgive us for the wrong and the injustice that we have caused you. We took part of your country. We ignored you. We pretended that you did not exist or, even worse, that you did not matter. We stereotyped you, convincing others that you are all terrorists. We have refused to recognize that you have any rights, while we insisted that you should recognize and legitimate *our* right to *your* land. We have insisted, and convinced the United States and others to insist, that you recognize our claim to your land. And amazingly, many governments in the world have agreed with us. We have refused to negotiate with your representatives, rejecting them as terrorists. Here, too, we have extracted a pledge from the United States government that it will not negotiate with your representatives.[7] We have done this and much more. We have wronged you. Now, we recognize that the healthiest solution to any conflict is the use of negotiation and compromise, as opposed to power, repression, and control. We are willing to negotiate with your representatives, the PLO, and we choose to live in peace with you. We want to stay a part of the Middle East. We want to live among you, Muslims and Christians. Your own country of Palestine today used to be our country two thousand years ago. We still have many cherished historic memories that keep pulling us to it. It is our "holy land," too, our "promised land." There is room for both of us here.

Such an attitude does not deny the link of the Jews with the past, but it acknowledges the realistic historical and demographic changes that have taken place in Palestine over the last two thousand years.

These two attitudes would immediately lay the right foundation for a new life for the whole of the Middle East, and would initiate the dynamic process toward peace and reconciliation.

In some parts of the Middle East there are strong traditions that provide solutions for communal disputes. One person is killed by another. The families are locked in a bitter feud. People of good repute and leaders of adjoining communities are called to mediate. Through their wisdom and clever maneuverings they start the feuding parties on the path of peace.

A number of years ago, the men of a Druze village in the Galilee went on a rampage in a nearby Christian and Muslim town. They pillaged the town, burning houses and cars and killing people. A traditional *sulha* (process of reconciliation) ensued.

I am not suggesting that this is what needs to take place between the Palestinians and the Jews. The scope of the problem is more regional and international. In today's world, the best *sulhas* are done when people allow international law and the international community to operate and arbitrate. The example above shows that humans have the capacity to deal with the worst disputes, even when innocent blood has been spilled. So, in spite of all the bitterness and hatred that have resulted from Israeli policies against the Palestinians, the Palestinians still have inherent Semitic values of honor, magnanimity, and hospitality that allow them to find viable solutions and live in peace with their neighbors, even if they were once their bitter enemies. Indeed, it will take many years to forget the hate and the harm, but it is possible to live together in spite of it all. This is not wishful thinking. Those who know the Arabs well know that this is a reality of life in the Middle East. Israeli Jews could be assured of this if they would change their attitude. I believe that the attitudinal changes I have proposed can be a catalyst, setting in motion the dynamic process: a foundation on which to build peace in our region.

To reiterate what I have said thus far: There is a need for new attitudes to the Israel-Palestine conflict from both the Palestinians and the Jews—the Palestinians' acceptance of Israel's right to exist within secure borders, and Israel's acceptance of a Palestinian state on the West Bank and in Gaza. What I have proposed is but one basis for a solution. In my view it is only the viable syllogism that provides us with a realistic solution to the conflict. Building on that, the dynamic process should point to the creation of a federation of states in the Middle East. I envision this federation as a coming together of two or more sovereign states in order to create a dynamic relationship among them. Some people have suggested the idea of a confederation between Israel and Palestine. That is a wonderful idea. But I would like to suggest the even more challenging idea of a federation that would eventually include the sovereign states of Lebanon and Jordan. Such a Federated States of the Holy Land could widen the base for economic cooperation among the partners. It could create a mutual feeling of interdependency, the life of peaceful neighbors, not enemies. It would bring together four countries small in population that perhaps cannot be viable on their own, but which, when joined together in a dynamic, healthy federation, could be a blessing to themselves and to the entire Middle East.[8]

For Israel and Palestine, in such a federation, boundaries and borders would be respected because people live as neighbors and not as enemies. Even the awkward boundaries of the future state of Palestine, which would link the West Bank with Gaza, could be accepted because they are the borders of a friendly neighbor and not an enemy.

Israel, Palestine, Jordan, and Lebanon are all part of the Holy Land. Each would guard its sovereignty, but they are all interdependent and belong together in a dynamic federated relationship. Each has a sizable number of Palestinian refugees, who can benefit from the federation. The chain of development will have to be set in motion. Repatriation of all refugees will have to take place. The Jewish settlements on the West Bank and in Gaza would provide new towns for the returning Palestinian refugees. Israelis, with their expertise in "making the desert bloom," can be partners in building the country. The whole world community will come to the aid of the Federation. Most of the money that each partner had designated for arms will now be diverted to the development and building of the Federation.[9] And Israel would have to give up its nuclear weapons.[10]

Such a federation could also help address the problem of Jerusalem, perhaps the thorniest of all issues in the Arab-Israeli conflict. It is the key to peace. Once a solution is found for the governance of Jerusalem, the solution of the whole country ensues.

SHARING JERUSALEM: THE KEY TO PEACE

The problem of Jerusalem would have to be approached with the same basic major premise in mind. The minor premise would have to be changed in order to preserve the unity of the city rather than to divide it. It would be an omen to the people of Israel and the Palestinians, and indeed to the world community, if Jerusalem did not remain united. It would also be tragic if Jerusalem were placed unilaterally under the full control of either the Palestinian state or the State of Israel.

Throwing all biased arguments aside, one needs to recognize that Jerusalem is a city holy—equally holy—to Judaism, Islam, and Christianity. It is futile to argue to which of the three it is most holy. It cannot be controlled by any one of them. Jerusalem's future should not be determined by military power. It is unique, a city belonging not only to the nations of the Middle East but to the world. Jerusalem must be shared.

Many ideas have been proposed for the governance of Jerusalem. Most of them fall short because they are biased in favor of one side over another. To date, the concept fairest to Jerusalem and to the different sides of the conflict is that suggested by the United Nations and the Vatican: internationalization, Jerusalem as *corpus separatum*. It has many merits to commend it, and could be considered for a transitional period; but I do not see it as the permanent solution. I believe that eventually the people of both Israel and Palestine are capable of running their own affairs without the tutelage of the United Nations. Although the U.N. would have to play the major role in creating and keeping peace in the Middle East, acting at different stages as the interim force that facilitates a smooth transition, it would be left for the indigenous peoples, the Arabs and the Jews, to see that the dynamic process is both initiated and sustained.

Therefore, my proposal issues from the federation scheme I have discussed. Jerusalem can be the federal capital of a United States of the Holy Land, belonging not to any one state alone, but to all. Lebanon's capital is Beirut, Jordan's is Amman. The Palestinians could choose a capital from the existing cities of the West Bank, or create one. Israel, for the sake of peace, will have to accept Jerusalem as its federal capital, but not as its national capital. It will either keep Tel Aviv, which is still recognized as its capital by the world community, or choose another. To give up Jerusalem as a national capital will be difficult for many Jews and for many Palestinians. But peace is paramount, and Jerusalem will still be theirs on a higher platform. (Even at the height of the Israelites' history, Jerusalem was not the capital for most of the Children of Israel. Ten of the twelve tribes gave their allegiance to Samaria rather than to Jerusalem.)

Jerusalem as the federal capital would again be given the dignity, honor, and holiness it deserves. The Holy City will not be Judaized, Islamized, or Christianized: it will be the city of the One God.

One of the obvious weaknesses of this scheme is that Israel as a Jewish state would be only one of a federation of four, and the three other states would be Arab. I am afraid there is no way around this, unless one goes back to the idea of a confederation between Israel and Palestine only. The federation of the four states could conceivably give Israel a unique, positive position rather than being a disadvantage.

Perhaps with such a vision, Israel can discover fresh meaning in the apocalyptic vision of Micah:

> It shall come to pass in the latter days
> that the mountain of the house of the Lord
> shall be established as the highest of the mountains,
> and shall be raised up above the hills;
> and peoples shall flow to it,
> and many nations shall come, and say:
> "Come, let us go up to the mountain of the Lord,
> to the house of the God of Jacob;
> that he may teach us in his ways
> and we may walk in his paths."

For out of Zion shall go forth the law,
and the word of the Lord from Jerusalem.
He shall judge between many peoples,
and shall decide for strong nations afar off;
and they shall beat their swords into plowshares,
and their spears into pruning hooks;
nation shall not lift up sword against nation,
neither shall they learn war any more;
but they shall sit every man under his vine and under his
      fig tree,
and none shall make them afraid;
for the mouth of the Lord of hosts has spoken.[11]

Surely, the Palestinians would share in this vision and prayer for peace.

8

Justice, and Only Justice: A Final Plea

> Look carefully then how you walk, not as unwise
> men but as wise, making the most of the time,
> because the days are evil.
>
> Ephesians 5:15–16

I have tried to lay down the foundation of a Palestinian theology of liberation, a theology that will help Palestinian Christians in particular to come to terms with the most excruciating issues of the Israel-Palestine conflict. It is a proposal that will offer hope to Jews and Muslims as well. I have also suggested that the role of the Church in Israel-Palestine should be that of the dual imperative: the prophetic and peacemaking responsibility. As an instrument of the dual imperative, I have suggested the creation of a Center for Peacemaking in Israel-Palestine. Furthermore, I have tried to point to a possible resolution of the conflict, grounded in my understanding of God in history, the insistence on justice, and the responsibility of loving our neighbor as ourself.

PEACE IS KNOCKING AT OUR DOOR

As I write this concluding chapter, I have mixed feelings of hope and fear. Hope, because I am convinced that peace is possible in our area. Peace is knocking at our door, but the door has not been opened. The door of peace is reached only through the door of justice. Once that door opens, peace lies inside. Where peace is, a meal is prepared; it is the feast of reconciliation ready to be celebrated. There is, however, no entrance except through the door of justice.

This hope is not imaginary. It is real. It is accessible. It is within reach. It demands courage on the part of Israeli Jews, and the persistent encouragement of American Jews and the United States government.

There is a Jewish interpretation of Deuteronomy 16:20, "Justice, and only justice, you shall follow. . . ." The word "justice" is used twice. The first "justice," it is said, applies to the Jews; the second applies to other people.[1]

The creation of the State of Israel, after the tragedy of the Holocaust, has rendered some justice to the Jewish people by giving them a home where they can live in peace. Although this home was built on the ashes of other peoples' homes, on their pain and suffering, it has gradually come to be accepted by the Palestinians. It is time now to go further and implement the second "justice," justice to the Palestinians. If this justice is not done, Israel will go on living unjustly. This injustice will be like a worm eating at Israel's core; Israel will forfeit its own justice. Justice to the Palestinians means the creation of a Palestinian state.

ISRAEL'S DANGEROUS DREAM

It is important that Israel be convinced that "Greater Israel" is an unrealistic and dangerous dream that some Jews are striving for. If they achieve it, it will be the result of the power of their guns. But they should know, as the past forty years have shown, that their military victories will not result in peace and security. On the contrary, they will heighten their sense of insecurity. The 150 million Arabs in the Middle East will not go away; they will not suddenly disappear. The nightmare will persist. Israel cannot live forever behind walls of its own making, committing injustice unresisted. It has to accept itself as being a small state in the Middle East, surrounded by largely Islamic countries. There was a time in the ancient Israelites' history when the area of Jewish sovereignty was very small.[2] To live in peace on the land was of more importance than the size of the territory. Israel must accept its true size. Expansion will only bring renewed conflict and insecurity. Israel's worst enemy today is neither the Palestinians nor the Arabs, but Israel itself. "Justice, and only justice, you shall follow. . . ." is an injunction that Israel needs to heed if it is ever to be free.

My realistic hope is mixed with fear. I am afraid that Israel is characterized today by two words: intransigence and arrogance. The arrogance has taken a heavy beating since the *Intifada,* but it has not disappeared. The intransigence, however, has intensified. Some Israeli Jews have advocated harsher measures against the Palestinians. Extremists have been urging mass expulsions, and indeed, many Palestinians have already been deported. Among them is Mubharak Awad, director of the Palestinian Center for the Study of Non-violence, based in East Jerusalem. Mubharak has been a strong advocate of nonviolence, but that did not deter the Israeli government from deporting him (on June 13, 1988) "in spite of America's objection." The tragic position of the State of Israel is that both violent and nonviolent protests are perceived as threats. The goal of both is self-determination for the Palestinians. Israel adamantly rejects this "end." Therefore, any "means," whether violent or nonviolent, has to be rejected. In fact, nonviolent resistance is more potent than violence, because Israel is better equipped and trained to deal with the latter. Mubharak, therefore, had to go. This is indeed tragic, since it shuts the door to any positive and legitimate resistance.[3]

"NEVER AGAIN" OR "YES, AGAIN"?

"Never again" became the Jews' moral imperative after the Holocaust, and we all shared that imperative with them. But in Israel it has become "yes, again" because of Israel's own intransigence. Israel has not been successful in achieving peace and security for its own people. Instead of listening to reason and accepting the reality of the rights of the Palestinians to their own land and state, it continues to oppress and uproot them even further. Its actions stem from frustration, defiance, greed, and megalomania. Israel's oppressive policies cannot sow the seeds of peace; they are only setting the stage for another holocaust whose instigators and executors are the Israeli Jews themselves. Israel's "never again" is no

longer the sorrowful cry of a moral nation beleaguered and struggling to survive. It is the frustrated cry of a nation trying to commit
suicide, whose leadership reflects both a Samson and a Massada
complex: if they do not achieve what they want, they will bring
down everything and everyone with them when they go.

During the first few days of the 1973 war, Israel felt threatened,
and threatened, in turn, to use its nuclear arms, in order to oblige
the United States government to start a massive supply of weapons.[4] Given the mentality of some of its leadership, one cannot rule
out the use of nucelar arms by Israel. Those who love Israel and
are concerned about its welfare should stop its madness. The country and its leaders must be brought back to their senses.

Since the *Intifada* on the West Bank and in Gaza, the centuries-
old hatred of some Jews for Gentiles has been incarnated in their
hatred of the Arabs, particularly the Palestinians. The Palestinians
have become the vicarious sufferers for humanity's guilt toward the
Jews. But what is the real guilt of the Palestinians? Does it lie in
the mere fact that they had been living in their country, Palestine,
for hundreds of years when the Zionists came to claim it? Are they
to be blamed for refusing to surrender their rights, hand over their
house keys, pack up and leave in order to turn over the country to
its "original owners"? The Palestinians did not initiate the conflict,
yet today they are being dehumanized simply because they resist
occupation by a foreign power and demand independence, freedom,
and dignity. It is ironic that some of the oppressive methods em-
ployed by the State of Israel against the Palestinians have been
compared with those used by the Nazis against the Jews.[5] The oppressed have indeed become the oppressors. One cannot help but
be reminded of what the Austrian Jewish psychiatrist Viktor Frankl
wrote after he survived the death camps of Nazi Germany. Frankl
noticed that the inmates who had been freed from the camps began
to behave like their tormentors:

> Now, being free, they thought they could use their freedom
> licentiously and ruthlessly. The only thing that had changed
> for them was that they were now the oppressors instead of
> the oppressed. They became instigators, not objects, of will-
> ful force and injustice. They justified their behavior by their
> own terrible experience.[6]

Israel wants the world to remember the atrocities of the Holocaust, yet its actions against the Palestinians mock the sacredness of that great human tragedy, making a sham of it. Israeli Jews need to be reminded of the moving words of Frankl:

> Only slowly could these men be guided back to the common-place truth that no one has the right to do wrong, not even if wrong has been done to him.[7]

Maybe the day will come when Israel's Holocaust memorial, Yad va-Shem, will include scenes of the Palestinians' sufferings to remind the world of the extent, the depth, and the mystery of evil in our world.

A CAUSELESS HATRED

In the *Yoma* one reads,

> Why was the first Sanctuary destroyed?
> Because of three [evil] things which prevailed
> there: idolatry, immorality, bloodshed. . . .
> But why was the second Sanctuary destroyed. . . ?
> Because therein prevailed hatred without
> cause. That teaches you that groundless
> hatred is considered as of even gravity with
> the three sins of idolatry, immorality, and
> bloodshed together.[8]

It is significant that the rabbis did not blame the Romans or anti-Semitism or anti-Jewishness, or anything else, for the destruction of Jerusalem; they blamed "causeless hatred." There is a "causeless hatred" operating in Israel-Palestine today, endangering both the Palestinians and Israel.

Those who are concerned must do all in their power to save the Palestinians from Israel and to save Israel from itself. The movement toward destruction can be redirected; the two nations deadlocked in conflict can still live in peace as good neighbors. They will either have to live as cousins in peace or die estranged as fools. "By three things does the world endure: justice, truth and peace.

. . . The three are one, because if justice is done, truth has been effected and peace brought about; and all three are mentioned in one verse, as it is stated, *Execute the judgment of truth and peace in your gates,* [indicating that] wherever justice is done peace is to be found.''[9]

These words from *Perek HashShalom* are addressed to all people of goodwill, who need to join together in making our part of the world endure on the pillars of justice, truth, and peace. By so doing, hope will be increased and fear diminshed and we can all, Jews and Palestinians, become recipients of that blessedness pronounced by Jesus Christ: ''Blessed are the meek, for they shall inherit the earth.''[10]

THE CHRISTIAN CHALLENGE: LOVE YOUR ENEMIES

My final plea, however, is directed to my own people, the Palestinians. Let me introduce it with a story.

It happened after ten o'clock one cold night in February 1988, in one of the suburbs of East Jerusalem. Their two little girls were already asleep, and my friend Issa and his wife were watching TV in their pajamas, when they heard a loud banging on their front door. The soldiers did not wait for the door to be opened; they had started breaking the glass windows on the front porch when Issa, frightened, opened the door. The troops shoved him aside and dashed into the house, searching it. The little girls awoke and clung to their parents. The soldiers broke a few things in their wild search, but they did not find whatever they were looking for. Worst of all, they were using very bad language. They ordered my friend to go with them, not even allowing him to change into his street clothes. So Issa went with them, in his pajamas. His wife managed to quickly give him his identity card. Then, shocked and scared, she called her relatives, who hurried over to stay with her and the children.

Issa was taken to a dark open area where dozens of other people, young and old, were detained. They, too, had been grabbed from their homes during the cold winter night. They were ordered to sit there and wait. Their identity cards were taken from them. Every few minutes one of the soldiers would come, scream at them, threaten them, curse at them, and then leave. This scene was repeated often until 2 o'clock in the morning, when one soldier came, flung all the ID cards into the dark night air, and told the gathered men to each look for his card and walk home. In the early hours of the morning, my friend reached his house.

A few days later, Issa came to my office and told me his story. I have known him for a number of years, and he has always struck me as a peaceful and gentle man, a hard worker who tries to make a good living for his young family. He has never been involved in politics and has never belonged to a political party. He loves his country and his people. He is honest and truthful. I listened very carefully to him while he told me his story. I remember him saying at the end, "I never hated the Jews; even after they occupied the West Bank, I never felt much hate for them. But now it is different. Hate is building up in me. I hate them. I know it is wrong to hate, but they are making me hate them."

This young man is not anti-Semitic; he is, after all, a Semite himself. His ancestors have lived in the Jerusalem area for hundreds of years. He was expressing a phenomenon of hate that, since the *Intifada*, is slowly spreading to engulf most of the Palestinian community on the West Bank and in Gaza.

Neither in 1948 nor in 1967 has so much hatred and resentment been generated as since the beginning of the *Intifada*. The Israeli army feels helpless in the face of rioting Palestinians and it has turned brutal. Every change in the military policy takes a turn for the worse—beatings, tear gassing, crushing of bones, live ammunition . . . the iron-fist policies generate more and more hatred. And the Palestinians stand unshaken in their determination to resist the occupation. People who are oppressed and have no freedom easily learn to hate.

In *The Yellow Wind,* David Grossman tells the story of a thirty-year-old man who lives in the Balata refugee camp near Nablus on the West Bank. The man spent ten years of his life in jail for belonging to one of the PLO organizations. This man's Palestinian identity was awakened and strengthened while in jail. "Before I went to jail, I didn't even know I was a Palestinian. There they taught me who I am. Now I have opinions. Don't believe the ones who tell you that the Palestinians don't really hate you. Understand: the average Palestinian is not the fascist and hating type, but you and the life under your occupation push him into hatred." [11]

In the face of such mounting hatred, what should be the attitude of the Palestinian Christian? Some Christians would deny the possibility of love and forgiveness in such circumstances. They would say that the hatred that is being bred is too much for the human spirit to endure and deal with constructively. So they succumb to hatred. And hatred, when used as a weapon, destroys its users as well as their victims.

Others would pronounce pious platitudes about love and forgiveness. Their words are unreal and superficial. They have not suffered themselves, and so they can detach themselves from the suffering of others and live in their own spiritual realm while repeating those sweet words from the New Testament.

I believe that neither of these two groups is being faithful to the true Christian calling. Christians are conscious of their full and real life in the world. They do not live a shadowy existence, pretending that they are not affected by what is going on around them. Life is real. In fact, for Christians, life should be as real as it can be. Jesus said, "I came that they may have life, and have it abundantly." [12] Christians are supposed to have a heightened level of consciousness, sensitive to all that is going on around them in the world. They recognize that this is God's world and that they are called to be faithful stewards of it. Furthermore, they are their brothers' and sisters' keepers. To be sensitive is to care, to be concerned, and to become involved in the real world of people. On the one hand, Christians know the depth and extent of sin and evil in the world. Therefore, nothing comes as a shock or a surprise to them when people are living without God; when people allow their selfish desires to control them; when, guided by greed, people manipulate and subjugate others. On the other hand, Christians should try not to dilute or compromise the Christian way of life, which is in essence the truly human life—the human values of the good life as they have come to be understood through Christ. They do not succumb to generalities. The ideal remains lifted up and not watered down. They will constantly aspire to that ideal and try to live up to it. It should not create frustration, because they should be realistic in their life with God. Indeed, they are conscious of their weak and frail humanity, but very much aware of the power of God at work in them. Therefore, in the midst of so much hate and bitterness, they cannot forget the words of Jesus: "You have heard that it was said, 'You shall love your neighbor and hate your enemy.' But I say to you, Love your enemies and pray for those who persecute you, so that you may be sons of your Father who is in heaven. . . ."[13]

Christians know how difficult these words are. But they are fully cognizant that the words of Jesus reflect the genuinely human, and they should remain for them the standard of the truly authentic life.

Therefore, the challenge to the Palestinian Christians, and indeed of all Christians faced with situations of bitterness and hate, is to keep up the struggle and never to succumb to despair and hate. I am speaking out of my own experience with Israel since 1948. I have learned much from my father, who had to come to terms with the hate and resentment in his life after he lost everything to the Israelis in Beisan. His struggle was real but he did not succumb to hate. For when people hate, its power engulfs them and they are totally consumed by their hatred. So I consider the challenge to my fellow Palestinians to be three-fold:

Keep struggling against hate and resentment. Always confess that the struggle goes on and the battle is not over. At times you will have the upper hand, at times you will feel beaten down. Although it is extremely difficult, never let hatred completely overtake you. By the power of God the struggle will go on until the day comes when you begin to count more victories than defeats.

Never stop trying to live the commandment of love and forgiveness. Do not dilute the strength of Jesus' message: do not shun it, do not dismiss it as unreal and impractical. Do not cut it to your size, trying to make it more applicable to real life in the world. Do not change it so that it will suit you. Keep it as it is; aspire to it, desire it, and work with God for its achievement.

Remember that so often it is those who have suffered most at the hands of others who are capable of offering forgiveness and love.

THOSE WHO SUFFER CAN FORGIVE

Laurens van der Post was imprisoned during World War II by the Japanese, suffered torture, and almost died. In the introduction to *Venture to the Interior,* he describes the Boer War in South Africa at the turn of this century and his father's bitterness after the war. Then one of the Afrikaner leaders made a gesture of reconciliation to the English, and his father's bitterness was somehow taken away. Van der Post goes on to write of people who have not suffered themselves but can only imagine suffering. Those who suffer can forgive, he says, but those who only participate in suffering through imagination are angry, bitter, and vengeful.

> It has always been to me one of the more frightening ironies of Afrikaner life that people like my father, who with Smuts and Botha had actually fought and suffered in the war, could forgive and begin anew, whereas others, alive today, who were never in the heart of that conflict, can still find it so hard to forgive an injury that was not even done to them. And how can there ever be any real beginning without forgiveness?
>
> I noticed something similar in my own experience when I met War Crimes officers, who had neither suffered internment under the Japanese nor even fought against them. They were more revengeful and bitter about our treatment and our suffering in prison than we were ourselves.
>
> I have so often noticed that the suffering which is most difficult, if not impossible, to forgive is unreal, imagined suffering. There is no power on earth like imagination, and the worst, most obstinate grievances are imagined ones. Let us recognize that there are people and nations who create, with a submerged deliberation, a sense of suffering and of grievance, which enables them to evade those aspects of reality that do not minister to their self-importance, personal pride, or convenience. These imagined ills enable them to avoid the proper burden that life lays on all of us.
>
> Persons who have really suffered at the hands of others do not find it difficult to forgive, nor even to understand the people who caused their suffering. They do not find it difficult to forgive because out of suffering and sorrow truly endured comes an instinctive sense of privilege. Recognition of the creative truth comes in a flash: forgiveness for others, as for ourselves, for we, too, know not what we do.[14]

These last words bring to mind Christ, who, in the midst of his great anguish and suffering on the cross, was able to forgive his enemies.

The challenge for Christians will always be to imitate their Lord and opt for forgiveness instead of revenge. There is probably no finer characteristic of God in the New Testament than forgiveness and love—and note that the exhortation to love our enemies is followed by the words, "so that you may be sons of your Father who is in heaven."

Van der Post's words ring true. I am amazed that many Jews in Israel-Palestine rationalize their harsh treatment of the Palestinians by identifying with the sufferings of the Jews during the Holocaust, which they did not themselves endure. Indeed, those who suffer forgive, and those who imagine the suffering are often angry and resentful. One is reminded here of Etty Hillesum, a Dutch Jew who in 1943 was taken with her parents and brother to Auschwitz, where they all met their deaths. In spite of the great suffering she herself endured and the suffering that she saw around her in the camps, she never gave in to hate. In her diary she mentions how cruel and merciless the Nazis were, adding, "we must be all the more merciful ourselves." [15] On another day she entered in her diary:

Do not relieve your feelings through hatred, do not seek to be avenged on all German mothers, for they, too, sorrow at this very moment for their slain and murdered sons. Give your sorrow all the space and shelter in yourself that is its due, for if everyone bears his grief honestly and courageously, the sorrow that now fills the world will abate. But if you do not clear a decent shelter for your sorrow, and instead reserve most of the space inside you for hatred and thoughts of revenge—from which new sorrows will be born for others—then sorrow will never cease in this world and will multiply.

And if you have given sorrow the space its gentle origins demand, then you may truly say: life is beautiful and so rich. So beautiful and so rich that it makes you want to believe in God. [16]

To keep struggling against hate and to practice forgiveness need not mean abdicating one's rights or renouncing justice. This should be emphasized over and over again. It is part of loving one's enemy that Christians must remind the "enemy" of justice and right. It is part of loving to speak the truth. It is part of our responsibility to ourselves and to God's people in the world to expose injustice. What is wrong is wrong. What is unjust is unjust. And the Palestinian Christians should stand on these principles and insist that justice must be done. They should never give up their rights, but neither should they give in to hate. Booker T. Washington, who as a black had good reason to be bitter and hateful toward whites, said, "I shall never permit myself to stoop so low as to hate any man." [17]

The challenge to Palestinian Christians, and indeed to all Palestinians and to all people in this conflict in Israel-Palestine, is: do not destroy yourself with hate; maintain your inner freedom; insist on justice, work for it, and it shall be yours.

A POSTSCRIPT

The pastor in me prompts me to conclude my remarks with three prayers. This book has touched on history, politics, religion, and theology. The prayers are offered, therefore, as a way of lifting its main issues of concern to God, and praying also for all the peoples who are caught up in the Middle East conflict. And let us be mindful that a prayer, once uttered, opens us up before God and allows God to work on us so that we might become God's instruments for the furtherance of justice, peace, and reconciliation in the world.

Two of the prayers are well known. The first, the prayer of St. Francis, is a personal prayer of commitment to peace and its implication for the person. The second is a general prayer for justice and peace in our world. The third, which is usually attributed to Reinhold Niebuhr, has been a favorite of many groups. I find it relevant as a prayer for the Middle East conflict since it petitions God for real human integrity and the maturity to accept what must be accepted and to change what must be changed.

May the God of justice, mercy, and peace accept these prayers we offer.

> Lord, make me an instrument of your peace.
> Where there is hatred, let me sow love,
> Where there is injury, pardon;
> Where there is doubt, faith;
> Where there is despair, hope;

Where there is darkness, light;
Where there is sadness, joy.
O divine Master, Grant that I may not so much seek
to be consoled, as to console,
To be understood, as to understand,
To be loved, as to love,
For it is in giving that we receive;
It is in pardoning that we are pardoned;
It is in dying that we are born to eternal life.[18]

Lord, we pray for the power to be gentle; the strength to be forgiving; the patience to be understanding; and the endurance to accept the consequences of holding to what we believe to be right.

May we put our trust in the power of good to overcome evil and the power of love to overcome hatred. We pray for the vision to see and the faith to believe in a world emancipated from violence, a new world where fear shall no longer lead men to commit injustice, nor selfishness make them bring suffering to others.

Help us to devote our whole life and thought and energy to the task of making peace, praying always for the inspiration and the power to fulfill the destiny for which we and all men were created.[19]

God grant me the serenity to accept the things I cannot
change,
the courage to change the things I can,
and the wisdom to distinguish the one from the other.[20]

Notes

CHAPTER 1

1. Beisan/Beth Shean has a very rich history that dates back to the early Bronze Age (c. 3,000–2,400 B.C.). During the time of Christ it was called Scythopolis and was once the chief city of the Decapolis. More recent excavations have revealed the great significance of Beisan. See "Return to Eden," by Abraham Rabinovich, *Jerusalem Post Magazine* (May 6, 1988).

2. The Eastern Orthodox Church is usually referred to as the Greek Orthodox Church. The term "Greek" can be misleading. In the Patriarchates of Antioch and Jerusalem almost all the members of the Greek Orthodox Church are Arabs.

3. See chapter 2, p. 31

4. Rudyard Kipling, *Sixty Poems* (London: Hodder & Stoughton, 1976), p. 112.

5. Psalm 42:11.

6. For a more detailed study of the stereotyping of Arabs in the American media, see Edmund Ghareeb, ed., *Split Vision*.

7. See chapter 3.

8. For a study of the PLO, see Helena Cobban, *The Palestinian Liberation Organization: People, Power, and Politics* (Cambridge University Press, 1985).

9. For a study of early Arab Christianity, see J. Spencer Trimingham, *Christianity Among the Arabs in Pre-Islamic Times* (London and New York: Longman Librairie du Liban, 1979).

10. For a study of Arab nationalism, see George Antonius, *The Arab Awakening;* see also Sylvia G. Haim, *Arab Nationalism.*

11. Acts 16:37–39 and 22:25–29.

12. See chapters 2 and 3.

CHAPTER 2

1. Sharif Kanana, *Ataghyeer Al-ijtimaᶜi wa-tawafuq Annafsi ᶜind As-sukan Alᶜarab fi Israil* [Socio-Cultural and Psychological Adjustment of the

Arab Minority in Israel] (Birzeit University, 1978), p. 45.

2. Fayez A. Sayegh, "A Palestinian View," in Sayegh et al., *Time Bomb in the Middle East*, pp. 44–45.

3. Max I. Dimont, *Jews, God and History*, p. 312.

4. Moshe Menuhin, *The Decadence of Judaism in Our Time*, p. 25.

5. Ibid., p. 26.

6. Uri Avnery, *Israel without Zionism*, p. 45.

7. Ibid., pp. 173–74.

8. E. I. J. Rosenthal, "Judaism," in *Religion in the Middle East*, ed. A. J. Arberry, vol. 1, p. 7.

9. Dimont, p. 196.

10. Rosenthal, p. 12.

11. Ibid. At the end of his life, Heine insisted that although he had been baptized, he had never been converted.

12. Dimont, pp. 324–28.

13. Avnery, p. 48.

14. Edward Said, *The Question of Palestine*, p. 96.

15. Ibid., p. 69.

16. Menuhin, p. 42.

17. Sayegh, p. 59.

18. Rosenthal, p. 35.

19. Avnery, p. 51.

20. After World War II, Libya was suggested as a location for a Jewish home, but was rejected by the Zionists.

21. Avnery, p. 66.

22. Edwin Hodder, *The Life and Work of the Seventh Earl of Shaftesbury, K.G.*, p. 14.

23. Ibid.

24. Ibid.

25. A. L. Tibawi, *British Interests in Palestine 1800–1901*, p. 34.

26. Avnery, p. 66.

27. Rosenthal, p. 28.

28. Avnery, p. 107.

29. Dimont, p. 393. Herzl entertained the idea of being a messiah himself. Menuhin, p. 40.

30. Rosenthal, pp. 44–45.

31. Said, p. 70.

32. Avnery, p. 56.

33. Ibid., p. 59.

34. Alfred M. Lilienthal, *The Zionist Connection: What Price Peace?* p. 13.

35. Avnery, p. 64. Hagop A. Chakmakjian writes that during Herzl's

visit with the sultan, the latter "offered a charter of autonomy in Palestine for the price of Jewish influence and support against the Armenians, whose plight as a result of the Turkish massacres of 1894–1896 had aroused considerable compassion in Europe. . . ." Hagop A. Chakmakjian, *In Quest of Justice and Peace in the Middle East,* pp. 32–37.

36. Menuhin, pp. 43–49. On January 23, 1904, Herzl asked the king of Italy for a Jewish state in Libya. The king's answer was "Ma e encora casa di altri!" [But, it is still someone else's home!] *The Diaries of Theodor Herzl,* Marvin Lowenthal, ed. (New York: Dial, 1956), p. 56, quoted in Menuhin, p. 49.

37. Ibid., pp. 48–49.

38. C. H. Dodd and M. E. Sales, *Israel and the Arabs,* p. 63.

39. Lilienthal, pp. 16–17.

40. Ibid., p. 17.

41. Ibid., p. 18.

42. Menuhin, pp. 83–84.

43. Ibid., p. 236.

44. Sayegh, p. 48.

45. Walter Laquer, ed., *The Israel-Arab Reader,* p. 56.

46. Pierre Rondot, *The Changing Patterns of the Middle East,* p. 125.

47. Laqueur, pp. 45–58, 62–75, 84–94.

48. Ibid., pp. 113–22.

49. Sayegh, p. 49.

50. Ibid.

51. See Alfred Lilienthal (pp. 56–59) for a more detailed account of the way bribes and threats were used to pressure the delegates to vote in favor of partition.

52. Sayegh, p. 44. (Italics in the original.)

53. Ibid., p. 51.

54. Ibid., pp. 51–52.

55. Menachem Begin, *The Revolt: Story of the "Irgun,"* pp. 32, 163, 337.

56. Menuhin, pp. 118–20.

57. According to the partition plan, the area allotted to Israel was 14,400 square kilometers. When the fighting ceased, Israel encompassed an area of 20,662 square kilometers. Ian Lustick, *Arabs in the Jewish State,* p. 283.

58. Sayegh, p. 53. The reader will recall from chapter 1 that the Palestinian Arabs of Beisan, including my family, were displaced on May 26, 1948.

59. Ibid., pp. 53–54.

60. Menuhin, p. 126. In *Palestinian Self-Determination,* p. 37, Hassan

bin Talal writes that only 17,500 Arab soldiers actually entered Palestine to help their Palestinian neighbors. He puts the number of the Israeli combined armies at 62,500: 3,500 Palmach, 55,000 Haganah, and 4,000 Irgun.

61. Lustick, p. 28.
62. Menuhin, pp. 220–21.
63. Lilienthal, p. 115.
64. Sayegh, pp. 59–60. One *dunum* is about one-quarter of an acre.
65. Lustick, p. 48.
66. Don Peretz, *Israel and the Palestine Arabs,* p. 143.
67. Lustick, p. 40.
68. Ibid., p. 124.
69. This occurred on November 21, 1961; quoted in Menuhin, p. 193.
70. Lilienthal, p. 117.
71. Ibid., p. 118.
72. Ibid., p. 115.
73. Lustick, p. 59.
74. Menuhin, p. 194.
75. Lustick, p. 57.
76. Lilienthal, p. 116.
77. Lustick, p. 59.
78. Avnery, p. 179.
79. Lilienthal, p. 109.
80. Menuhin, p. 237.
81. Lustick, p. 41.
82. Ibid., p. 64.
83. June 15, 1969; quoted in Avnery, p. 262.
84. Lustick, pp. 135–36.
85. Avnery, p. 113.
86. Lilienthal, p. 762.
87. Lustick, p. 24.
88. Ibid., p. 25.
89. Laqueur, p. 127.
90. Lustick, pp. 25–26 and 77.
91. For a detailed study of the subject, see Elia T. Zureik, *The Palestinians in Israel.*
92. Avnery, p. 211.
93. Ibid., p. 37.
94. Cheryl Rubenberg, *The Palestine Liberation Organization: Its Institutional Infrastructure* (Belmont, Mass: Institute of Arab Studies, 1983), pp. 58–59.
95. Kanana, p. 78.
96. Lilienthal, p. 122.

97. Kanana, p. 81.

98. Lustick, p. 143. The latest statistics show the Arabs in Israel comprising 18 percent of the population.

99. Approximately 77 percent of eligible Arab voters participated in the 1984 election. About 34 percent of these voted for the Democratic Front for Peace and Equality, while 18 percent went to the Progressive List for Peace. The remaining 25 percent went to other Israeli parties. Uri Davis, *Israel: An Apartheid State,* p. 138.

100. Lilienthal, p. 125.

101. Ibid., p. 124; Lustick, pp. 68–69.

102. David Shipler, *Arab and Jew.* Shipler mentions (p. 84) that between June 1, 1978, and June 4, 1982, Palestinian guerrillas killed a total of 29 Israelis in their attacks on northern Israel. To prevent such attacks, Israel launched a war that cost it 654 lives.

103. Ibid., pp. 46–48.

104. Hanna Siniora, "A Palestinian Perspective: Lessons the U.S. Must Learn," *In These Times,* vol. 12, no. 16 (March 16–22, 1988): 16.

CHAPTER 3

1. Stephen Neill, *Christian Missions,* pp. 420–21.

2. Timothy Ware, *The Orthodox Church,* p. 12.

3. Since I am most familiar with the life of the Christian community in Israel after 1948, I have intentionally chosen to focus on it. When I refer to the Palestinian Christians in all of geographic Palestine, I use the designation Israel-Palestine.

4. Steven Runciman, "The Christian Arabs of Palestine," p. 3.

5. Moshe Menuhin, *The Decadence of Judaism in Our Time,* p. 236.

6. Saul P. Colby, *Christianity in the Holy Land,* p. 124.

7. Robert Brenton Betts, *Christians in the Arab East,* p. 212.

8. Ibid., p. 69.

9. The Druze are a Middle Eastern religious sect that separated from Islam in the 11th century. They trace their origins to a Fatimid caliph of Egypt, al-Hakim. Most of the Druze live in Syria and Lebanon. About 70,000 live in Israel.

10. Colby, p. 131.

11. The Arab Muslim community in Israel, lacking professional clergy, was not as organized as its Christian counterpart. The loss of its *Waqf* (religious endowment property) to the State crippled its influence and effectiveness.

12. Betts, p. 173.

13. Ibid., p. 175.

14. Alfred M. Lilienthal, *The Zionist Connection,* pp. 112–114; see also Elias Chacour, *Blood Brothers,* pp. 73–83.

15. Betts, p. 174.

16. Lilienthal, p. 133.

17. Ibid., p. 112.

18. To give some examples from the Episcopal Church: St. John the Evangelist Church in Haifa had the largest Anglican congregation in Palestine, its membership exceeding 1,200. After the 1948 war and the large exodus of Arabs from Haifa, the congregation's size shrank to 150. St. Peter's Church of Jaffa had a membership of over 400, which dwindled to 15 after the war.

19. Howard A. Johnson, *Global Odyssey,* p. 192.

20. Ibid., p. 188.

21. Psalms 22, 25, 71, 72, 98, 115, 118, 121, 122, 125, 128, 130, 131, 147, and 148.

22. Psalms 6, 7, 10, 17, 20, 21, 29, 35, 44, 45, 48, 55, 58, 60, 70, 74, 75, 77, 79, 87, 94, 99, 108, 109, 120, 126, 132, 133, 137, and 144.

23. Paul M. van Buren, *Discerning the Way,* pp. 181–82.

24. Paul M. van Buren, "Discerning the Way to the Incarnation," p. 197.

25. I asked van Buren in London in 1981 how many visits he had made by then to Israel and was told that he had visited there once, several years before. One would have presumed that before writing his theology of the "Jewish-Christian reality," and venturing to make categorically one-sided statements, van Buren would have made several visits to Israel and spent some time probing the complexities of the political situation and the relationship of Israel to the Arabs.

26. Paul M. van Buren, *A Christian Theology of the People Israel.*

27. Ibid., p. 200. For a more detailed study of his support of Israel, see Lilienthal, "Christians in Bondage," pp. 486–512.

28. From an article ("Christian Zionism") written by Joel Barber in preparation for and as an advertisement of the First International Christian Zionist Leadership Congress, held in Basel, Switzerland, in 1985.

29. For an excellent study of the history and beliefs of the fundamentalists, see Dewey Beegle, *Prophecy and Prediction.*

30. Krister Stendahl, "Toward a New Generation."

31. Kenneth Cragg, "The Anglican Church," in *Religion in the Middle East,* ed. A. J. Arberry, vol. 1, p. 588.

32. Rosemary Radford Ruether, *Faith and Fratricide.*

33. Michael D. Ryan of Drew University reviewed Ruether's book in *Journal of Ecumenical Studies,* vol. 12, no. 4 (Fall 1975): 603.

34. "Middle East Peace Means Restoring an Old Arab's Farm," *National Catholic Reporter* (June 5, 1987): 12.

35. Rosemary Radford Ruether, "Peace Doesn't Mean Putting Palestinians in Their Place," *National Catholic Reporter* (April 8, 1988): 14–15; see also Ruether's article "Listening to Palestinian Christians," *Christianity and Crisis*, vol. 48 (April 4, 1988): 113–15.

36. Rosemary Radford Ruether's review of van Buren's book in *Christianity and Crisis*, vol. 47 (October 12, 1987): 34.

37. See statements on the Middle East by the World Council of Churches, National Council of Churches, and others. For more on those who have shown the courage to make their views known see Paul Findley, *They Dare to Speak Out.*

38. Marc Ellis, *Toward a Jewish Theology of Liberation*, p. 114.

39. Ibid., pp. 25–26.

40. Ibid., p. 114.

41. Ibid., p. 116.

42. Roberta Strauss Feuerlicht, *The Fate of the Jews.*

43. Ibid., p. 220.

44. Ibid., p. 283.

45. Ibid., p. 287; see also Earl Shorris, *Jews without Mercy.*

46. Shoki Coe, "Contextualizing Theology," in *Mission Trends No. 3*, ed. Gerald H. Anderson and Thomas F. Stransky, pp. 21–22.

47. Cited by E. W. Fashole-Luke, "The Quest for African Christian Theologies," in *Mission Trends No. 3*, ed. Gerald H. Anderson and Thomas F. Stransky, pp. 21–22.

48. Luke 4:16–30.

49. Quoted in Samuel M. Garrett, "An Anglican View of Ethics," pp. 36–37.

CHAPTER 4

1. Luke 1:68.

2. Elmer Berger, *Prophecy, Zionism and the State of Israel*, Introduction by Arnold J. Toynbee.

3. I have intentionally used the word "beliefs" here rather than "faith." Although the beliefs of many have been shattered, their faith in God has been sustained. Beliefs—referring primarily to the mind, reason, and knowledge—can be updated with new information. Faith, on the other hand, is the response of the whole being of a person to God.

4. I have chosen to use the terms "Hebrew Scriptures" and "Old Testament" interchangeably, as each seemed appropriate. For Christian

readers, the term "Old Testament" is the most familiar, while for Jews the more appropriate designation is "Hebrew Scriptures." When either term is used the reference is always to the same body of material.

5. By hermeneutics, we generally mean the interpretation of ancient texts. The concern in hermeneutics is with the development of criteria for text interpretation. It begins with determining the original meaning of a text and leads to the elucidation of its sense for modern readers.

6. Charles Harold Dodd, *The Meaning of Paul for Today,* pp. 131–32. On Paul's understanding of the knowledge of God, Dodd cites 1 Corinthians 2, 12:8; 2 Corinthians 10: 3–6; 1 Thessalonians 1:5; Philippians 1:9–10; Colossians 2:2–3; Ephesians 1–17; 1 Corinthians 8:1–3; Galatians 4–9; and 1 Corinthians 13:12.

7. There are two important truths to remember about a developing and maturing understanding of God. On the surface they might seem contradictory, but they are actually complementary. First, there is a sense in which the message of the prophets and other people of faith in the Bible was a call to a *return* to the source, to the faith of the Patriarchs and/or to the Covenant of Sinai. In other words, what God wanted to say God had already said. People need only to rediscover it, listen to it, and obey it. Second, there has in a sense been a deepening maturity, a growing understanding by humans of what God is. One can point, for example, to developing concepts of monotheism, the resurrection of the dead, or life after death. Oftentimes this developing understanding reached back to the past—to the source—for nourishment, yet pressed on in the present and into the future for a fuller and deeper knowledge of what God is. Jesus, for example, was able to argue the resurrection of the dead to the people of his day by appealing to the relationship of God to the Patriarchs (Matthew 22:31–32). Yet, the belief in the resurrection did not emerge chronologically until the intertestamental period. Moreover, this developing understanding was not always systematic and consistent. At times, one could detect tension, struggle, and even regression. One vivid illustration is to be seen in the contrast between Isaiah and Joel on the concept of war and peace. Isaiah, in the eighth century B.C., could envision a time of peace when the nations "shall beat their swords into plowshares and their spears into pruning hooks" (Isaiah 2:4); Joel, in the fifth century B.C., advocated precisely the reverse (Joel 3:10). In spite of this unsystematic development, there is a growing maturity in the concept of God that eventually found its culmination in Jesus Christ.

8. This is the opposite of the view held by John Bright *(The Authority of the Old Testament,* pp. 151–52), who maintains that the whole of the Old Testament is valid and authoritative because the whole is theological. For me, the whole of the Old Testament is material for theological reflec-

tion and, therefore, valuable; however, the validity and authority of any part of it is determined by the hermeneutic of the knowledge of God in Christ.

9. 2 Timothy 3:16.

10. Joshua 6:21. Similarly, in the Exodus story, it is the Lord who inflicts disease and plagues on the Egyptians (Exodus 7–12); it is the Lord who kills every firstborn in the land of Egypt (Exodus 12:29); and it is the Lord who fights for Israel and brings total destruction to the Egyptian army (Exodus 14–15).

11. Joshua 6:17.

12. 2 Kings 2:23–24.

13. See Exodus 17:14–16 and Deuteronomy 25:17–19.

14. 1 Samuel 15:1–3.

15. Robert I. Friedman, "No Land, No Peace for Palestinians," *The Nation* (April 23, 1988): 563.

16. Ibid.

17. Ibid.

18. Until 1948 there was an Arab village, Zir'in, in the same area.

19. See 2 Kings 9:26.

20. Galatians 6:7.

21. Gerhard von Rad, *Old Testament Theology,* vol. 2, p. 23.

22. Ibid.

23. 1 Kings 22:8.

24. John Ferguson, *War and Peace in the World's Religions,* p. 80.

25. Amos 9:7.

26. For an illustration of this point see page 96.

27. G. Ernest Wright, *The Old Testament against Its Environment,* pp. 110–112.

28. S. G. F. Brandon, *Jesus and the Zealots,* p. 326.

29. Isidore Epstein, *Judaism,* p. 111. Several other Jewish sects during the first century A.D. had their own political or religious ideologies—in fact, the Talmud suggests that there were twenty-four of these parties and sects. The Pharisees were chosen for this study because they represent the only sect that survived the national cataclysms of A.D. 70 and 135 and thus were responsible for the development of Rabbinic Judaism.

30. Guenter Lewy, *Religion and Revolution,* p. 74.

31. Sanhedrin 97a, cited by Lewy, p. 92.

32. Daniel 8:25.

33. Max I. Dimont, *Jews, God and History,* pp. 103–4.

34. Lewy, p. 86.

35. Jakob J. Petuchowski, "Judaism Today," in *Religion in the Middle East,* ed. A. J. Arberry, vol. 1, p. 44.

36. Dimont, p. 372.

37. There are also some profound insights in the Torah, as well as in the Writings that are included in this tradition, as I intend to illustrate later.

38. Isaiah 45:22–23.

39. Jonah 4:1–4.

40. Amos 2:1–3.

41. John Shae, *Stories of God,* p. 108.

42. John Yoder, *The Politics of Jesus,* pp. 26–63. See also Oscar Cullmann, *Jesus and the Revolutionaries.*

43. Matthew 23:23. See also Micah 6:8 and Luke 11:42.

44. Matthew 3:12. See also Luke 3:17.

45. Matthew 11:2–6. See also Luke 7:18–23.

46. Jack L. Stotts, *Shalom*, p. 92.

47. See, for example, Luke 4:16–30.

48. John 3:16.

49. Matthew 1:3, 5–6.

50. Matthew 2:1.

51. Matthew 2:13–15.

52. Matthew 8:5–13.

53. Matthew 15:21–28. In his exegesis of this point, Sherman E. Johnson writes, "There are rabbinical sayings which designate godless people and heathen as dogs. One must, of course, remember that this is not the invariable attitude of the ancient Jews and that there are in rabbinical literature many sayings and anecdotes exhibiting friendliness to Gentiles." Sherman E. Johnson, "St. Matthew," in *The Interpreter's Bible,* ed. George A. Buttrick, vol. 7, "New Testament: Matthew, Mark," pp. 441–43.

54. Luke 4:25–29.

55. John 4.

56. Luke 17:11–19.

57. Luke 10:29–37.

58. Acts 1:6.

59. Acts 1:6; 28:16. Some of the many important passages that illustrate the inclusive nature of God in Acts are the sermon of Stephen (chapter 7), the ministry of Philip in Samaria (8:4–25), the conversion of Cornelius (chapter 10), and the preaching of Paul (chapters 13 and 17, for example).

60. Galatians 3:26, 28–29.

61. Ephesians 3:3–6.

62. John 1:12–13.

63. In the last few years a number of Jewish organizations and political parties identifying themselves as religious Zionists—among them Oz VeShalom and Netivot Shalom—have appeared in Israel. Such groups insist that they are full-fledged Zionists, drawing their inspiration from the

Torah and the Prophets. Although their constituency is small, they provide a good corrective to the policies of the State and a promise of hope for the future. In spite of their encouraging presence, I still feel that Zionism reflects in essence a retrogression in Jewish history rather than a developing movement; and only history will tell whether, out of an act of retrogression, some lasting good might be achieved.

64. For the sake of clarity, I must emphasize again that I am giving here an interpretive view of what has happened in the twentieth-century Zionist movement and the establishment of the State of Israel in our time. I am not saying that the Jewish community that opted for Zionism consciously voted to adopt the nationalistic tradition, while being equally conscious that by doing so it was rejecting and abandoning the Torah-oriented and prophetic traditions. The facts are that the Zionist movement was created and the State of Israel was established. The most salient features have been that of the nationalistic tradition. The Torah-oriented, as well as the prophetic, traditions have been put at the service of naked nationalism. Certain portions of the Torah and the Prophets that give credence to Zionist views have been cited and exploited. Ezekiel's vision of the valley of dry bones, for example, has become to Zionists a specific prophecy that was intended to be fulfilled by the ingathering of Jews and their return to Israel after 1948 (Ezekiel 37).

65. Walter Laqueur, ed., *The Israel-Arab Reader,* p. 127.

66. See chapter 2, pp. 25–26.

67. See chapter 2, p. 43.

68. Grace Halsell, *Journey to Jerusalem,* p. 57.

69. *Jewish Chronicle* (London: 30 October 1967): 13, quoted in Berger, *Prophecy, Zionism, and the State of Israel,* p. 15.

70. Norman Bentwich, "Judaism in Israel," in *Religion in the Middle East,* ed. A. J. Arberry, vol. 1, p. 105.

71. A clear articulation of this racially exclusive concept of Israel and its God is found in Rabbi Meir Kahane's *They Must Go.*

72. See Genesis 15:19–21 and Joshua 12 and 13.

73. See Genesis 12:7; 13:15, 17; 15:18; 17:8; 24:7; 26:3f.; 28:13f.; 35:12; 48:4; 50:24.

74. See Arthur Koestler, *The Thirteenth Tribe.*

75. W. D. Davies, *The Gospel and the Land.* See also Walter Brueggemann, *The Land.*

76. The Hexateuch is a name given by modern biblical scholars to the first six books of the Bible, i.e., Genesis to Joshua, in the belief that all derive from a single set of literary sources.

77. See 1 Samuel 13:19; Ezekiel 40:2; 47:18; 1 Chronicles 22:2; 2 Chronicles 2:17; 34:7. It also occurs in 2 Kings 5:2, 4; 6:23; Ezekiel 27:17;

and in 2 Chronicles 30:25, where it refers to North Israel only.

78. Davies, pp. 27–29.

79. Ibid., p. 31.

80. Numbers 35:34.

81. Jeremiah 2:7.

82. Jeremiah 16:18.

83. Deuteronomy 4:25–26. See also 28:63; Leviticus 20:22; Joshua 23:15–16.

84. Davies, p. 31. The term "holy land," which suggests that the land itself was inherently "holy," seldom appears in the Hebrew Scriptures. See Psalm 78:54 and Zechariah 2:16. It is the proximity of God alone that lends holiness to a place or a land.

85. Joshua 24:13.

86. Psalm 24:1.

87. Isaiah 45:18.

88. Davies, p. 115.

89. Ibid.

90. Ibid., p. 110.

91. Ibid., p. 154.

92. Psalm 95:3–5.

93. Amos 1 and 2.

94. Exodus 3:5.

95. Isaiah 44:3–4.

96. Ernest Renan, *The Life of Jesus* (New York: Modern Library, 1927), p. 61.

97. Cyril of Jerusalem, *Catechetical Lectures*, X.19, tr. E. H. Gifford. *Library of Nicene and Post-Nicene Fathers*, 2nd series, vol. 7 (New York: Christian Literature Co., 1894), pp. 62–63.

98. Luke 2:14.

99. Matthew 5:9.

CHAPTER 5

1. Quoted in John Rawls, *A Theory of Justice*, p. 10.

2. *Webster's New World Dictionary of the American Language*, College Edition (Springfield, Mass.: Merriam-Webster, 1955), under "Justice."

3. In Deuteronomy the people are asked to constantly remember that they were slaves in Egypt. Such a reminder was supposed to keep them from mistreating others. See Deuteronomy 5:15; 15:15; 16:12; 24:18; and 22.

4. Deuteronomy 30:19.

5. Abraham J. Heschel, *The Prophets,* pp. 198–219.

6. John Shae, *Stories of God,* p. 106.

7. Isaiah 30:18; Psalm 119:137.

8. Isaiah 28:17.

9. Deuteronomy 32:4.

10. Jeremiah 9:23–24.

11. Psalm 9:7–9.

12. Isaiah 5:16.

13. Amos 5:22–24.

14. Isaiah 56:1a; 2a.

15. Shae, pp. 108–9.

16. Paul Tillich, *Systematic Theology,* vol. 3, p. 264.

17. Rawls, pp. 22–27.

18. Some examples are the annexation of occupied East Jerusalem after the 1967 war, (under the Jerusalem law of 1980) and the annexation of the Golan Heights in 1982.

19. By international law is meant the set of uniform principles and norms that requires at least a minimum standard of reasonable and humane conduct in the world community.

20. This does not imply that international law is perfect. One could point to certain provisions in some of the international agreements that are subject to flexible interpretations. Nations wishing to avoid their obligations can easily do so. For example, the International Covenant on Civil and Political Rights, 1966, article 12:3, states: "The above-mentioned rights shall not be subject to any restrictions except those which are provided by law, are necessary to protect national security, public order. . . ." The magic words "national security" leave a door opened wide to discriminatory abuse. See Walter Laqueur and Barry Rubin, eds., *The Human Rights Reader,* p. 220.

21. Tillich, vol. 3, p. 265. Moshe Menuhin has written *(Decadence of Judaism,* pp. 473–85) that Adolf Eichmann's trial should have been held before an international tribunal rather than exploited by Ben-Gurion to serve his political ends.

22. Lesley Lempert, "A Legal Note," in *American-Israeli Civil Liberties Coalition, Inc, Newsletter* (March 1988): 3.

23. Raja Shehadeh, *Occupier's Law,* p. 97.

24. Ibid., pp. 97–99.

25. Ibid., pp. 12–13, 100.

26. N. T. Mallison Jr. and S. V. Mallison, "The Role of International Law," p. 1.

27. Ibid., p. 2.

28. See chapter 2, pp. 27–28.

29. Laqueur and Rubin, pp. 113–26.

30. Henry Cattan, *Palestine and International Law*.

31. Mallison and Mallison, p. 4.

32. Ibid., p. 5. Only Israel, Malawi, and Costa Rica abstained from this vote.

33. Ibid., p. 7.

34. Reinhold Niebuhr, *Moral Man and Immoral Society*, p. 6.

35. James Luther Mays, *Micah*, p. 63.

36. Micah 2:1–2.

37. Proverbs 3:27.

38. Robert B. Coote, *Amos among the Prophets*, p. 39.

39. This vicious circle is well described in Dom Helder Camara's book, *The Spiral of Violence*.

40. One of the most popular sayings of the late President of Egypt, Gamal Abdel Nasser, still remembered by many Palestinians, is "What has been taken by force cannot be claimed back except by force."

41. An example of direct intervention would be Russia's invasion of Afghanistan in 1979. Indirect intervention is illustrated in places like El Salvador and, supremely, the Middle East. A classic case occurred during the 1973 Middle East war. Henry Kissinger, then United States secretary of state, saw it as a showdown between his country and the Soviet Union, a war between American and Russian arms. "If the Arabs did well, the credit would go to Soviet arms." Henry Kissinger, "Years of Upheaval," pp. 33–37, 40, 49–50.

42. The balance of power between the superpowers in the nuclear age has its ambiguities and dangers. It has, for example, produced the phenomenon of overkill: in a possible war, the United States and the Soviet Union could kill every citizen of the opposing country fifty times over. Between them, the Americans and the Russians could kill every citizen of the world ten times over. In order to maintain the balance of power, it is necessary to manufacture more nuclear arms continuously. Their presence, however, threatens the world. Is it possible that by increasing the sum of uncertainty one's own certainty is increased?

43. Niebuhr, *Moral Man and Immoral Society*, p. 6.

44. Ibid., p. 3.

45. Since the *Intifada*, more Western Jews have become critical of Israel's policies. Some have been appalled at the draconian measures that the State has used against the Palestinians. For example, see Darrell Turner's "Severe Criticism of Israel by Jews Seen as Unprecedented," *National Catholic Reporter* (April 1, 1988): p. 22. Prominent American Jews have compared Israeli policies with "pogroms," denouncing them as "inhuman and indefensible" and as violating "every principle of human de-

cency.'' See also Albert Vorspan, ''Soul-Searching,'' *New York Times* (May 8, 1988): 40f.

46. Niebuhr, *Moral Man and Immoral Society,* p. 29.

47. Ibid., p. 17.

48. Ibid., p. 121.

49. Ibid., p. 199.

50. To the extreme Zionists, Greater Israel fulfills the biblical promise that *Eretz Yisrael* will extend ''from the river of Egypt to the greater river, the river Euphrates'' (Genesis 15:18). See Grace Halsell, *Prophecy and Politics,* p. 110.

51. Extremist groups like the Popular Front for the Liberation of Palestine still insist on regaining the entire country. The Palestine Liberation Organization (PLO) as a whole, however, has stated its willingness to accept a Palestinian state on the West Bank and in Gaza. Meetings of the Palestinian National Council (PNC) in 1974 and in 1977 committed the Palestinians to this idea, and to the implicit recognition of Israel as a neighbor. See Edward Said, *The Question of Palestine,* p. 224.

On November 12–15, 1988, The PNC met in Algiers in an extra-ordinary session called ''The Intifada Session,'' and on November 15th declared the establishment of a Palestinian state. By basing the declaration of independence on the UN General Assembly Resolution 181, the PNC again gave implicit recognition to the State of Israel. It was Resolution 181 of 1947 that called for the partition of Palestine into two states—one Arab and one Jewish—giving the establishment of the State of Israel international legitimacy at the time. Moreover, in declaring the State of Palestine, the PNC relied on the resolutions of the United Nations since 1947, which certainly include the recognition of the State of Israel.

52. This is a good definition of fanaticism—when any means is justified in order that a desired end may be achieved.

53. Niebuhr, *Moral Man and Immoral Society,* p. xii.

54. Ibid., p. 1.

55. Ibid., p. 42.

56. Ibid., p. 16.

57. Ibid., p. 19.

58. Ibid., p. 31.

59. Ibid., p. 20.

60. Ibid., p. 22.

61. The concern of the Deity for justice to the poor was not peculiar to ancient Israel but is found in other Near Eastern religions. The Egyptian god Amon Re is addressed: ''Thou art Amon, the Lord of the silent man, who comes at the voice of the poor man. If I call to thee when I am distressed, thou comest and thou rescuest me. Thou givest breath [to] him

who is weak; thou rescuest him who is imprisoned." James B. Pritchard, ed., *Ancient Near Eastern Texts,* p. 380. In a Babylonian hymn, Shamash, the sun god, is praised for punishing the unrighteous judge, the receiver of a bribe who perverts justice, and for being pleased with him who "intercedes for the weak" (Quoted in Heschel, p. 200). See also J. Pederson, "The Role Played by Inspired Persons among the Israelites and Arabs," *Studies in Old Testament Prophecy,* ed. H. H. Rowley (Edinburgh: T & T Clark, 1950), pp. 127–42.

62. Exodus 22:21–22; 23:9; Deuteronomy 14:29; 26:12; Proverbs 14:21, 31; 15:25; 19:17; 23:10–11; Isaiah 1:17; Jeremiah 7:6.

63. Exodus 23:10–11; Leviticus 23:22; Deuteronomy 24:19–22.

64. Exodus 23:6; Leviticus 24:22; Deuteronomy 1:16; 24:17–18; 27:19.

65. Proverbs 22:22–23.

66. Isaiah 10:1–2.

67. Amos 2:6; 5:16. Coote, pp. 35 and 45.

68. Psalms 76:8–9.

69. Coote, pp. 39–40.

70. Exodus 20:2; 22:21–24; Deuteronomy 4:37–40.

71. Coote, p. 41.

72. Karl Barth, *Church Dogmatics,* vol. 2, p. 386.

73. John C. Bennett, *The Radical Imperative,* pp. 13–14.

74. Reinhold Niebuhr, *Pious and Secular America,* p. 92.

75. Rawls, p. 302.

76. Barth, vol. 2, p. 387.

77. Deuteronomy 7:7–8.

78. Barth, vol. 2, p. 387.

79. Matthew 5–7.

80. For a detailed study of the three theories, see Roland H. Bainton, *Christian Attitudes Toward War and Peace,* p. 14.

81. Matthew 5:13–16.

82. For one description of the massacre of over 250,000 Assyrian Christians by the Turks, see the moving story of Rev. Joseph Naayem, *Shall This Nation Die?*

83. From "Statement Issued by the Heads of the Christian Communities in Jerusalem," January 22, 1988.

84. *The Kairos Covenant,* ed. Willis H. Logan, pp. 20–21.

85. Ibid.

86. Psalm 97:2.

87. Shae, p. 106.

88. Barth, vol. 2, p. 369.

89. Matthew 18:23–35.

90. It is only in light of the wholeness and comprehensiveness of the

unity and harmony of God's being that we can talk about the Resurrection as an expression of the justice of God. Strictly speaking, the cross is the expression of God's justice against sin and evil. The Passover, therefore, finds a parallel in Good Friday. Easter has become for the Church the focal point from which everything receives evaluation and meaning. Paul can triumphantly declare, "For Christ, our paschal lamb, has been sacrificed. Let us, therefore, celebrate the festival." (1 Corinthians 5:7–8).

91. For example, the story of Naboth and Ahab (1 Kings 21). See chapter 4, pp. 86–89.

92. Although *siddik* in Arabic is the transliteral word for the Hebrew *tsadik*, it is not the same word that is translated "righteous" in English. The word most often translated "righteous" in Arabic is *bar*.

93. Psalm 143:1–2. See also Psalm 143:11.

94. Psalm 98:9—righteousness, expressed concretely as kindness. The combining of God's mercy and justice is also expressed in Isaiah 30:18. Reinhold Niebuhr has suggested that in later Hebrew the word *tsedakah* is linked with *hesed*. Psalms 36:10. Quoted in Heschel, p. 201.

95. Proverbs 14:31. See also Proverbs 17:5.

96. Exodus 22:22–23, 27.

97. Genesis 4:8–16.

98. One of the great sayings in the Talmud carries this same meaning: "Whoever sheds blood diminishes God's presence in the world." (*Gen. Rabbah* 34, 14).

99. Heschel, p. 220.

100. Amos 9:7 (New English Bible).

101. The Revised Standard Version translates it "Ethiopians."

102. Coote, pp. 117–18. See Genesis 10:8–11.

103. Shae, p. 114.

104. Quoted in John Macquarrie, *The Concept of Peace*, p. 24.

105. Jeremiah 6:6.

106. Jeremiah 6:14.

107. Jeremiah 6:15. Jerome J. Shestack has written that "leaving the West Bank and the Gaza Strip may, indeed, pose a threat to Israel's physical security; staying there may pose a threat to its moral values" ("Human Rights Issues in Israel's Rule of the West Bank and Gaza," in David Sidorsky, ed., *Essays on Human Rights in Contemporary Issues and Jewish Perspectives*, p. 207).

108. Isaiah 1:17.

109. Jeremiah 22:15–16.

110. Isaiah 32:16–17. Peace is also linked with righteousness in Psalms 85:10; 72:7; Isaiah 48:18; 57:2; 60:17; and James 3:18.

111. Isaiah 48:22.

112. Dom Helder Camara, *Revolution through Peace*, p. 130.

113. Robert McAfee Brown, *Making Peace in the Global Village*, p. 15.

114. Pope John XXIII, *Pacem in Terris*, p. 76.

115. Zechariah 8:19.

116. Boake Carter quoted in *Reader's Digest Treasury of Modern Quotations*, p. 706.

117. *Thomas Merton on Peace*, p. 45.

118. Isaiah 39:8.

119. Isaiah 59:8. See also Luke 1:79.

120. Zechariah 8:12.

121. Psalm 34:14.

122. Matthew 5:9.

123. Ferguson, *War and Peace in the World's Religions*, p. 86.

124. Sanhedrin 38a. Quoted in Ferguson, p. 87.

125. *Gen. Rabbah* 38, 6. Quoted in Ferguson, p. 87.

126. Gen. 14:14; Nedarim 32a. Quoted in Ferguson, p. 88.

127. Genesis 48:22.

128. Ferguson, p. 88. For more examples see Ferguson, pp. 86–96.

129. *Theological Dictionary of the New Testament*, ed. Gerhard Kittel, under "Eirene," by Gerhard von Rad, vol. 2, p. 406.

130. One text that might be understood as expressing an inward reality is Romans 14:17. This can only be so understood if the Kingdom of God is seen as an inner reality and not as a social entity.

131. In black liberation theology, liberation is emphasized as a prerequisite to reconciliation. See, for example, J. Deotis Roberts, *Liberation and Reconciliation: A Black Theology*, p. 47.

132. Ephesians 2:14–18. The peace of Christ should also bring about the reconciliation of humans with their neighbors. "It is the ending of hostility and the beginning of mutuality. It is the relationship that God intends and provides for his creation." Stotts, *Shalom: The Search for a Peaceable City*, p. 107. (See Colossians, 1:19–20).

133. 2 Corinthians 5:17.

134. John 1:12.

135. Peace on earth is a possibility if humans are willing to give the glory to God (Luke 2:14). The song of the angels has been reversed. When humans give the glory to themselves, war rather than peace results. Peace, then, becomes eschatological, when God's purposes will be fulfilled that "every knee should bow . . . and every tongue confess that Jesus Christ is Lord, to the glory of God the Father" (Philippians 2:10–11). Christians can have only a taste of peace on earth. They might experience it in full momentarily, or in part over longer periods of time.

136. See Micah 4:1–4; Isaiah 11:6–9; Revelation 21:2–4.

137. Quoted in Macquarrie, *The Concept of Peace*, p. 13.

CHAPTER 6

1. John 8:32.

2. Quoted in Robert McAfee Brown, *Making Peace in the Global Village*, p. 19.

3. There are certain similarities to the church situation in Latin America. José Comblin, in *The Church and the National Security State*, pp. 172–73, has said that the church people in Latin America are very conscious of the price of the prophetic word:

> The church runs the risk of losing many material and cultural goods, including many opportunities of acting on behalf of its own people. The cost of the prophetic word is pressure, persecution, threat, and finally death. In the present situation the church is realizing that the word of God may be dangerous to its own security. If Christians speak, the power of the state reacts against them, and may silence them forcibly. If they choose to remain silent, they choose survival, but they feel they may be betraying their own mission.

4. "When one speaks of the vision of peace, one has in mind its ideal character . . . eschatological character . . . a peace of such depth and comprehensiveness that it can only lie at the consummation of history. . . . A concept implies recognizable and describable structures. . . ." John Macquarrie, *The Concept of Peace*, pp. 12–13.

5. An excellent illustration of the exercise of Christian responsibility in response to the Arab-Israeli conflict can be seen in the National Council of Churches of Christ in the USA, *Middle East Policy Statement*.

6. Thomas Merton, "Pacem in Terris," p. 70.

7. In February 1852, Sultan Abdul Mejid issued a *firman* authoritatively determining the rights of the historical churches in the disputes over the Holy Places. This *firman* in essence confirmed the de facto situation of the Holy Places that had existed since 1757 with certain minor amendments. At the Congress of Berlin in 1878, the de facto rulings of the *firman* of 1852 were confirmed. In article 62 of the Treaty of Berlin the expression "status quo" was used for the first time to describe the facts and existing situation of the Holy Places.

From the strictly legal point of view, the status quo applies to five shrines only: the Church of the Holy Sepulchre, Deir el-Sultan (near the Holy Sepulchre), the sanctuary of the Ascension of the Mount of Olives, the

Tomb of the Virgin Mary in the Valley of Jehosaphat, and the Church of the Nativity in Bethlehem. The denominations affected by the status quo are the Greek Orthodox, the Latins, and the Armenians. (The Copts, the Syrians, and the Ethiopians are grouped with the Armenians.) Strictly speaking, these Holy Places are not a part of the State of Israel, but the sensitivities among the churches are not confined to strict geographical boundaries.

For a more detailed discussion of the status quo, see Saul P. Colby, *Christianity in the Holy Land,* pp. 75–76, 171–180.

8. *Reader's Digest Treasury of Modern Quotations,* p. 725.

9. One of the best places to begin indoctrinating children in justice and peace is the Christian school. There are over eighty Christian primary and secondary schools in Israel-Palestine that serve both Christians and Muslims.

10. Matthew 5:9.

11. See chapter 5, pp. 134–135.

12. Charles Habib Malik writes that when the Church is oppressed and persecuted it ceases to be evangelical and turns liturgical, "preserving the entire deposit of faith behind symbol and song. It dies, so to speak, that the faith may live." Charles Habib Malik, "The Near East," in *The Prospects of Christianity throughout the World,* ed. M. Searle Bates and Wilhelm Pauck, p. 87.

13. The term "Levantine" denotes those people who live in two worlds—the Christian and the Muslim—at the same time, without fully belonging to either. The first world reflects their qualitative, personal, and spiritual existence, the second their quantitative, economic, social, and political existence. These people, on the one hand, are attached emotionally and existentially to their home and country; on the other hand, they feel somehow strangers among their own people. They live at times in ambiguity and frustration and resign themselves to a status of social and political inferiority even though they possess the capacity for greater achievements. For a detailed description of Levantinism, see Malik, in *Prospects of Christianity throughout the World,* ed. Searle and Pauck, 88–93.

14. In spite of Levantinism, the Christians of the Middle East have played a significant role and have contributed much to the development and progress of the area, including the rise of Arab nationalism. Pierre Rondot has said, "without them [the Christians] the Middle East would have less character, less flavor, and less charm, for they are the salt and the leaven." Pierre Rondot, *The Changing Patterns of the Middle East,* p. 58.

15. In addition to what the churches in Israel-Palestine could give, I believe that the greatest monetary support would come from various agencies, organizations, and churches abroad, including some governments and

such international bodies as the World Council of Churches. I have been amazed at the amount of money that certain groups have received when they engage in some (oftentimes not too serious) peacemaking activities.

16. So far as I know, no parallel to this Center has been set up in Israel-Palestine. This does not mean, however, that no individuals or groups have been active in peacemaking. To name only two: An organization called *Shutafut* (Partnership) has in the last few years brought Arab and Jewish youth together. Neve Shalom has also developed into a sort of cooperative settlement near Jerusalem, bringing Jews, Muslims, and Christians together in a model of Arab-Jewish coexistence. In contrast to these limited, peripheral, and rather symbolic attempts, the Center for Peacemaking, if set up and supported by the major Christian churches in Israel-Palestine and guided by the fundamental vision expressed in this chapter, could make a more permanent and substantial contribution to justice and peace.

17. According to Thomas Hobbes (1588–1679), the natural state of humankind is one of war. Human life is "solitary, poor, nasty, brutish, and short." Peace is a secondary condition based on fear. John Locke (1632–1704) offered a different view. The state of nature for humankind, he wrote, is "men living together according to reason." I believe that Locke is closer to the biblical tradition. Humans are by nature rational and sociable. Peace is more fundamental than war. By stressing this latter view, the Christian promotes a positive attitude for peace. (Thomas Hobbes, *Leviathan,* pp. 21–128; John Locke, *Two Treatises of Government,* pp. 121–28.)

18. A good illustration of this point is found in "An Open Letter to North American Christians," signed by thirteen Christians from Latin America. (Quoted in Brown, p. 26):

> If in the past you felt it to be your apostolic duty to send us missionaries and economic resources, today the frontier of your witness and Christian solidarity is within your own country. The conscious, intelligent, and responsible use of your vote; the appeal to your representatives in Congress; the application of pressure by various means on your authorities, can contribute to changing the course of our governments toward paths of greater justice and brotherhood, or to accentuate a colonialist and oppressive policy over our peoples. In this sense you must ask yourselves if you will or will not be "your brother's keeper" in these lands of America, from which the blood of millions of Abels is clamoring to heaven.

19. National Council of Churches of Christ, *Middle East Policy Statement,* p. 1.

20. Walter Rauschenbusch (1861–1918), one of the great representatives of the liberal social gospel, has written that "the life of humanity is infinitely interwoven, always renewing itself, yet always perpetuating what has been. The evils of one generation are caused by the wrongs of the generations that preceded, and will in turn condition the sufferings and temptations of those who come after." Quoted in John C. Bennett, *The Radical Imperative*, p. 18.

21. G. H. Jansen *(Militant Islam,* pp. 49–68) has argued that Islam as a religion was little affected by 350 years of Christian missionary endeavor; and as a policy, it was little affected by the 150 years of colonial conquest and imperial rule.

22. The assassination of Anwar Sadat, President of Egypt, by Muslim militants on October 6, 1981, is a case in point.

23. Judah Halevi in *Al Khuzari* (11,44) in the twelfth century wrote that Israel has a mission of suffering. "Israel, the heart of humanity, the suffering servant, bears the ills of all, and by this very fact allows God to be revealed on earth." Rabbi Joshua ben Levi said, "He who gladly accepts the suffering of this world brings salvation to the world." Quoted in John Ferguson, *War and Peace in the World's Religions*, p. 96.

24. Baba Kamma 93a. Ibid.

25. Ferguson, pp. 96–97.

26. Menachem Begin, *The Revolt*, introduction and p. 32.

On the surface, the phenomenon of the "fighting Jew" might be interpreted, and understandably so, in light of and as a reaction to the Holocaust. So can a person understand the often repeated insistence on "never again"; however, this has developed into a Massada complex. Unless peace is achieved on Israel's terms, the door of compromise and flexibility will be closed. This means Israel clinging to and obsessed by power as the only alternative that ensures the survival of the State. The will that is obsessed with power prefers to destroy itself and everyone else with it rather than admit and concede to others their legitimate rights and by so doing save itself and live with its neighbors in peace.

27. National Council of Churches of Christ, *Middle East Policy Statement*, p. 13.

CHAPTER 7

1. Matthew 7:12.

2. Mark 12:31.

3. At the beginning of World War I, the Assyrian Christians numbered between 700,000 and 800,000, scattered in Iraq, upper Syria, Iran, and Turkey. These included members of what we refer to today as the

Ancient Church of the East, the Chaldeans, the Syrian Orthodox, and the Syrian Catholics. About 250,000 were killed at the hands of the Turks, Kurds, and Iranians. (See the historical essay on the Assyro-Chaldean Christians by Rev. Gabriel Oussani, in Joseph Naayem, *Shall This Nation Die?* (pp. xv–xxvi.)

During 1894–6, nearly two hundred thousand Armenians were killed by the Turks. The killing resumed in 1909, but the worst massacres took place during World War I. More than one million Armenians were exterminated; thousands converted to Islam to escape death; and about a million survived (*Encyclopedia Americana,* International Edition [Danbury, Conn.: Grolier, 1984], p. 333).

4. See pp. 27–28 of chapter 2. When Britain issued the Balfour Declaration on November 2, 1917, Palestine was still under Turkish rule. The utter absurdity of the declaration is exposed when people realize that Britain was promising a country that was not its own to a people whose country was not theirs. It is as ridiculous as if I were to promise to give another person your home.

5. Evan M. Wilson, *Jerusalem, Key to Peace,* p. 140.

6. Ibid.

7. It was Henry Kissinger who, while U.S. secretary of state, established the policy that the United States would not deal with the PLO until it accepted two important conditions—Israel's right to exist and U.N. Security Council resolutions 242 and 338. These conditions were formally adopted on September 1, 1975, to the annoyance of many U.S. officials who felt that they should open negotiations with the PLO. See Wolf Blitzer, *Between Washington and Jerusalem,* pp. 206–207.

8.

Country	Population	Area
Israel	4,449,000 (1987)*	7,992 sq. miles†
Jordan	2,853,000 (1987)	34,443 sq. miles
Lebanon	2,762,000 (1987)	3,950 sq. miles
West Bank and Gaza	1,342,000‡	2,031 sq. miles

Country	Religion			
	Muslim	Christian	Jewish	Other
Israel	13.5%	2.4%	82.5%	1.6%
Jordan	93.0%	4.9%	–	2.1%
Lebanon§	53.0%	39.0%	–	8.0%
West Bank and Gaza	96%	4.0%	–	–

*Includes population of East Jerusalem and about 25,000 Israeli residents living in the occupied territories.

†Excluding West Bank, Gaza Strip, Golan Heights, and East Jerusalem.

‡Israel Central Bureau of Statistics Report, 1986, 1988.

§No official data exist subsequent to the 1932 census, when Christians (predominantly Maronite) were a slight majority. It is estimated today that the Muslims constitute a majority, but by what margin is uncertain. An unofficial estimate (1984) indicated that the main religious groups were distributed as follows: Shiite Muslims 32%; Sunni Muslims 21%; Maronites 24.5%; Greek Orthodox 6.5%; Greek Catholics 4.0%; Armenians 4%; Druze 7%; Other 1%.

Statistics from *1988 Britannica Book of the Year* (Chicago: Encyclopedia Britannica, 1988).

9. The Middle East leads the world in the purchase of arms. Of the eighteen leading arms importing countries of the world in 1984, seven were from the Middle East: Iraq, Saudi Arabia, Iran, Libya, Egypt, Syria, and Israel. *World Almanac and Book of Facts, 1988* (New York: Pharos Books), p. 340.

10. A 1968 CIA report estimated that Israel possessed between twelve and twenty nuclear bombs. According to the *Christian Science Monitor,* Mordechai Vanunu, the Israeli nuclear technician who in October 1986 informed the *Sunday Times* of London of Israel's large nuclear arsenal, revealed that Israel may have one hundred to two hundred nuclear weapons of varying strength (reported in the *Christian Century* [April 13, 1988]: 362). So far, Israel has refused to sign the Nuclear Nonproliferation Treaty. See Halsell, *Prophecy and Politics,* p. 198.

11. Micah 4:1–4.

CHAPTER 8

1. Reuven Moscovitz mentioned this interpretation of Deuteronomy 16:20 during a panel discussion, "People, Land, and Faith," at the Ecumenical Theological Research Fraternity in Israel meeting in Jerusalem, February 10, 1977.

There are other interesting commentaries on this verse in the Jewish tradition. Rabbi Abraham Ibn Ezra (Spain, 1089–1164) said that the word "justice" is mentioned twice "in order to indicate that one should pursue justice whether it would be to his advantage or loss." See Ramban (Nachmanides), *Commentary on the Torah—Deuteronomy,* Charles B. Chavel, ed. (New York: Shilo, 1976), pp. 195–96. In the Babylonian Talmud, R. Ashi (France, 1040–1105) wrote, "The first mention of justice refers to a decision based on strict laws; the second, to a compromise." (*Sanhedrin,* 32b).

2. After the Babylonian Exile, the existing borders were only between Bethel and Hebron. In fact, at no time in Jewish history did the "land of Israel" have the "promised borders." In the Hebrew Scriptures, there are various definitions and descriptions of borders; one definition extends them

from the Nile to the Euphrates. Another includes the area of Palestine and eastern Jordan. The problem of borders was simply not very much discussed or worried about in the Bible. In fact, at the height of Solomon's reign, parts of the western coastal area were not even part of Israel.

3. See Elias Haddadin's letter to the editor in the *Atlanta Constitution* (June 14, 1988): p. 18A.

4. Grace Halsell, *Prophecy and Politics,* p. 199.

5. See the work of Professor Israel Shahak of the Hebrew University, Jerusalem, chairperson of the Israeli League for Human and Civil Rights, who suffered under the Nazis himself. Shahak reproduces periodically in mimeograph form articles dealing with political, social, and religious issues that he collects from Hebrew newspapers. He and other Israeli writers have not hesitated to compare certain Israeli practices with those of the Nazis. Shahak introduces one of his mimeographed collections, "An example of anti-Arab racism in Israel," with the words,

> While the first three items here describe a particular incident, one of the many as the first item makes clear, the fourth gives some examples of how much Nazi-like violence is employed all the time by the Police, Borderguards and the (volunteer) Civil Guards against Arabs in Tel Aviv and in all other places in Israel. The first simple conclusion, which, as this collection shows, is accepted by many in Israel but can not be mentioned in the Western countries, is that Jewish chauvinism, racism, and in many cases Jewish Nazism, exist. The second conclusion is that, in part, they have social patterns similar [to] other forms of racism and in particular [to] anti-Semitism, and in extreme cases they resemble German Nazism."

In another collection, "Transfer and Holocaust," Shahak refers to the "Nazification of the State of Israel and the expulsion or extermination of the Palestinians." In the same collection, Shahak includes an article by Hayim Baram entitled "Transfer will lead to civil war," which appeared in *Kol Ha'ir* on February 26, 1988. In opposing the idea of the mass deportation of Palestinians, Baram says, "I personally will fight, also with arms, against individuals who will take here steps against an entire population, which would remind me, and the rest of the world, of the crimes of the Nazis." For further reading, see the *Report on the Violations of Human Rights in the Territories During the Uprising, 1988,* published by the Israeli League for Human and Civil Rights, P. O. Box 14192, Tel Aviv, Israel.

6. Viktor E. Frankl, *Man's Search for Meaning,* p. 143.

7. Ibid., p. 144.

8. Abraham Cohen, ed., *The Babylonian Talmud,* "Yoma" (London: Soncino, 1984), p. 59a (3).

9. Ibid., "Perek HashShalom," 2.

10. Matthew 5:5.

11. David Grossman, *The Yellow Wind,* p. 11.

12. John 10:10.

13. Matthew 5:43–45a.

14. Laurens van der Post, *Venture to the Interior,* pp. 30–31.

15. Quoted in Marc Ellis, *Toward a Jewish Theology of Liberation,* p. 98.

16. Ibid., p. 102.

17. David Kin, ed., *Dictionary of American Maxims* (New York: Philosophical Library, 1955), "Hate," p. 227.

18. St. Francis of Assisi, 1181–1226. See *The Oxford Book of Prayer,* ed. George Appleton (Oxford: Oxford University Press, 1985), number 217, p. 75.

19. Week of Prayer for World Peace, 1978. Ibid., number 227, p. 78.

20. Reinhold Niebuhr, *Prayers for Peace* (Mount Vernon, N.Y.: Peter Pauper Press, 1962), p. 18.

Bibliography

American Friends Service Committee. *A Compassionate Peace: A Future for the Middle East*. New York: Hill and Wang, 1982.

Anderson, Gerald H., and Thomas F. Stransky, eds. *Mission Trends No. 3*. New York: Paulist Press, 1976.

Antonius, George. *The Arab Awakening*. London: Hamish Hamilton, 1955.

Appleton, George, ed. *The Oxford Book of Prayer*. Oxford: Oxford University Press, 1985.

Arberry A. J., ed. *Religion in the Middle East*. 2 vols. Cambridge: Cambridge University Press, 1969.

Atiya, Aziz Suryal. *A History of Eastern Christianity*. Notre Dame, Ind.: University of Notre Dame Press, 1968.

Avnery, Uri. *Israel without Zionism*. New York: Collier, 1971.

Bainton, Roland H. *Christian Attitudes toward War and Peace*. Nashville, Tenn.: Abingdon, 1960.

Barth, Karl. *Church Dogmatics*. 4 vols. Edinburgh: T & T Clark, 1957.

Bates, M. Searle, and Wilhelm Pauck, eds. *Prospects of Christianity throughout the World*. New York: Scribners, 1964.

Beegle, Dewey M. *Prophecy and Prediction*. Ann Arbor, Mich.: Pryor Pettengill, 1978.

Begin, Menachem. *The Revolt: Story of the "Irgun."* New York: Abelard-Schumann; London: W. H. Allen, 1951.

Bennett, John C. *The Radical Imperative*. Philadelphia: Westminster, 1975.

Benson, Arthur Christopher. *The Life of Edward White Benson (Sometime Archbishop of Canterbury)*. 2 vols. London, 1899.

Berger, Elmer. *Judaism or Jewish Nationalism: The Alternative to Zionism*. New York: Brookman, 1957.

——. *A Partisan History of Judaism*. New York: Devin-Adair, 1951.

——. *Prophecy, Zionism and the State of Israel*. Introduction by Arnold J. Toynbee. New York: American Alternative to Zionism, n.d.

Betts, Robert Brenton. *Christians in the Arab East*. Atlanta, Ga.: John Knox, 1978.

Blitzer, Wolf. *Between Washington and Jerusalem: A Reporter's Note-

book. New York: Oxford University Press, 1985.

Blyth, George Francis Popham. *The Primary Charge*. London, 1890.

――――. *The Second Charge*. London, 1893.

――――. *The Third Triennial Charge*. London, 1896.

Brandon, S. G. F. *Jesus and the Zealots*. Manchester: University Press, 1967.

Bright, John. *The Authority of the Old Testament*. Nashville, Tenn.: Abingdon, 1967.

Brown, Raymond E. *The Critical Meaning of the Bible*. New York: Paulist Press, 1981.

Brown, Robert McAfee. *Making Peace in the Global Village*. Philadelphia: Westminster, 1981.

Brueggemann, Walter. *The Land*. Philadelphia: Fortress, 1977.

Buttrick, George A., gen. ed. *The Interpreter's Bible*. Vol. 7, "New Testament: Matthew. Mark." Nashville, Tenn.: Abingdon, 1951.

Camara, Dom Helder. *Revolution through Peace*. Translated by Amparo McLear. New York: Harper & Row, 1971.

――――. *The Spiral of Violence*. London: Sheed and Ward, 1975.

Cattan, Henry. *Palestine, the Arabs and Israel: The Search for Justice*. London: Longman Group, 1970.

――――. *Palestine and International Law*. London: Longman Group, 1973.

Chacour, Elias. *Blood Brothers*. Grand Rapids, Mich.: Chosen, 1984.

Chakmakjian, Hagop A. *In Quest of Justice and Peace in the Middle East: The Palestinian Conflict in Biblical Perspective*. New York: Vantage, 1980.

Colby, Saul P. *Christianity in the Holy Land: Past and Present*. Tel Aviv: Am Hasefer, 1969.

Comblin, José. *The Church and the National Security State*. Maryknoll, N.Y.: Orbis, 1979.

Coote, Robert B. *Amos among the Prophets*. Philadelphia: Fortress, 1981.

Cullmann, Oscar. *Jesus and the Revolutionaries*. Translated by Gareth Putnam. New York: Harper & Row, 1970.

Davies, J. G. *Christians, Politics and Violent Revolutions*. Maryknoll, N.Y.: Orbis, 1976.

Davies, W. D. *The Gospel and the Land*. Berkeley: University of California Press, 1974.

Davis, Uri. *Israel: An Apartheid State*. London and New Jersey: Zed Books, 1987.

Dimont, Max I. *Jews, God and History*. New York: Signet, 1962.

Dodd, C. H., and M. E. Sales, *Israel and the Arabs*. London: Routledge and Kegan Paul, 1970.

Dodd, Charles Harold. *The Meaning of Paul for Today*. New York: Meridian, 1957.

Donnelly, Lewis, ed. *Justice First*. London: Sheed and Ward, 1969.

Ellis, Marc. *Toward a Jewish Theology of Liberation*. Maryknoll, N.Y.: Orbis, 1987.

Elon, Amos. *Herzel*. New York: Holt, Rinehart, and Winston, 1975.

Epstein, Isidore. *Judaism*. Harmondsworth, U.K.: Penguin, 1977.

Ferguson, John. *War and Peace in the World's Religions*. London: Sheldon, 1977.

Feuerlicht, Roberta Strauss. *The Fate of the Jews*. New York: Times Books, 1983.

Findley, Paul. *They Dare to Speak Out*. Westport, Conn.: Lawrence Hill, 1985.

Fishman, Hertzel. *American Protestantism and a Jewish State*. Detroit, Mich.: Wayne State University Press, 1973.

Frankl, Viktor E. *Man's Search for Meaning*. New York: Washington Square, 1963.

Garrett, Samuel M. "An Anglican View of Ethics: The Investigation of a Context." *Anglican Theological Review* 61 (January 1979).

Ghareeb, Edmund, ed. *Split Vision*. Washington, D.C.: American-Arab Affairs Council, 1983.

Grossman, David. *The Yellow Wind*. New York: Farrar, Straus and Giroux, 1988.

Hadawi, Sami. *Christianity at the Crossroads*. Ottawa: Jerusalem International Publishing House, 1982.

———. *The Jews, Zionism, and the Bible*. Toronto: Arab Palestine Association, 1981.

Haim, Sylvia G. *Arab Nationalism: An Anthology*. Berkeley: University of California Press, 1976.

Halsell, Grace. *Journey to Jerusalem*. New York: Macmillan, 1981.

———. *Prophecy and Politics*. Westport, Conn.: Lawrence Hill, 1986.

Heschel, Abraham. *The Prophets*. New York: Harper & Row, 1962.

Hillesum, Etty. *An Interrupted Life: The Diaries of Etty Hillesum, 1941–43*. New York: Pocket, 1985.

Hobbes, Thomas. *Leviathan*. Edited by Michael Oakeshott. New York: Crowell-Collier, 1962.

Hodder, Edwin. *The Life and Work of the Seventh Earl of Shaftesbury, K.G.* London: Cassell, 1887.

Holland, Joe, and Peter Henriot. *Social Analysis: Linking Faith and Justice*. Washington, D.C.: Center of Concern, 1980.

Isaacs, Stephen D. *Jews and American Politics*. New York: Doubleday, 1974.

Jaeger, David-Maria A., ed. *Papers Read at the 1979 Tantur Conference on Christianity in the Holy Land*. Jerusalem: Franciscan Printing Press, 1981.

Jansen, G. H. *Militant Islam*. London: Pan, 1979.

Jiryis Sabri. *The Arabs in Israel*. New York: Monthly Review, 1976.

John XIII, Pope. *Pacem in Terris*. New York: Paulist, 1963.

Johnson, Howard A. *Global Odyssey*. London: Geoffrey, 1963.

Kahane, Rabbi Meir. *They Must Go*. New York: Grosset and Dunlap, 1981.

Kanana, Sharif. *Ataghyeer Al-ijtimaʿi wa-tawafuq Annafsi ʿind Assukan Alʿarab fi Israil* [Socio-Cultural and Psychological Adjustment of the Arab Minority in Israel]. Birzeit University, 1978.

Kee, Alistair, ed. *A Reader in Political Theology*. Philadelphia: Westminster, 1974.

Kissinger, Henry. "Years of Upheaval." *Time,* March 1, 1982, 30–56.

Kittel, Gerhard, ed. *Theological Dictionary of the New Testament*. Vol. 2. Grand Rapids, Mich: Eerdmans, 1964.

Koestler, Arthur. *The Thirteenth Tribe*. New York: Random House, 1976.

Laqueur, Walter, ed. *The Israel-Arab Reader*. London: Lowe and Brydone, 1969.

Laqueur, Walter, and Barry Rubin, eds. *The Human Rights Reader*. New York: Meridian, 1979.

Lewy, Guenter. *Religion and Revolution*. New York: Oxford University Press, 1974.

Lilienthal, Alfred M. *The Zionist Connection: What Price Peace?* New York: Dodd, Mead, 1978.

Limburg, James. *The Prophets and the Powerless*. Atlanta: John Knox, 1977.

Locke, John. *Two Treatises of Government*. Thomas I. Cook, ed. New York: Hafner, 1973.

Logan, Willis H., ed. *The Kairos Covenant*. New York: Friendship Press, 1988.

Lustick, Ian. *Arabs in the Jewish State*. Austin: University of Texas Press, 1980.

Macquarrie, John. *The Concept of Peace*. New York: Harper & Row, 1973.

Mallison, N. T., Jr., and S. V. Mallison. "The Role of International Law in Achieving Justice and Peace in Palestine-Israel." Paper presented at the Conference on Human Rights in Palestine for the World Conference of Christians for Palestine. Geneva, January 11–14, 1974.

Mays, James Luther. *Micah*. Philadelphia: Westminster, 1976.

Menuhin, Moshe. *The Decadence of Judaism in Our Time*. New York: Exposition, 1965.

Merton, Thomas. "Pacem in Terris." In ". . . *Therefore Choose Life.*" Santa Barbara, Calif.: Center for the Study of Democratic Institutions, 1965.

Moltmann, Jurgen. *The Church in the Power of the Spirit*. New York: Harper & Row, 1977.

Naayem, Joseph. *Shall This Nation Die?* New York: Chaldean Rescue, 1921.

National Council of Churches of Christ in the USA. *Middle East Policy Statement.* New York: 1980.

Neill, Stephen. *Christian Missions.* Harmondsworth, U.K.: Penguin, 1964.

Niebuhr, Reinhold. *Moral Man and Immoral Society.* New York: Scribners, 1960.

————. *Pious and Secular America.* New York: Scribners, 1958.

Nielsen, Jorgen S., gen. ed. *International Documents on Palestine, 1974.* Beirut: Institute for Palestine Studies, 1977.

————, gen. ed. *International Documents on Palestine, 1975.* Beirut: Institute for Palestine Studies, 1977.

Peretz, Don. *Israel and the Palestine Arabs.* Washington, D.C.: Middle East Institute, 1958.

Pritchard, James B., ed. *Ancient Near Eastern Texts.* Princeton, N.J.: Princeton University Press, 1950.

Rawls, John. *A Theory of Justice.* Cambridge, Mass.: Harvard University Press, 1971.

The Reader's Digest Treasury of Modern Quotations. New York: Crowell, 1975.

Roberts, J. Deotis. *Liberation and Reconciliation: A Black Theology.* Philadelphia: Westminster, 1971.

Rondot, Pierre. *The Changing Patterns of the Middle East.* Translated by Mary Dilke. London: Chatto and Windus, 1961.

Rose, Norman A. *The Gentile Zionists: A Study in Anglo-Zionist Diplomacy, 1929–1939.* London: Frank Cass, 1973.

Ruether, Rosemary Radford. *Faith and Fratricide.* New York: Seabury, 1974.

Runciman, Steven. "The Christian Arabs of Palestine." Paper presented at the Second Carreras Arab Lecture, University of Essex. Essex, U.K., November 26, 1968.

Said, Edward. *The Question of Palestine.* New York: Random House/Vintage, 1980.

Sayegh, Fayez A., John Coventry Smith, Yehoshafat Harkabi, and Elizabeth Monroe. *Time Bomb in the Middle East.* New York: Friendship, 1969.

Shae, John. *Stories of God: An Unauthorized Biography.* Chicago: Thomas More, 1978.

Shehadeh, Raja. *Occupier's Law: Israel and the West Bank.* Washington, D.C.: Institute for Palestine Studies, 1985.

Shipler, David K. *Arab and Jew.* New York: Times Books, 1985.

Shorris, Earl. *Jews without Mercy.* New York: Anchor, 1982.

Sidorsky, David, ed. *Essays on Human Rights in Contemporary Issues and*

Jewish Perspectives. Philadelphia: Jewish Publication Society of America, 1979.

Stendahl, Krister. "Toward a New Generation." Paper presented to the Consultation on the Church and the Jewish People. London, June 22, 1981.

Stotts, Jack L. *Shalom: The Search for a Peaceable City*. Nashville, Tenn.: Abingdon, 1973.

Talal, Hassan bin. *Palestinian Self-Determination*. New York: Quarter Book, 1981.

Tibawi, A. L. *British Interests in Palestine, 1800–1901*. Oxford: Oxford University Press, 1961.

Tillich, Paul. *Systematic Theology*. 3 vols. Chicago: University of Chicago Press, 1963.

Torres, Sergio, and John Eagleson. *The Challenge of Basic Christian Communities*. Maryknoll, N.Y.: Orbis, 1981.

Trimingham, J. Spencer. *Christianity Among the Arabs in Pre-Islamic Times*. New York: Longmans, 1979.

van Buren, Paul M. *A Christian Theology of the People Israel*. New York: Seabury, 1983.

———. *Discerning the Way*. New York: Seabury, 1980.

———. "Discerning the Way to the Incarnation." *Anglican Theological Review*, 63 (July 1981).

van der Post, Laurens. *Venture to the Interior*. New York: William Morrow, 1951.

Von Rad, Gerhard. *Old Testament Theology*. Vol. 2. New York: Harper & Row, 1965.

Ware, Timothy. *The Orthodox Church*. Harmondsworth, U.K.: Penguin, 1964.

Wilson, Evan M. *Jerusalem, Key to Peace*. Washington, D.C.: Middle East Institute, 1970.

Wright, G. Ernest. *The Old Testament against Its Environment*. London: SCM, 1962.

Yoder, John. *The Politics of Jesus*. Grand Rapids, Mich.: Eerdmans, 1972.

Zahn, Gordon Z., ed. *Thomas Merton on Peace*. New York: McCall, 1971.

Zureik, Elia T. *The Palestinians in Israel*. London: Routledge and Kegan Paul, 1979.

General Index

221

Scripture Index